# SEDUCED
## — BY —
# SUCCESS

**How the Best Companies Survive
the 9 Traps of Winning**

# Robert J. Herbold

McGraw-Hill
New York   Chicago   San Francisco
Lisbon   London   Madrid   Mexico City   Milan
New Delhi   San Juan   Seoul   Singapore
Sydney   Toronto

## *To Patricia*

The **McGraw·Hill** Companies

1 2 3 4 5 6 7 8 9 0   DOC/DOC   0 9 8 7

ISBN-13: 978-0-07-148183-0
ISBN-10:     0-07-148183-4

Design by Lee Fukui and Mauna Eichner

The apple image in the interior is used courtesy of Leander/Alamy.

This publication is designed to provide accurate and authoritative information in regard to the subject matter covered. It is sold with the understanding that neither the author nor the publisher is engaged in rendering legal, accounting, or other professional service. If legal advice or other expert assistance is required, the services of a competent professional person should be sought.

> *—From a Declaration of Principles jointly adopted*
> *by a Committee of the American Bar*
> *Association and a Committee of Publishers*

McGraw-Hill books are available at special quantity discounts to use as premiums and sales promotions, or for use in corporate training programs. For more information, please write to the Director of Special Sales, Professional Publishing, McGraw-Hill, Two Penn Plaza, New York, NY 10121-2298. Or contact your local bookstore.

This book is printed on acid-free paper.

# CONTENTS

# ACKNOWLEDGMENTS

First, I would like to thank Bill Leigh of the Leigh Bureau, the individual who got me thinking about how successful organizations often fall prey to certain traps that lead to serious business problems. Bill is a real thinker and has the ability to stimulate fresh ideas and excite people about pursuing them further.

Next, I want to thank Wes Neff who runs the day-to-day activities of the Leigh Bureau. I've worked with Wes for several years. He helped me launch my first book called *The Fiefdom Syndrome; the Turf Battles That Undermine Careers and Companies—and How to Overcome Them.* Wes is the person who continually probed me as to how successful companies often stumble, and why that occurs.

Also, I want to thank Jeffrey Krames, Leah Spiro, and Ruth Mannino of McGraw-Hill. Jeffrey was very helpful in the early stages of the book's development, while Leah applied her superb skills and experience in the later stages. Ruth was a great help in getting the book through production. I should also mention how much I appreciate the efforts of Philip Ruppel for his help with the McGraw-Hill sales folks and of Tara Cibelli and Lydia Rinaldi in the McGraw-Hill marketing and publicity areas.

Most important, I would like to acknowledge the work of Kim McGee, my administrative assistant here at the Herbold Group, LLC. Kim does it all. This book simply would not have been pulled together on schedule without her constant assistance. She is greatly appreciated. Anis Ithnin, my assistant at INSEAD in Singapore, was also very helpful.

# SUCCESS IS A
# SERIOUS
# BUSINESS
# VULNERABILITY

**When leaders of** organizations experience meaningful levels of success or periods of stability, they tend to believe that they are entitled to continued success into the future. In many cases, managers become complacent, comfortable, and mediocre when, in fact, they should be building on all the things they have done well in the past. They should be probing to uncover fresh approaches, improving their products and services, and staying lean and agile. Unfortunately, the business pages are filled with sad stories of once successful organizations that, after reaching the top, could not keep it going, could not sustain their success.

I've observed this phenomenon over and over again. Success is a huge business vulnerability. It can destroy an organization's or an individual's ability to understand the need for change and can also destroy the motivation to creatively attack the status quo. Organizations and people become trapped by what I call *legacy* practices and thinking. The implicit assumption here is that your current practices have made you a winner; you're at the top of your game, and no one can beat you. Individuals lose themselves in the approaches they used in their glory days and are unable to see that they are not building on their best practices but merely trying to repeat old successes. They don't notice that the world is changing around them. I believe that this fall-out from success is one of the most crippling problems that individuals and organizations face.

It is important to realize that people and companies fall into this success trap. It happens to entire companies and departments, to small groups within organizations, and to individuals. All are susceptible to the perils of success.

> *I am writing this book to help individuals and organizations become successful and stay successful.*

The classic example of a company that has been seduced by success is GM, which has enjoyed a storied past but is plagued by a troubled present. Or consider a company with an impeccable reputation in the kitchen and the front yard: Rubbermaid. For ten years, from 1985 to 1994, Rubbermaid was among the top ten in *Fortune* magazine's annual list of most admired companies, and, in 1993 and 1994, it was rated number one.[1] This producer of household products like plastic trashcans and dish drainers looked invincible. It was riding high based on its knack for continuously spotting unmet household needs and innovating to fill those needs. It produced highly predictable and very impressive financial results year after year.

But serious problems emerged in the mid-1990s. Legacy practices were setting in and Rubbermaid simply passed along to customers its fast-growing costs and hung on to outdated production techniques.[2] This resulted in lagging earnings and a decision in 1995 to shut down nine plants and lay off 9 percent of its workforce.[3] Problems continued to get worse, and in late 1992, Rubbermaid was acquired by the relatively unknown Newell.[4] As reported by *Fortune* magazine in 1998, "they became terrible at the basics of manufacturing and marketing."[5] A major retail customer added "they've been such lousy shippers. Not on time, terrible fill rates, and their products cost too much." Amazingly, in the midst of these problems back in 1995, CEO Wolfgang Schmitt down-played the situation saying, "We hit a bump . . . and will be back on our usual growth path by the end of the year."[6]

Rubbermaid had a great run, but could not sustain it.

On the flip side, some companies have achieved tremendous success and not only sustained it, but broadened it. Consider the case of Michael Dell. His personal computer company was almost an instant success when he launched it in 1984. He ignored all the accolades and personally led his company to continual success for two decades, with Dell as number one in the personal computer business globally and as *Fortune*'s Most Admired Company in 2005. In 2006, Dell's business weakened significantly as competition caught up, but the company's 20 years of impressive growth remains a success story.

The key observation here is that whether you are talking about individuals, small groups, or large organizations, success generates the risk of falling prey to the mind-set of becoming proud, to being very comfortable with your current practices, and to losing your sense of urgency.

Success is not an entitlement; it does not prolong itself. In fact, in my almost 40 years in business I have learned that the legacy of success all too often is failure. Yes, winning and achieving great success is often the start of a long, painful journey to disaster. I'm not alone in making this observation. Bill Gates, one of the most successful businessmen of all times said it well:

> *Success is a lousy teacher. It seduces smart people into thinking they can't lose.*[7]

Dieter Zetsche, the Daimler Chrysler CEO and the person responsible for the recent turnaround at Chrysler, has had a similar insight into the dangers inherent in winning:

> *If you are very successful, you start thinking you can walk on water.*[8]

Walter Winchell said it quite succinctly:

> *Nothing recedes like success.*[9]

Not surprisingly, Peter Drucker probably summarized it the most eloquently:

> *Success always makes obsolete the very behavior that achieved it. It always creates new realities. It always creates, above all, its own and different problems. Only the fairy tale ends, "They lived happily ever after."*[10]

Far too many once dominant individuals and organizations can speak to the truth of these observations. But I believe it doesn't have to be that way.

I am writing this book to help individuals and organizations become successful and *stay successful.* I will show you how to look past your current success or stability and constantly probe for new and better ideas and ways to do things. I'll show readers how to put their past successes in perspective so they don't rely too heavily on what worked yesterday or what's working today. It's too easy to be trapped in the exhilaration of the present and to believe you've found the true and everlasting formula for sustained success. Well, I can assure you that doesn't exist.

# 1

# A CLASSIC EXAMPLE: GENERAL MOTORS

The vulnerabilities resulting from success can bring down individuals and organizations of all sizes. Let's take a look at what has happened to one of America's most treasured business icons of the twentieth century.

General Motors is a 98-year-old company that took the leadership of the automobile business away from Ford in the 1920s. In the 1950s, it became the largest employer in the free world and the first firm to make $1 billion in a year.[1] In the mid-1970s, General Motors had almost a 50 percent market share in the United States. It had the bestselling model in America, the Oldsmobile Cutlass. The favorite saying about GM in those days was, "As GM goes, so goes the nation."

For the next 30 years, it was all downhill for General Motors. By early 2006, its financial problems were staggering. It had lost $8.6 billion in the prior year, and its market value was down to $11 billion.[2] That was roughly equal to the market value of Sara Lee and two-thirds of the value of Electronic Arts, the computer game company.

How could such an incredibly successful company experience a three-decade-long decline? While we have all read many stories about GM's problems recently, let's go back to the start of that 30-year period and take a snapshot every few years to see what was happening and what we can learn.

## GM: The Vulnerabilities Begin to Emerge

As far back as the late 1970s and early 1980s, it cost GM far too much to manufacture a car. For example, the Japanese could make cars for an estimated $1,500 to $2,000 less in production costs than similar models produced in U.S. factories by General Motors. GM also had severe quality problems. It was reported by *Consumer Reports* in 1983 that every GM model it reviewed had a "worse than average" rating for frequency of repair.[3]

In 1983, *Fortune* magazine reported that the Japanese had an approach to creating high quality and producing efficiency that was totally different from GM's.[4] For example, when Japanese engineers began to design a car, they worked closely with the suppliers who would eventually be providing parts for that car. Consequently, they could take any constraints or needs that those suppliers had into account while they were designing the car. In essence, they were designing out a lot of problems before they ever occurred.

This was in stark contrast to the way GM was doing things. Specifically, it would get the car completely designed and ready to go and then go to its suppliers and ask them to place bids for supplying the components of that car. It was too late to react to some of the issues the suppliers brought up or to incorporate any suggestions they might have for making things less expensive and easier to produce.

The Japanese practices just described were common knowledge, and obviously GM's legacy practices and legacy people prevented it from adopting the Japanese approach. While GM claimed in the early 1980s that it was working hard to improve its production capabilities, it was clearly clinging to the past. At the time, a GM executive commented that the majority of the company's managers never really grasped the need to change their old ways of operating.[5] The comment by one writer at the time was, "Over-confidence dies hard, particularly in an organization as conservative as GM."[6]

## GM: The Decline Gains Momentum

By 1986, GM's problems were beginning to affect its business very seriously. Its U.S. market share had fallen from 48 percent in 1980 to 41 percent in August of 1986. While Ford and Chrysler were just about holding their own, imports, particularly those from Japan, were gaining market share.[7]

Anne Fisher of *Fortune* summarized the situation in 1986 by observing, "GM's biggest hurdle may be its humdrum styling. With a smattering of exceptions, the company's cars are unexciting."[8] Ron Glantz, a GM watcher with Montgomery Securities at the time, said, "GM's mammoth bureaucracy—layer upon layer of managers, departments, and committees—has had to approve, re-approve, and cross-approve the car divisions every move." Even its own people were criticizing the company. Chief Financial Officer F. Alan Smith was quoted at the time as saying, "for the forty billion dollars GM had invested in plants and equipment, GM could have bought Toyota and Nissan. Instead, the company lost market share. Something is obviously wrong."[9] The person in charge of Buick-Oldsmobile-Cadillac at the time said that the biggest impediment to change at General Motors could be summed up in one word: "history."

## GM: Serious Design, Cost, and Labor Issues

By 1989, GM's market share had declined from the 41 percent of 1986 to 36 percent.[10] The core problem during this time period was that the cars produced by GM were looking more and more alike. Financial consultant John Schnapp said at the time, "The differentiation that existed in GM's glory days has virtually disappeared." Six decades earlier, Alfred P. Sloan had driven the creation of Chevrolet, Pontiac, Oldsmobile, Buick, and Cadillac, which were to represent progressively higher rungs on the economic ladder of life. Step by step, GM was dismantling that differentiation. For example, all the subcompact models from Chevrolet, Pontiac, Buick, and Oldsmobile that were on the market were built on a common chassis and had the same mechanical components. Eventually, this

*Six decades earlier, Alfred P. Sloan had driven the creation of Chevrolet, Pontiac, Oldsmobile, Buick, and Cadillac, which represented progressively higher rungs on the economic ladder. Step by step, GM was dismantling that differentiation.*

approach was also used for Cadillac. While this gave manufacturing some flexibility, it forced the cars to look very much the same and, most importantly, drive pretty much the same. As Alex Taylor of *Fortune* stated in his summary of this situation, "Instead of developing unique cars for Buick customers, Buick engineers spent their time devising minor alterations in trim and handling qualities on a platform also used by Chevrolet."[11]

In 1992, Taylor summed up the status of GM: "GM must restructure radically if it is to survive."[12] The fiscal year that had just been completed saw General Motors lose an average of $1,500 on every one of the vehicles it produced in North America. Its market share continued to decline, and it was clear that the old Sloan model of distinctive nameplates was in serious trouble. Oldsmobile's sales had declined from over 1 million vehicles in 1983 to slightly more than 400,000 in 1991.

In the early 1990s, many of GM's manufacturing plants were generating huge deficits because they were running at only 50 percent of capacity. Unfortunately, back in 1990, GM's CEO had made a three-year agreement with the United Auto Workers (UAW) that required GM to pay its over 300,000 blue-collar workers even if they were temporarily laid off because of slow demand for cars. That behavior still exists today, as GM has job banks with thousands of idle workers.[13]

Those UAW contracts also provided a defined-benefit pension plan that required GM to pay retired workers for life.[14] The Japanese automakers used defined-contribution plans, where contributions were made to a worker's retirement account while he or she worked and the balance was handed to the employee upon retirement, protecting the company from huge pension liabilities.

Throughout the 1980s, Toyota had built numerous automobile manufacturing facilities in the United States, and, as noted by Reuters, these facilities had "more efficient manufacturing operations, lower benefit costs, and a mostly nonunion work force."[15] In the 1980s and early 1990s, everyone knew that GM's labor contracts were a huge problem, but GM went ahead and signed them anyway. Why didn't GM observe the superior model of the Japanese and make the painful, but clearly necessary, changes? It was stuck in its legacy practices.

Not only was GM ignoring the more efficient and flexible Japanese labor practices, it was also ignoring what companies like Caterpillar were doing, namely, abandoning the punishing UAW contracts and emerging with Japanese-style operations. Specifically, back in 1984, Caterpillar's CFO Jim Owens, who eventually became CEO, recalled: "The Japanese were killing us."[16] Union contracts gave Caterpillar minimal flexibility to deal with the natural ups and downs in its industry. As explained by Joann Muller of *Forbes*, "Caterpillar began spreading its manufacturing base into nonunion regions of the southeastern U.S., building 20 smaller, more specialized factories with lower wage rates" and flexible benefits.[17]

Naturally, these new Caterpillar facilities massively upset the UAW. Owens's point of view at the time was, "Well, we might as well get it over with now."[18] Years of labor unrest followed, but the eventual result was new contracts at Caterpillar's remaining legacy plants that achieved a 42 percent lower wage rate for new hires, capped retiree health-care costs, had employees share in the cost of health care, and gave Caterpillar the ability to identify up to 15 percent of its workforce as "supplemental," defined as receiving 30 percent less pay and reduced benefits. Stepping back, the obvious question is, why didn't GM take this learning from Caterpillar and apply it in the late 1980s?

## GM: The Organization Fragments

In the early and mid-1990s, GM was fragmenting organizationally and the legacy practices were clearly in control. Functional resources such as marketing, engineering, human resources, and planning existed in each division, with no coordination across divisions. Consequently, GM suffered from a lack of overall leadership in these areas. An analysis showed that less than 0.1 percent of employees were being let go for performance reasons, and no one was really aggressively tackling the problems.[19] In fact, a GM memo at the time said, "Our culture discourages frank and open debate. The rank and file of GM personnel perceives that management does not receive bad news well."

At the beginning of 1997, GM's market share had slipped to 30 percent. All of the same problems were continuing to devastate the company's business. As Alex Taylor put it, "Lacking unity and direction, the divisions became easy prey for powerful independent constituencies: suppliers, dealers, and labor unions."[20] The organization operated without any kind of centralized leadership of manufacturing, purchasing, data processing, advertising, or market research.

This lack of discipline hurt most in the manufacturing area. For example, GM allowed each of its truck and car divisions to do its own stamping of sheets of metal into body parts. This meant that each division bought its own press system, and consequently, these extremely expensive systems ran at less than 50 percent capacity, since they were serving the needs of only one division.

### GM: Hope Seems Lost

By the year 2000, GM was continuing to lose market share and, as Susan Jacobs, president of an automotive consulting firm, put it: "There's a lack of realism at GM about the company's potential in a crowded market."[21] *Fortune* described a core problem in its February 21, 2000 issue when it noted, "Few of its products excite anyone under the age of 60. It's practically a prisoner of its unions. It has nimble, more creative competition in Detroit (Ford, Daimler-Chrysler) and across the Pacific (Toyota, Honda). Despite constant reorganization over the past decade, it remains complex, bureaucratic, and highly politicized."[22]

In the fall of 2005, a full 30 years after the start of this long and consistent decline, GM's market share stood at a record low for that three-decade period of 22 percent.[23] While GM was hopeful about its new models for late 2004, the Pontiac G6, Buick LaCrosse, and Chevrolet Cobalt, these models were simply incapable of stopping the long but consistent slide. As Alex Taylor put it when he described those models, "They turned out to be simply too timid to excite consumers."[24]

> *GM went blindly along, producing unexciting cars and signing union contracts that were clearly economic suicide over the long run.*

In considering GM's market share, it's important to understand that by 2005, GM was highly dependent on sales to rental car agencies and to its own employees and their families. Specifically, those customers represented one-third of all GM's sales.[25] As you would imagine, sales to rental car agencies and company employees are the lowest-margin sales that GM makes.

Another problem was the fact that it took GM so long to redesign its models. For example, it took nine years for GM to replace the Chevrolet Cavalier with the updated model called Cobalt. In contrast, the Honda Civic was completely redesigned every four to five years.[26] In the United States, GM also suffers from having too many brands (eight: Chevrolet, Pontiac, Buick, Cadillac, Saab, GMC, Saturn, and Hummer) compared to Toyota (three: Toyota, Lexus, and Scion) and too many dealers (7,500 versus 1,422 for Toyota).[27] Those 7,500 GM dealers sell an average of 587 cars per year, compared with 1,617 per year for the Toyota dealars.[28]

To give people a feel for just how much confusion and compromising was going on at General Motors, David Welch provided an eye-opening example in a *BusinessWeek* article.[29] Specifically, when General Motors decided to build the more compact Hummer H3, it wanted it to have the same wide, aggressive stance that the big Hummer had ridden to success. But to make the H3 more cost-effective, GM forced the designers to use the same narrow platform that GM's small pickups were built on. This decision obviously saved some engineering dollars and helped the company get more use out of its pickup manufacturing lines, but it dealt a serious blow to the Hummer H3. Specifically, the engineers couldn't use the popular I-6 truck engine that they wanted to in the Hummer, and consequently, the car was underpowered. In essence, people were buying a pickup truck that was dressed like a Hummer. For most consumers, a test drive revealed that and dampened their enthusiasm.

For 30 years, General Motors watched Japanese car companies come to America and build nonunion plants that turned out distinctive-looking cars with world-class quality and industry-leading efficiencies. Over those decades, GM never came to grips with the enormous constraints that were put on the company by its rigid legacy practices and thinking. Besides having models described as "too timid to excite consumers," the company's inaction on the labor front was killing it. By 2005, it had almost 700,000 retirees and their dependents that relied on General Motors for pensions and health care.[30] Pension and health-care spending came to roughly \$2,200 for every vehicle that GM built and was the key reason that GM lost \$1,227 on each vehicle it sold in North America.[31] Year after year, decade after decade, GM went blindly along, producing unexciting cars and signing union contracts that were clearly economic suicide over the long run. It was clearly captured by its legacy practices.

# 2

## WHY DOES THIS HAPPEN?

When you step back from all this GM history, it is absolutely shocking to see America's premier corporation of the 1970s spiral downward for three straight decades. Joseph White of the *Wall Street Journal* summarized the 30-year period well in 2005 when he reported that GM's "current woes are aggravated by legacies that go back to their days when they were an icon of America's industrial power. The mindset of the old days persists despite decades of attempts to adapt to the new reality."[1]

What's ironic is that the former head of General Motors, Alfred P. Sloan, who really drove the company to its incredible level of success, is famous for saying, "Any rigidity by an automobile manufacturer, no matter how large or how well established, is severely penalized in the market." He wrote that in his 1965 memoirs, *My Years with General Motors*. As David Welch explained in a *BusinessWeek* article, Sloan was actually referring to Henry Ford, who in the 1920s refused to change his business model to build different cars that would suit different tastes in America.[2] Little did Mr. Sloan know that the comment would be so applicable to GM decades later.

The story of General Motors over the last 30 years is a classic lesson in how companies can be absolutely captured by legacy practices from periods of prior success, causing very serious problems in the business. After seeing this phenomenon year after year, I believe it is ultimately a human behavior problem. In reviewing hundreds of case studies, I have identified three destructive behaviors that are created and nurtured by success. These behaviors lead to the constant clinging to legacy thinking and legacy practices. They are as follows:

**1. Lack of urgency.** Andy Grove described this behavioral problem well in his book *Only the Paranoid Survive.*[3] Success seems to lead to the avoidance of any kind of stress in favor of basking in the glory of prior times. Individuals, companies of all sizes, government agencies, nonprofits, and education groups are all vulnerable to this kind of behavior.

Take Kodak. Back in the mid-1990s, it was the absolute king of the photography business with its highly profitable film business. Digital photography was emerging, but Kodak didn't pay much attention to it. After the technology started to get some press coverage, the company did launch a weak effort to learn about this revolutionary new approach to photography by developing and marketing a clumsy system called Advantix that attempted to combine elements of digital and film technologies.[4] Clearly Kodak was thinking defensively, with its goal being to protect its film business.

For the next six years, Kodak saw its business decline, and its stock price plummeted from $80 in 1997 to $30 by 2003. Management demonstrated no sense of urgency in grabbing digital technology and transforming its business around it.

In 2003, Kodak announced a 72 percent decrease in its dividend and revealed plans to invest $3 billion in digital photography. The stock market read this as too little too late, and the stock price decreased 14 percent further right after the announcement.

By late 2005, the stock price was $24 per share, and outgoing CEO Dan Carp, who had spent his entire career at Kodak, made an amazing statement. He said: "I saw my first digital camera 20 years ago. . . . I knew right then that this company was going to transform itself."[5] The lack of urgency in those 20 years was incredible.

**2. Protective and proud.** Success and stability seem to breed a loss of curiosity and a defensive attitude toward any kind of new thinking that is critical of the current approach. This is sometimes called the "not invented here" problem.

A classic example of this occurred at Sony. Sony basically invented and owned the portable music market in the 1980s and 1990s with the Walkman. If any company should have invented the iPod, you would have thought it would be Sony. Unfortunately, Sony was wedded to its prior success.

In fact, in 2005, when Apple's iPod and iTunes Store had clearly established portable music leadership, Takashi Fukushima, the head of the Walkman division, was asked why the Walkman didn't incorporate a hard drive that could store thousands of music files. He responded that hard-drive gadgets "aren't interesting because anyone can make them." It is a classic example of prior success causing an individual to be protective and proud.

Strong leaders know the importance of avoiding the proud and protective attitude. In 1999, Carlos Ghosn was appointed CEO of Nissan Motor Company, and Nissan was in deep trouble.[6] Between 1992 and 1999, it had generated $10.5 billion in losses and accumulated $19 billion in debt, and its worldwide market share had dropped from 6.9 percent to 4.9 percent. When Ghosn arrived, there was nothing exciting happening. Nissan had created some great cars in the past, such as the Maxima and the 300Z, but all that was left was pride in its prior glory.

Ghosn immediately tackled all aspects of the business. He restored profitability by 2000 and cut debt in half by 2001, and by 2002 he was getting some excitement back into the cars. By 2005, Nissan's market share was up to 6.3 percent, volume was growing 10 percent per year. For the fiscal year ending March 2006, it had $7.7 billion of before-tax income. His senior vice president of global marketing, Steven Wilhite, reported, "Ghosn functions as if collapse lurks around the next corner. He is absolutely tenacious in fighting complacency and the notion that we are in good shape." Joann Muller of *Forbes* notes, "He is fueled by a sense of crisis mixed with passion."[7] Clearly Ghosn busted through the proud and protective attitude that had gripped Nissan.

3. **Entitlement mentality.** Once you achieve some degree of success or stability, the world does not owe you lifelong success. Many individuals and organizations are so impressed with themselves and their achievements that they can no longer imagine a world where they are in decline.

A classic example of the ravages of an entitlement mentality is Digital Equipment Corporation (DEC). Its founder and CEO, Ken Olsen, revolutionized the computer industry in the late 1970s and early to mid-1980s with the minicomputer. This midsized computer was ideal for departments within companies and at long last freed division managers from the mainframe computer and allowed them to do their own independent computing. Because of this success, Olsen was viewed as a visionary and a legend in the computer industry.

By the mid-1980s, however, the personal computer was emerging, and it made the minicomputer obsolete. Olsen refused to acknowledge this. When market pressures eventually forced DEC and Olsen to launch a PC in the late

1980s, it was incompatible with IBM's PCs and died a few years later. Also during this period, DEC was slow in implementing reduced-instruction-set-computing (RISC) technology, and its commitment to the emerging industry standard Unix operating system was weak.

In the third quarter of 1990, earnings were off 83 percent, and the company's almost 125,000 employees caused it to have half of the revenue per employee as its competitor Sun Microsystems and two-thirds that of IBM. The stock price was $54, off 73 percent from its 1987 high of $198.

> *The question Gates kept asking was, "How can we ever truly lead this business if the most discriminating users think we are inferior?" This led us to discuss intricate features of Word, and the group hammered out a timetable for fixing those issues.*

In the face of all these problems, CEO Olsen made the statement, "This is still a growth company. We have always had strategies that are long term and quite different from the rest of the industry."[8] Olsen was forced out as DEC's chairman in mid-1992, coincident with the announcement of a $2.8 billion loss and the layoff of 20,000 employees.[9] DEC and Olsen are a classic case of an entitlement mentality.

Just to show that this doesn't have to happen to a successful organization, in late 1994, when I had been COO of Microsoft for only a few months, Bill Gates asked me to attend a product review for Microsoft Word. That product was in a major market share battle with the word processing leader, WordPerfect from Novell. I thought the meeting would just be a big love fest, since, in the past several months, Word had cut WordPerfect's market share lead in half, and clearly Microsoft Word had the leader on the run.

Middle manager Steve Sinofsky, who was in charge of the product group responsible for Word, led the presentation. He started out with a chart labeled "Low Lights," which I had quickly learned was standard practice at Microsoft and a requirement of Bill Gates. We ended up spending the entire meeting on that chart, which noted that while Word was gaining market share overall, it had made no progress in its user ratings among the legal profession (very heavy and sophisticated users of word processors), which was an area that WordPerfect dominated. The question that Gates kept asking was, "How can we ever truly lead this business if the most discriminating users think we are inferior?" At the meeting, this led us to discuss intricate features of Word that were causing the lack of progress, and the group hammered out a timetable for fixing those issues. I noticed that there was a "High Lights" slide at the end of the presentation, but we never got to it.

You would have thought that the amazing success of Windows and the major progress of Microsoft Office and Microsoft Word would have generated a euphoria that would lead to an entitlement mentality, but instead, the total focus was on consistent improvement.

Of course, even with Bill Gates's intensity, staying current in the brutally competitive personal computer arena is a constant struggle. There is no doubt that at times, Microsoft's strong focus on its core areas causes it to be late in new areas. This has certainly happened in the Internet search area, with Google jumping out in front and Microsoft hustling to catch up. Even in basic areas like browsers, where recently Mozilla's Firefox has been making claims of superiority and Microsoft is countering with Internet Explorer 7, it is always a battle.

# 3

## LEGACY THINKING AND BEHAVIOR CAN BE AVOIDED: TOYOTA

There are individuals and companies that have achieved tremendous success and sustained it. Let's take a detailed look at Toyota and see how it has avoided these problems.

In the mid-1970s, when General Motors was truly *the* U.S. automotive giant, with a market share of almost 50 percent, Toyota was a struggling exporter. Its first export effort to the United States was the Toyota Crown.[1] It fizzled because it was too slow for American highways. Being persistent, Toyota then started exporting the compact Corolla. Toyota was working hard during this period to improve the quality and reliability of its products because it wasn't really being taken seriously in the U.S. car market.

So how did this minor exporter of automobiles to the United States continually grow its market share for 30 years, here in the United States and elsewhere in the world, winding up with close to global auto sales leadership and forecasts suggesting that it will take the lead in 2007? The answer is a principle called *kaizen*. To the Japanese, this means "continuous improvement." Applying this ap-

> *All Toyota's employees are constantly focusing on refining all aspects of its business to make it simpler, more effective, and more efficient.*

proach to all aspects of the business, Toyota, year after year and decade after decade, keeps doing things better and better all the time. All of its employees are constantly focusing on refining all aspects of its business to make it simpler, more effective, and more efficient. This corporate mindset was explained well by Fujio Cho, the CEO of Toyota in 2004.[2] He described the continual push to improve everything in the following way: "Trying to pull a handcart up a steep hill—there's always tremendous danger that if we relax, even for a moment, we could lose momentum and be thrown to the bottom."

Such continual refinement of processes has led to incredible precision and masterful automation on the factory floor. You get a feel for this high level of precision when you read Clay Chandler's 2005 description in *Fortune* magazine of what goes on at the Tsutsumi plant in Toyota City: "It is a ballet of astonishing precision—workers fastening parts beneath a dashboard straddled on mechanized chairs that enable them to bounce in and out of the passenger compartment with a minimum of squatting and bending . . . robots guide air conditioners into optimum position for manual installation . . . an incredible engineering mechanism of coils and magnets lifts bolts from a parts bin in the exact size and sequence required."[3]

Toyota intuitively understands the risks of legacy practices. Teruo Suzuki, the general manager of Toyota's human resources department, said, "Our greatest fear is that as we keep growing, our ability to maintain the discipline of kaizen will be lost."[4]

## Toyota: Extensive Training in Kaizen for New Employees

Toyota was slow in starting up U.S. production. As its constantly improving export models became popular in the United States, generating sufficient demand to warrant manufacturing them locally, it cautiously entered into a joint venture with GM in 1983 to build Corollas in Fremont, California. Its biggest issue was instilling all the Japanese practices into an American facility. It didn't want to simply adopt the legacy practices of U.S. manufacturers; it wanted to instill the kaizen culture in its workers. This required massive amounts of training. Toyota made training its number one priority in launching itself as a manufacturer in the United States. There was a stringent nine-month training period for any management employee. It focused on instilling the culture of kaizen and continuous improvement. College graduates who joined the company spent their first four weeks working in a factory and then spent three months selling cars. They got a continuous stream of lectures from top management and plenty of instruction on problem solving and kaizen.

The amount of detail in this training is incredible, and the company uses this thorough approach wherever it builds a plant. Recently, *Fortune*'s Clay Chandler reported on a class of 1,500 workers who were being taught the excruciating details of how things should work.[5] For example, workers from Indonesia were practicing a series of deep knee bends holding a paint spray gun filled with water in order to improve their body painting techniques. They were also getting training at the cylinder insertion station, where they were practicing fitting a sequence of progressively larger metal cylinders into a row of corresponding holes. Few were able to complete the task within the required 60 seconds. The trainer, who could complete the task in 24 seconds, stopped the students periodically to show them how to position their feet, distribute their weight, and hold each cylinder to get it right. With that kind of detailed training, it quickly became clear to a new employee just how deeply kaizen is driven into this culture.

## Toyota: Relentlessly Driving for Efficiency

In 1990, when Shoichiro Toyoda was president, he launched a major effort to streamline Toyota's organization even further. He removed two layers of management, made major cuts in staffing, and put himself in charge of product development. He explained: "We felt we suffered from large-corporation disease. It had become extremely difficult for top executives to convey their feelings to workers. So we embarked on a cure. We have a saying 'a large man has difficulty exercising.' We wanted to recertify that customer satisfaction is our first priority."[6] What's interesting is that this campaign was being initiated in 1990, when Toyota was absolutely tops in quality, productivity, and efficiency. It was turning out luxury sedans with Mercedes-like quality while using one-sixth the labor that Mercedes used per car. Most organizations would have basked in their glory rather than launch yet another belt-tightening exercise.

## Toyota: Just-in-Time Model

The legacy practice followed by most car manufacturers is to produce large batches of cars to match some sales forecast. Then the automobiles are put into various stages of inventory, ending up on dealer lots to sell to customers. Not only does that inventory cost money, but you can also get stuck with large batches of models that have fallen out of favor with consumers. Toyota's famous "just-in-time" production avoids most of that inventory. Toyota car dealers use online computers to order cars directly from the factory. Thomas Hout, a vice president of Boston Consulting Group, commented: "Their system works like airline reservations. In placing an order, the dealer essentially reserves a portion of factory capacity. Rather than wait several months, the customer can get his built-to-order car in a week to ten days. That leads to savings all along the line. The factory can balance production and stay in touch with shifting demand; the dealer keeps almost no inventory."[7]

## Toyota: The Chief Engineer Idea

To avoid bureaucracy, committees, and clumsy coordination, each time Toyota updates a model, it assigns a chief engineer to oversee the task. This engineer has responsibility for everything associated with the development of the new model.[8] He makes the final decisions about its suitability for the potential market, its physical dimensions, how it is made, and who the suppliers will be. He even helps develop the marketing strategies.

This is far different from Detroit's traditional product development practices. There, the person in charge of a new model works to implement the plans received from the product planning and marketing organizations. This individual has no final authority over product decisions, manufacturing plans, supplier selection, marketing, or manufacturing issues related to the vehicle that is being designed. All that is dependent upon a variety of different groups that often use consensus decision making.

## Toyota: The Global Body Line

The first trials of an ingenious, highly flexible automobile assembly idea occurred in 1996 at a small, labor-intensive plant in Vietnam that assembled Camrys. Toyota called it the Global Body Line, and it is a standardized automobile manufacturing line where you can swap robots, change the software in the robots, and exchange people for robots or vice versa, giving you the ability to produce almost all of the Toyota models on that same manufacturing line.[9] Between 2002 and 2004, Toyota rolled out this idea broadly in its plants. For perspective, at Toyota's Georgetown, Kentucky, plant, workers build Toyota Camrys, Toyota Solara Coupes, and Avalon sedans on the same manufacturing line. Traditional automobile manufacturing practices would simply prohibit you from mixing models that way on a particular line. Where's the advantage? Toyota can add yet another body type to an existing line at 70 percent lower cost than the traditional method of revamping an old line or building a new one.

In a 2004 *Fortune* article, Stuart Brown describes how traditional inflexible manufacturing lines can lead to missed opportunities.[10] Back in 2000 and 2001, Chrysler's PT Cruiser was a big hit. Demand for it quickly exceeded the capacity of the Mexican plant where it was built. But Chrysler was unable to shift the overflow to its other plants, which had plenty of spare capacity. The PT Cruiser was based on the chassis of Chrysler's Neon compact car. Once the demand was clearly outpacing its forecast, Chrysler tried to move some PT Cruiser production to one of several Neon plants. Unfortunately, the PT Cruiser was taller than the Neon, and that size difference prevented Chrysler from using the Neon lines. This mistake cost Chrysler $480 million in forgone pretax profits, Prudential's car analyst Michael Bruynesteyn estimated.[11]

## Toyota: Great Products

We have discussed Toyota's constant innovation with respect to production capabilities, but it has been equally aggressive in generating great product initiatives. In 1989, Toyota announced the Lexus LS 400, the first luxury car it had launched. With a price tag of $45,000, this was the first Japanese car to compete directly with Mercedes-Benz, BMW, and Jaguar. It took the Lexus LS 400 only 14 months to outsell the competing models from those three manufacturers. Its conservative but stylish look coupled with impeccable quality and reliability made it a huge and instant success.[12]

In the mid-1990s, Toyota executives became concerned that the industry was quite vulnerable to environmental activists and to the political instability of oil-producing regions. This caused them to begin a serious effort to develop a hybrid gas/electric car.[13]

Toyota launched its hybrid product, called the Prius, in 1997 in Japan. Toyota's senior engineer, Takeshi Uchiyamada, commented, "We wondered if anybody would want one." Such uncertainty represents quite a risk for an automobile company. But, on the other hand, Toyota engineers kept the assembly simple so that these Prius cars could be made on the same production line as mainstream models such as the popular Camry.[14]

A few years later, Toyota began marketing the Prius in America, and it was an instant hit. Electric cars had been marketed for a few years in the United States, but not with much success. They had to be plugged in overnight to recharge them, and they had a limited range. That's not the case with the Prius. The gasoline engine kicks in when it is needed, and it also re-charges the battery while it's running. The Prius is an egg-shaped vehicle that gets about 50 miles per gallon and has been an incredible hit, particularly with technology enthusiasts and environmentally oriented customers.

*Toyota launched its hybrid product, called the Prius, in 1997 in Japan. Toyota's senior engineer, Takeshi Uchiyamada, commented, "We wondered if anybody would want one."*

It's another example of Toyota doing a thorough job of reading the marketplace and making aggressive bets even during its long run of success.[15] While the company wondered back in 1997 whether it would sell any, 230,000 of the Prius were sold in 2005, and the company expects to sell 400,000 in 2006.[16] Toyota stayed ahead of the market and invented a product before its customers even knew they wanted it.

## Toyota: The Marketplace Results

With the incredible success of its hybrids, Toyota is clearly viewed as the most influential global car company at this point in time. Also, it's the most profitable, as measured by total earnings. For perspective, in the fall of 2006, Toyota's past 12 months' income was $12.3 billion. The combined income of General Motors, Ford, DaimlerChrysler, and Volkswagen was actually a loss of $6.2 billion. In 2005 Toyota sold 8.3 million vehicles, and that figure grew to 9.0 million in 2006. This puts the company on track to be the worldwide leader in 2007.[17]

Toyota has stated its intention of being totally global, and it is continuing a very aggressive campaign to build cars on every continent. In 2004 it opened factories in the Czech Republic and China. It has plans for production facilities in Canada, Russia, and Thailand. Toyota now has 47 plants in 26 overseas markets (that is, outside Japan), a significant increase from its 20 plants in 14 foreign countries in 1990. Currently Toyota generates more than 70 percent of its profits from its overseas operations.[18]

Stepping back from all of this, it's a remarkable record over the past 30 years. Recently Katsuaki Watanabe, Toyota's president, stated that he views job number one as fighting complacency as Toyota gets bigger and bigger. He said, "I feel that being successful may make us arrogant and want to stay in a comfort zone."[19] Toyota understands the ravages of legacy practices very well!

# 4

## BEWARE OF THE NINE SUCCESS-INDUCED TRAPS

uccess leads to the damaging behaviors of a lack of urgency, a proud and protective attitude, and entitlement thinking. This leads to the tendency to institutionalize legacy thinking and practices. Essentially, you believe that what enabled you to become successful will enable you to be successful forever. After reviewing this problem in many companies, I believe there are nine dangerous traps into which successful people and organizations often stumble.

### TRAP 1: NEGLECT
#### Sticking with Yesterday's Business Model

By business model, I mean what you do and how you do it. It includes such issues as deciding what industry you will be competing in and what approaches you will use in carrying out all the processes necessary to compete in that industry. Will we manufacture something or contract it out? How will we sell our products or services?

> *You believe that what enabled you to become successful will enable you to be successful forever.*

Do we go through retail channels? How should we organize our sales force? Which segments of the industry do we want to ignore, and which do we want to compete in? What is the structure of our support staff? Which parts of the organization do we outsource? What are our approaches to distribution and inventory management? What are the cost targets of the various components of the organization, like information technology costs and human resources costs? Does our model leave us satisfied with our gross margins, profit margins, and other such figures?

Organizations should be consistently reviewing all aspects of their business model, looking for areas that are weak and need to be overhauled. By weak, we mean out of date, too costly, too slow, or not flexible. In which areas of the business model are you at parity? In those areas, are there any bright ideas on how to achieve a competitive advantage?

Let's consider Dell Computer. At the start, Michael Dell looked at the personal computer industry and asked himself if there was a unique business model that could be developed in that industry. Since the products are made from components purchased from other vendors, such as the hard drive, the microprocessor, and the software, he probably could develop unsurpassed products but not superior products. He also observed that all the personal computer manufacturers were using the retail channel as the way to get the products into consumers' hands. Dell believed that there was potential for a business model that sold unsurpassed products using a direct-to-the-customer sales approach and a just-in-time manufacturing approach, avoiding the costs and complexity of both a sales force and inventories. He was right. He created distinctiveness and uniqueness in what looked like a commodity business.

Southwest Airlines also built a successful company around several unique aspects of its business model, such as no seat reservations, buying only Boeing 737 aircraft to keep maintenance simple and low cost, having somewhat zany flight attendants who generate fun, and avoiding the hub-and-spoke model of airline routes. All of this adds up to a low-cost, convenient, enjoyable travel alternative compared with other airlines. Southwest operates with a unique business model.

The question that is always in front of Dell, Southwest, and any other company is: how can the business model evolve to increase customer and shareholder value? What happens all the time is that once a company becomes successful, over time, its business model ceases to be better than its competitors' and is only at parity. Then its model becomes outdated and inferior, and the company doesn't even notice. When people at the company eventually do notice, they can't seem to generate the will to change.

## TRAP 2: PRIDE
### Allowing Your Products to Become Outdated

You may be super proud of your product or service today, but you have to assume that it is going to become inferior to the competition very soon. You need to hustle and beat your competition to that better mousetrap, and you need to do it over and over.

The amazing thing about success is that it leads to a subconscious entitlement mentality that causes you to believe that you no longer need to do all the dirty work of getting out and studying consumer behavior in detail, analyzing different sales approaches, jumping on the latest technology to generate improved products, and everything else that is required to stay ahead. The attitude is often one of believing that you have done all of that and have figured it out, and now things are going to be fine.

Until the early 1970s, typewriters were used to prepare documents. The IBM Selectric model was the standard. Then along came Wang Laboratories' word processor in 1976, providing a completely new approach. It displayed text on a cathode ray tube (CRT) screen that was connected to a central processing unit (CPU). In fact, you could connect many such screens to that CPU in order to handle many different users. Wang's device incorporated virtually every fundamental characteristic of word processors as we know them today, and the phrase *word processor* rapidly came to refer to CRT-based Wang machines. Then, in the early to mid-1980s, the personal computer emerged. Wang saw it coming but made no attempt to modify its software for a personal computer. PC-based word processors like WordPerfect and Microsoft Word became the rage, and Wang died. Wang fell into the trap of not updating its products, even though it basically invented the word processor industry.

We saw this behavior very clearly with the General Motors example. Its cars, while highly distinctive back in the 1970s, were allowed over time to look more and more alike, and the excitement factor for the customer disappeared.

## TRAP 3: BOREDOM
### Clinging to Your Once-Successful Branding after It Becomes Stale and Dull

Constantly achieving uniqueness and distinctiveness for a brand and also keeping it fresh and contemporary is hard work. Once a brand achieves some success, the tendency is to sit back and pat yourself on the back, allowing your brand to become dull and ordinary.

The Plymouth automobile was introduced by Chrysler for the 1928 model year as a direct competitor to Ford and Chevrolet. It was a sturdy and durable car that attracted a legion of loyal owners. Plymouth became one of the low-priced three from Detroit and was usually number three in sales, just behind Ford and Chevrolet. For almost two decades, Plymouth sold almost 750,000 cars per year and had a solid brand reputation in the low price range of being reliable but having a bit more flair than Chevrolet or Ford. Older readers may remember the 1957 Plymouth with the huge fins, as well as its Road Runner (beep beep!) model. Plymouth had a very clear brand positioning.

In the 1960s, the Plymouth brand began to lose its uniqueness. Chrysler decided to reposition the Dodge, reducing its price so that it was quite close to Plymouth's. Chrysler came out with low-priced compact and intermediate-size models under both the Plymouth trademark and the Dodge trademark. By 1982, Dodge was outselling Plymouth. Throughout the late 1980s and the 1990s, Plymouth offered nothing unique. Sales continued to decline, while Dodge was quite healthy. In 1999 Chrysler announced that the Plymouth brand would be discontinued. The lesson is simple: when you allow brands to get stale, they die.

> *Maintaining a vibrant brand requires constant hard work because the brand must be kept fresh and vital.*

Success often leads to companies putting aside the arsenal of market research approaches and tools used to help judge consumer attitudes toward their products and those of their competitors. The attitude is that we have done that and confirmed that all is well, so we are beyond that stage in life. Maintaining a vibrant brand requires constant hard work because the brand must be kept fresh and vital. Achieving a successful brand can easily lead people into the trap of believing that they have figured out the way to market the product and the job is done . . . they can just sit back and enjoy the fruits of their labor.

## TRAP 4: COMPLEXITY
### Ignoring Your Business Processes as They Become Cumbersome and Complicated

Successful organizations often reward themselves by adding more and more people and allowing processes to become fragmented and nonstandardized. This is often done under the banner of refining the management of the business. It is also caused by business units and subsidiaries seeking more autonomy, which leads them to develop their own processes and staff resources. Before you know it, getting any kind of change made is very complicated.

Over and over again you read stories about organizations experiencing weak financial results, then finally coming to grips with the problem, laying off thousands of people and simplifying the organization.

We saw in our Toyota case study how aggressive that company is at constantly improving each and every process. Keeping that mindset of constant improvement is very difficult. Success usually leads to a decrease in the intensity with which you tackle such challenges. Also, success leads to a belief that since we are doing so well, we probably need to reward the people in the organization who are asking for their own building and lots of extra people to get them to the next level. Unfortunately, all those extra costs often lead to bloated processes and further fragmentation of how work gets done.

## TRAP 5: BLOAT
### Rationalizing Your Loss of Speed and Agility

Successful organizations and individuals tend to create complexity. They hire a lot of extra people, since clearly things are going well, and those people find things to do, often creating layers of bureaucracy, duplicating capabilities that already exist in the organization, and making it very hard to react quickly to change.

Getting an organization to constantly think about retaining simplicity and flexibility is not easy. The account given in the previous chapter of Toyota's Global Body Line is a good example of doing it right. Toyota thought about agility ahead of time, and when it came time to build a brand-new car, such as the Prius, it didn't have to build a new plant or a new line. This enabled Toyota to get to market fast and save tens of millions of dollars compared with traditional approaches.

One area where agility can really get compromised easily is information technology. In successful companies, the various divisions are often allowed to go off and build large numbers of their own systems. Before you know it, finding the answer to a simple question, like how many people in the company work in finance, can become nearly impossible. The systems become fragmented, and different data standards emerge. Then, when you ask a simple question or go to integrate an acquisition, it can be an enormous systems nightmare.

Keeping the systems and processes you use to run the organization as simple as possible and requiring that all the basic systems be used companywide can go a long way in this area. That enables you to implement change quickly and integrate acquisitions easily. However, successful companies have trouble following that approach simply because of the tendency to reward themselves for their success with bigger and more costly approaches that create complexity and a resulting loss of agility.

## TRAP 6: MEDIOCRITY
### Condoning Poor Performance and Letting Your Star Employees Languish

When organizations are successful, they have a tendency to stop doing the hard things, and dealing with poor performance is a *really* hard thing. It also becomes hard to move new people into existing jobs, because there is the burden of getting the new person up to speed and the perception that you are losing valuable expertise. Also, the really strong performers tend to get ignored. Consequently, what happens in many successful organizations is that people are left in their jobs too long and poor performance is not dealt with as crisply as it should be. Unfortunately, this also leads to strong players not being constantly challenged.

Successful organizations are especially vulnerable to this trap, since companies that achieve success often have high morale and pride. And who wants to spoil the fun by dealing with the tough personnel issues, which is an onerous task for most managers? Any excuse to put it aside will be embraced.

## TRAP 7: LETHARGY
### Getting Lulled into a Culture of Comfort, Casualness, and Confidence

Success, and the resulting tendency to become complacent, often leads organizations and individuals to believe that they are very talented, have figured things out, have the answers to all the questions, and no longer need to get their hands dirty in the trenches. They lose their sense of urgency—the feeling that trouble might be just around the corner.

Considering our case studies on GM and Toyota, the contrast between their cultures is really striking. GM seems to exude pride

> *You become very proud of your successes and protective of the approaches that got you there.*

and an attitude of "we are the real pro in the industry," while Toyota has a more humble personality that is all about constant improvement.

The leader of a group really sets the tone on this cultural complacency issue. The tendency is to become very proud of your success and protective of the approaches that got you there. It is those very tendencies that lead to an insular, confident culture that makes people believe that they are on the winning team, while in reality, the world is probably passing them by.

## TRAP 8: TIMIDITY
### Not Confronting Turf Wars, Infighting, and Obstructionists

Success often leads to the hiring of too many people and the fragmentation of the organization. Business units and subsidiaries work hard to be as independent as possible, often creating groups that duplicate central resources. Staff groups fragment as similar groups emerge in the different business units. Before long, turf wars and infighting emerge, as who is responsible for what becomes vague.

Even worse, the culture gets very insular, with an excessive focus on things like who got promoted, why am I not getting rewarded properly, and a ton of other petty issues that sap the energy of the organization.

Another source of turf wars and infighting is lack of a clear direction for the organization and slow decision making on critical issues. When these kinds of management deficiencies occur, people are left to drift and end up pulling in different directions. That often leads to tremendous amounts of wasted time as groups argue to have it their way.

## TRAP 9: CONFUSION
### Unwittingly Providing
### Schizophrenic Communications

When an organization is successful or stable, its managers often fall into the trap of not making it clear where the organization is going from there. Sometimes this is because they don't know, but they don't admit that, and they don't try to get the company's direction resolved. They do everything they can to keep all options open, with no clear effort to get decisions made and a plan developed. Such behaviors lead to speculation by the troops, based on comments that they pick up over time. Often those comments are offhand remarks that the leaders have not thought through. Or the troops hear conflicting statements coming from a variety of folks in leadership positions in the organization.

When employees receive confusing and conflicting messages and don't have a clear picture of where the organization is going or whether progress is being made, they feel vulnerable and get very protective of their current activities. In late 1991, IBM's CEO, John Akers, announced that in the future, IBM would look more like a holding company and that "clearly it's not to IBM's advantage to be 100% owners of each of IBM's product lines."[1] During the next 12 months, everybody was trying to figure out what he meant. And IBM made no attempt to start publishing separate financial information by product line in preparation for possible spin-offs. IBM also ignored Wall Street's suggestion that it create separate financial entities, with their own stock exchange symbols, for the products that were to be spun off.[2] Employees and investors were confused. The IBM board of directors finally ended the drama in early 1993, announcing that Akers was leaving and a new CEO would be hired quickly. From 1987 to 1993, IBM shareholders lost $77 billion of market value.[3]

Communications from the head of the organization, be it a small group or an IBM, are critical. People want to know where they are headed and how things are going. When the words and actions don't match, confusion reigns.

In the remaining parts of this book, I will discuss these traps in detail. In each part, I will give detailed examples of companies and individuals that in some cases have been hurt and in other cases have avoided these problems. My objective in each part is to provide specific actions that people can take to avoid the particular trap, or to rid themselves of the problem.

### PART I

# TRAP #1

# NEGLECT: STICKING WITH YESTERDAY'S BUSINESS MODEL

**I've seen it** time and time again. Individuals and organizations experience the euphoria of winning. But seldom do these same talented people and superb organizations step back, review all the elements of their business model, and confront the question of whether or not they are improving. Are they superior to their competition in certain aspects of their model? Are there areas where they are behind, and if so, how quickly can they catch up? What are the new technologies and ideas that could enable them to strengthen their business model?

If you are Toyota, you decide to enter the luxury segment of the car business, and you launch Lexus. You worry about how the environmental and political factors will eventually affect the oil supply and the price and availability of gasoline, and you invent the Prius hybrid. If you are General Motors and it is the early 1980s, ideally you replace all your existing manufacturing facilities with factories that copy a lot of Toyota's manufacturing and workplace practices and then charge your people with beating Toyota's performance stats.

When you consider how businesses in a particular industry operate, the thing that is so striking is the wealth of opportunities that exist. Dive into a particular area and create unique advantages over your competition. We've seen companies emerge as unusually successful because of a unique logistics approach, a superior customer services model, or a significant new capability that expands products and services in a particular industry. What's important is to be constantly challenging your organization to imagine a different world from the one you are dealing with today. And you must really probe your potential to create some real advantages.

In Part I, we outline several approaches and ideas that will suggest how to avoid the trap of simply sticking with yesterday's business model. The key point is that you must continually step back from your set of current activities and ask the hard questions. Has your business model become stale and routine? Are you are putting enough effort into looking for ways to excel in the various aspects of how you do your business?

# 5

# FACE REALITY, THEN AGGRESSIVELY TACKLE YOUR VULNERABILITIES

I t is very hard for people who have enjoyed success to face reality and accept the fact that certain things they do could be significantly improved. It goes against their pride and their self-image. One of the most important things an individual or an organization can do is to develop a mindset that constantly assumes that things can be improved and aggressively pursues alternatives. Here are some good steps to follow to figure out where things stand:

1. **Review all aspects of your business model**. For each component, ask what the best players are doing and whether you have an advantage. If you have been doing things the same way for a long period in a particular area, force yourself to investigate alternatives thoroughly. This is the kind of exercise that typically never happens. People get so busy executing day-to-day activities that they rarely take time to step back and look at the big picture.

**2. Be objective.** This is the hard part. People who have experienced success and are experts in their legacy practices see things through very biased eyes. It takes energy and hard work to start with a clean piece of paper and create new approaches to things that you have become accustomed to doing in a certain way.

Let's look at an example of an industrial giant that was almost driven out of business because it couldn't see that it had become completely out of sync with its customers.

# IBM

As we saw in Chapter 4, "Beware of the Nine Success-Induced Traps," in the early 1990s, IBM was an example of a previously successful company whose top managers were simply not realistic. They were clinging to the ways in which IBM had operated for years, and they could not imagine any viable alternatives. When the board increased the pressure on the company's managers, they claimed that there was no better way to run the place and suggested that the company might as well be broken up into numerous smaller companies. But they never developed a specific plan to do so that looked compelling. The board of directors ran out of patience and hired a new CEO.

When Lou Gerstner became the CEO of IBM in 1993, he ran into some incredibly entrenched legacy practices. While Gerstner describes these in detail in his book *Who Says Elephants Can't Dance?* there are a few that are so classic that I want to point them out here.[1]

The first thing that infuriated Lou was IBM's process of strategic decision making, which consisted of groups within the company forwarding proposals to the Management Committee, often referred to as the MC. When Lou joined the company, there were six members of the MC, and it met once or twice a week, typically in a very formal, long meeting with lots of presentations. Being a member of the MC was the ultimate position of power that every IBM executive aspired to. Every major decision in the company was made by the MC.

The difficulty with this decision-making process was that over the years, IBM people had learned how to manipulate the system to get issues handled. Anything that was going to be truly contentious was worked out among the various groups in IBM to finally reach a compromise consensus. The consensus proposal, which reflected these compromises, was forwarded to the MC for presentation, discussion, and final decision. By the time the MC got a proposal, however, there really wasn't much to discuss because the compromises needed to appease possible dissenters had already been made. Unfortunately, such compromising also dilutes the impact.

*Lou uncovered how confusing IBM was from a customer perspective.*

As Lou explains in his book, he hated this watering-down process. He believed that the industry was moving so fast and the technology was so complex that risks had to be taken. A committee process based on compromise was no way to generate big, distinctive, disruptive ideas that could have a big payoff for IBM.

The second thing that was driving Lou nuts was IBM's complex financial management process. The difficulty was that each group in the complex matrix of geographical units and product divisions had its own set of financial systems and budgets. It was extremely difficult to pull together consolidated financial statements for all of IBM. Allocations were changing all the time, and accountability was almost completely absent. All of this made it very difficult to find out the real status of various projects and, most importantly, to set specific goals and hold people responsible for achieving them.

The third area where Lou uncovered flaws in the business model was how confusing IBM was from a customer perspective. IBM's product activities were fragmented, and the sales organization was very complex and internally focused, causing customers to be confused about how to deal with IBM. Customers were very disappointed by IBM's lack of responsiveness, undoubtedly because of this organizational complexity.

## IBM: The Gerstner Strategy

Given all these problems, Lou had to make some very fundamental changes in the company. He knew he had to clean up the complexity and point the entire organization in a specific direction that would get it focused and lead to success.

Within six months of his arrival, he announced to all IBM employees via e-mail that their new role in life would be to solve the customer's information technology (IT)–related business needs.[2] Basically, his mission was to transform IBM from a computer company to a much broader technology and services company. He totally reorganized the company around customers, and he made a huge push to increase IBM's services revenue. All of this involved some very tough decisions, such as massive layoffs, the sale of some operations, and the closing down of several manufacturing plants, many projects, and several offices. The prior business model had become massively bloated, fragmented, lethargic, and crammed full of legacy practices.

Once Lou decided on the direction in which to take the company, he used every opportunity to make sure that the industry, and IBM employees, knew what to expect from the company in the future. While IBM had typically been a very low-key player at the annual COMDEX show in Las Vegas, where well over 150,000 information technology professionals would gather once a year, Lou delivered a key speech to that group soon after his game plan was unveiled. He made sure everyone knew what IBM was attempting to achieve. This very high-profile speech was as much for the IBM employees as it was for the industry. Lou wanted to make it very clear that the name of the game for IBM was helping customers solve their IT-related business problems, and he talked about this new model for IBM whenever he had an opportunity, either externally or among employee groups.

In helping organizations solve their business-related IT issues, IBM also got very aggressive in offering them the opportunity to have IBM actually run the computer operations for that organization. In many cases, long-term contracts were signed, and former employees of the customer became IBM employees; IBM then ran their computer operations.

By 1995, Lou recognized that the Internet was a huge opportunity, and he integrated Internet capabilities and themes into IBM's customer-focused strategy. The company launched very effective television advertising that made it clear that IBM had been rejuvenated and was focused on solving customer problems, and that IBM could help organizations realize the enormous potential of the Internet. IBM's very successful ad campaign of the mid-1990s was led by IBM's top marketing executive and a long-time Gerstner compatriot, Abby Kohnstamm.[3] The ads created a very contemporary, fresh image for IBM and linked it tightly to the Internet and to solving customer problems. That advertising did a great job of portraying IBM's new business model and was in stark contrast to the image of an organization in a downward spiral that Lou inherited.

Replacing the complex, legacy-burdened business model with Lou's new model had a remarkable financial impact. When Lou arrived in 1993, IBM had generated $16 billion in losses over the prior three years. By 1999, the new business model was generating spectacular results. When Lou arrived, IBM's stock price was $40 per share. By 1999, the stock had gone up significantly: it had split twice, and it was trading at $120 per share. Revenue was growing at double-digit rates.

When you step back, what Lou Gerstner really brought to IBM was a willingness to admit that the current approach was totally broken and that the company needed to move with incredible speed to jump on a new business model that could pull it out of its serious tailspin. Half the task here was admitting the problem and getting all of the company's energy focused on fixing it.

## IBM: The Next Challenge

In March of 2002, Sam Palmisano took over from Lou Gerstner when Lou retired. While Lou was in charge, IBM's services revenue more than doubled, to $35 billion.[4] But during Sam's first two years as CEO, global services growth slowed down significantly; it grew

> *One thing that happens in successful companies is that the parts of the organization that are running well camouflage the parts that are consistently turning out mediocre results.*

only 4 percent in 2004. It became very clear to Sam Palmisano that the business model might once again need some important modifications.

Palmisano moved into action quickly and launched two major initiatives. First, he introduced the concept of on-demand computing, where customers could forget about buying computers and could instead rent computing power from IBM as if it were an electric company, paying for what they used. The second initiative he pushed was "business process transformation." This term was selected to represent IBM's interest in actually operating entire parts of a customer's business, such as personnel or accounting. For example, in late 2004, IBM took over the personnel department of Procter & Gamble, agreeing to sell its services back to P&G at a discount and hoping to sell those services to a myriad of other customers.

At the same time that Palmisano was launching these two efforts, he was also doing what Lou had done very well: eliminating things that were simply not working. He led the effort to sell the ailing $9 billion a year PC division of IBM to Chinese PC maker Lenovo. He also decided to get out of the disk drive business, selling the business to Hitachi.

The jury is still out on whether Palmisano's initiatives will pay off in the marketplace.[5] But you have to give Palmisano credit for facing reality, realizing that things were beginning to slow down, and rethinking ways in which IBM could continue to be a leader in its industry.

Once you face reality and isolate those areas of the organization that are vulnerable, you need to launch aggressive efforts to fix those things. One thing that happens in successful or stable companies is that certain parts of the organization that are running well camouflage the parts that are consistently turning out mediocre results. Put another way, certain vulnerabilities in your business model get ignored because things are generally going well. Unfortunately, many organizations don't face reality and don't aggressively tackle their vulnerabilities or weaknesses, and in some cases, these vulnerabilities become very significant marketplace disadvantages. Here are two guidelines that are important in this area:

1. **Treat every component of your business model as if you were totally dependent on it to be successful.** For each component, objectively assess what needs to be done to create significant improvement and a significant advantage. The key word here is *objectively*. In an environment where things are going fairly well, it's very hard to blow the whistle on a weak part of the organization, or on a gap in your consumer satisfaction, or on a product trend that may do you in. The intensity for spotting these things and going after them is significantly reduced when you are lulled into a belief that things are going well overall and you are feeling extremely proud of that. It's very important that your people understand that part of their job is to spot vulnerabilities and to make a lot of noise in bringing them to people's attention so that you can take action.

2. **Once you uncover potential vulnerabilities, organize to fix them.** Don't be fooled into believing that the current organization, which is implementing today's strategy and processes, will put a high priority on fixing vulnerabilities. That is, at best, that organization's second priority. Whenever there is a belief that vulnerability exists, people should be assigned to check it out and generate better ways of doing things. We are not talking about adding the task of fixing the vulnerability to someone who already has a full-time job. That typically leads to disappointing results. Make someone

> have as his or her one and only responsibility generating significant improvement in the area where the vulnerability exists.

Let's take a look at some companies that represent examples of dealing, or not dealing, with vulnerabilities. There are unique things to be learned from each of these cases.

# eBAY

This company has been enormously successful. Millions of people around the world have signed up for its services and buy and sell things on eBay's Internet marketplace. Early on, eBay spotted the fact that a significant percentage of Internet users are reluctant to buy and sell online because they are afraid to provide their bank account number or their charge card number to an online service. Even though eBay's business was extremely successful right out of the starting gate and was a very dominant player by the year 2002, in that year it spent $1.5 billion to acquire PayPal, an online payment company.[6]

PayPal addresses the key vulnerability of people who are reluctant to enter a credit card number to make a purchase. With a PayPal account, right at the outset you inform PayPal of your established bank accounts or credit cards that you may want to use to make an online purchase. That interaction between you and PayPal occurs only once, and from that point on, when you make a purchase through PayPal, no credit card or banking details are revealed at all. You simply select PayPal as your payment vendor and indicate which account or charge card you wish to use. It already has your options for paying for things on file, and it executes accordingly.

It's clear that eBay hit a sweet spot when it acquired PayPal. By early 2005, PayPal's worldwide number of accounts had increased to 72 million. That's more accounts than American Express has.[7] Also, PayPal achieved that result with virtually no marketing. Today, trades representing about 75 percent of the value of all eBay purchases are settled via PayPal.

There are added benefits for eBay. Specifically, PayPal is now going out and marketing its services to other online vendors. It is seeing great success. Its roster of customers is very broad.[8] It covers the spectrum from small merchants such as Saylor's Pizza in Hendersonville, Tennessee, to large accounts like Overstock.com and Apple Computer's iTunes Store.

One of the reasons why PayPal is meeting with so much success is the fact that its economics are superior to those of charge cards. For example, when Apple sells a 99-cent song via the iTunes Store, it pays either 16 cents in processing fees if the customer uses a credit card or 9 cents if a user pays via a PayPal account. It's clear which service Apple prefers its customers to use. Additionally, the security halo that PayPal offers users has helped eBay. It now has over 150 million registered users worldwide, which, as the *Economist* magazine pointed out recently, is about equal to the combined populations of France, Spain, and Britain.[9] Those registered users are buying and selling goods worth over $40 billion per year.

You have to give eBay credit for spotting the fact that people are inherently uncomfortable about the risk of fraud on the Internet. Its aggressive move to acquire PayPal demonstrates the kind of thinking that organizations need to exhibit in spotting vulnerabilities or opportunities. It would have been very easy for eBay to sit back in the comfort of what was already one of the most successful businesses on the Internet.

## AGILENT TECHNOLOGIES

Another example of facing up to problems in a business model comes from Agilent Technologies, on whose board I serve. Spun off from Hewlett-Packard in 1999, Agilent consisted primarily of HP's test-and-measurement activities and its semiconductor businesses.

Since the majority of Agilent employees had previously worked for HP, Agilent took on the HP culture. Under the HP ethos, it was extremely hard to kill projects. Consequently, it was hard to do anything about businesses that historically had not done well and were currently suffering. The same holds true for the processes used to run Agilent. Another negative factor was that successful companies tend to be more and more complex every year, and this was certainly a characteristic of HP in the 1990s.

## Agilent: Big Problems

For the first five years after Agilent was split off, it suffered significantly from the great volatility of the semiconductor business. First, that business wasn't as profitable as the test-and-measurement business. Second, it had wild fluctuations, with short periods of success followed by disastrous financial periods where the market dried up.

To make matters worse, Wall Street financial analysts had difficulty categorizing Agilent. Was it a test-and-measurement company, or was it a semiconductor company? Unfortunately, since it was in the semiconductor business, the analysts decided to classify it as such. The analysts' logic was that clearly Agilent would suffer from the same kind of wild swings as all the rest of the players in the semiconductor business, even though about two-thirds of Agilent's business was in test and measurement, which was more stable.

The bad news was that the price/earnings ratios for companies in the semiconductor business are not nearly as good as those for companies in the test-and-measurement business. This depressed Agilent's stock price.

For the first five years of Agilent's life, the board and the management team struggled with this issue. There was a lot of technical momentum within Agilent that favored keeping the semiconductor business. Several of the company's leaders had grown up in that area and were incapable of imagining Agilent getting out of the semiconductor business.

## Agilent: Facing Reality

The wild marketplace swings in the semiconductor business in 2004 convinced Agilent's management in early 2005 that the problem had to be confronted. Agilent knew that it hadn't been operating the business as efficiently as it could. On the other hand, it also knew that even if it were successful in making the business as lean as possible, it still would be operating under the burden of being seen by Wall Street as a semiconductor business.

In early 2005, the new CEO, Bill Sullivan, tackled this problem with gusto. His team delved into detailed financial analyses of what Agilent would look like with and without the semiconductor business and tested the hypotheses with Wall Street. Sullivan and his financial team quickly concluded that the semiconductor business needed to be jettisoned. He was also convinced that he could find a good buyer, since someone could take the business, streamline it significantly, and make not great but decent money.

> *Your people must understand that part of their job is to spot vulnerabilities and to make a lot of noise in bringing them to your attention.*

That's exactly what Bill Sullivan and his team did. They quickly found a buyer, which happened to be a joint purchase by two private equity firms, Kohlberg Kravis Roberts and Silver Lake Partners, and sold the semiconductor business for $2.6 billion. Agilent then quickly turned around and used that money to buy back Agilent stock.

## Agilent: The Results

These two moves had a dramatic financial impact on Agilent. First, Wall Street began to treat the company as a test-and-measurement company and gave it a higher P/E. Second, there were significantly fewer outstanding shares in the marketplace as a result of the enormous buyback executed by Agilent. This resulted in the stock price moving from the low $20 range up to the $35 range by early 2006.

This is a great story of an organization putting up with a problem for a long time, and finally realizing that enough is enough. In retrospect, the steps that Agilent took in 2005 should have been taken a lot earlier. On the other hand, let's give credit where credit is due. Bill Sullivan and his team did a great job of isolating a vulnerability, organizing to tackle it, and then executing quickly. That's a recipe for success.

# SONY

Sony's recent problems with its consumer electronics area provide a good lesson concerning how success in some areas may cause an organization to be too slow in tackling vulnerabilities in other areas. While Sony made $1.5 billion in profit in fiscal 2004, that overall result covered up a $300 million loss in consumer electronics. Sony's motion picture arm generated well over $500 million in profit in 2004, and Sony's financial arm, which sells insurance policies and online banking services, almost matched that result.[10] Sony's music business contributed a significant amount of profit as well. I suspect that the pressure on its consumer products group was not as intense as it would have been if it weren't for the comfort generated by the other parts of Sony.

The key point here for Sony or any other organization is that all components of the organization should be carefully scrutinized for vulnerabilities, and acceptable overall success should not moderate those efforts.

Sony's new CEO, Howard Stringer, faces the big task of tackling Sony's vulnerabilities aggressively and getting its consumer electronics business back into the leadership position it had in the golden years of Walkman devices and Trinitron TVs.

Facing reality can be very difficult, as we saw in the early 1990s with IBM. It requires great leadership, which we saw Lou Gerstner provide. Both eBay and Agilent demonstrate the value of tackling the vulnerabilities in your business model, while Sony shows that this can be tough to accomplish, as it tolerated a weak consumer electronics business way too long.

# 6

## REAPPLY WHAT
# WORKS

One of the hardest things to do is to keep a strong focus on leveraging those parts of the business that are running well. The tendency is to leave those things alone that are working well. In fact, what we should be doing is broadening the impact of what is working and adding new but related capabilities. While a company always needs to be experimenting in totally new areas, most successful organizations, over time, have developed the skill to constantly reapply what's working.

There are a variety of ways in which this can be done. There are geographical expansions, line extensions of the core products, new distribution channels to be opened up, and new advertising approaches that can show users new ways to use the product, just to name a few. What is important is to develop a culture that constantly asks the questions: "Where do we go from here with what is working? How do we broaden and deepen the impact of what is working?"

Let's review an example of a financial services company that has done a great job of constantly reapplying what works and moving ahead in new directions to satisfy a yet broader set of customers.

# FIDELITY INVESTMENTS

This privately held mutual fund company is a terrific example of taking a core set of products and capabilities and constantly pushing them out in all directions. It has become an incredible brokerage giant. By 2006, it had over $1.2 trillion of assets in its customer brokerage accounts, moving ahead of Charles Schwab and beginning to be a serious contender to Merrill Lynch, which had $1.4 trillion in assets.

## Fidelity: The Magellan Years

During the 1980s and 1990s, Fidelity's business was based on smart stock pickers who consistently beat the key market benchmarks. When you say Fidelity, most people think of Peter Lynch, who ran the incredibly successful Magellan fund for Fidelity.[1] Fidelity was wildly successful during this period, but it fully realized that if it was to keep growing, it needed to constantly broaden and deepen its impact. Edward C. "Ned" Johnson III has run Fidelity since 1972, and the Johnson family holds 36 percent of the voting stock.[2] His philosophy is fairly simple: spend whatever it takes on an ongoing basis to constantly improve your technology and your customer service, and make market share growth the first priority and profit growth the second priority.[3]

## Fidelity: Broadening Its Business

Despite the bursting of the Internet bubble, in 2001 Fidelity launched a major effort to take better advantage of the Internet. This is a classic case of taking your core set of products and pursuing a new avenue of distribution for those products. The firm spent significantly to improve its Web site for retail customers and launched very aggressive price cuts to attract users. For example, Fidelity charged its regular customers only $8 per trade.[4] This big push to take advantage of the Internet had a huge payoff for Fidelity. In 2004 it added over 1 million new retail accounts. Fidelity's total customers at the end of 2004 stood at 9.9 million. That was 40 percent higher than Charles Schwab Corp. and 10 percent more than Merrill Lynch, even though both Schwab and Merrill Lynch were also very aggressive with the Internet.

Fidelity also used the Internet as a tool to become a major player in index funds.[5] Vanguard had owned this turf for years, but given Fidelity's huge customer base, it got very aggressive behind its own index offerings. It reduced the management fees on its index funds to 10 basis points ($1 for every $1,000 invested). It wasn't abandoning its core strategy of having stock pickers who ran successful funds like Magellan; it was simply broadening its strategy to compete aggressively in another very successful part of the business.

Most Wall Street analysts didn't believe that Fidelity would ever get into index funds. They assumed that Fidelity customers were interested only in the high-profile funds like Magellan. Fidelity demonstrated its agility and interest in expanding its core product capabilities by recognizing that there was a lot of money going into index funds. It didn't want to miss that boat. As Jim Lowell, the editor of *Fidelity Investor* newsletter said at the time: "This is the most aggressive I have seen Fidelity be in the last 25 years."[6]

As another example of just how aggressive Fidelity has been with its core products, in 2002 it offered its customers the opportunity to generate significant tax savings when they redeemed shares. If you had bought shares regularly over the years at Fidelity, and you then asked Fidelity to sell part of your holdings, traditionally the basis cost would be the average purchase price of the various shares you had purchased over the years. Fidelity launched a new service that enabled you to look at specific lots of shares that you had bought, decide which lot you wanted to extract shares from, and then sell those shares. Naturally, you would probably want to pick the lots with the highest purchase price in order to minimize your tax burden.[7] This is another example of Fidelity just pushing and pushing to make its core franchise all the more attractive.

### Fidelity: Geographic Expansion

Many U.S.-based investment services have attempted to make it in Japan. Even during the tough period from 2000 to 2002, when the Nikkei Index dropped from a level of 20,300 down to 9,800, Fidelity made progress in Japan. In fact, at the end of that brutal period, Fidelity emerged as number one among foreign managers of equity funds in Japan, with a 23 percent market share of the foreign-managed funds market. It had a ranking of number six overall in Japan, with a 5.1 percent share. This is a remarkable achievement in extremely adverse conditions. At the end of that wicked two-year period, Fidelity was also managing $6.7 billion of Japanese pension money.[8]

## Fidelity: New Distribution Opportunity

In the 1980s, Fidelity spent $20 million developing its corporate 401(k) retirement service business.[9] It lost money on this business for several years, but eventually got it to a size where it was profitable. This was a natural for Fidelity. It looked at its core mutual fund offerings and recognized that if it could create menus of these offerings for participants in 401(k) plans, its volume would really increase. Fidelity's strategy worked perfectly after several years of technology investment. By late 2004, it was the largest 401(k) provider in the United States. By early 2005, almost 12 million employees throughout the United States had savings plans that were administered by Fidelity, and this represented 43 percent of the firm's mutual fund assets.

In 2005, Fidelity recognized the fact that its 401(k) business was huge, but that it would be tough going as the baby boomers retired. The company realized that its core capabilities of information processing and call centers made it an ideal candidate to also manage a broad set of health-care benefits, retirement benefits, and payroll processing for other companies. Fidelity won major outsourcing contracts at Bank of America and General Motors to administer their health-care and retirement plans. The reason these firms went that route is that they could administer these plans more cheaply through Fidelity than on their own. Fidelity was leveraging its incredible computerized transaction-processing facilities and customer call centers, built originally to support the mutual fund business.[10] Becoming a major supplier to the human resources organizations in large and medium-size companies was a gigantic step forward for Fidelity in increasing the size of its opportunities.

With the huge success of the Magellan mutual fund in the 1980s and 1990s, it would have been extremely easy for Fidelity to sit back and rely on its legacy practices to keep it successful in the future. Instead, the company has constantly taken what's working and used it to push into new areas, while keeping its core business the same—that is, offering financial alternatives to customers in an efficient manner

> *Observing how work is done in another industry or by a competitor can often spark creative ideas on how to use those same methods in your industry.*

and leveraging the massive computer transaction-processing facilities and customer call centers and the expertise in those areas that it has accumulated over the years.

As people look to leverage what's working in their organization, they also need to look outside their company. Ideas often emerge in startling places. For example, observing how work is done in another industry or by a competitor can often spark creative ideas on how to use those same methods in your industry. Naturally, intellectual property protection is important here, and you need to live within the patent laws. On the other hand, there are many good practices out there that are ripe for the picking. Here are a few ideas on how to take best advantage of these things:

1. **Practice creative plagiarism.** Study your industry and other industries for what's working well. Challenge your people to carefully analyze how other companies operate, probing areas like product supply and sales channels. Similarly, on the product and branding fronts, become a real student of what goes on in the marketplace; look for new, creative things that clearly are having an impact, and ask the question: how can that be modified to work hard in your industry and for your product?

**2. Don't listen to the folks who are frozen in their legacy practices.**
Often ideas seem bizarre at first, and you'll get a lot of criticism from those who are set in their ways. The "not invented here" syndrome is alive and well, and critics abound
when fresh, new approaches that are somewhat unortho-
dox are first discussed. It takes a lot of perseverance to
push your way through that kind of feedback and continue
on the search for improved practices and bright ideas.

**3. Make it clear to your people what you are looking for.** They
need to know that you expect them to observe what is going on, not only in your industry, but in other industries,
and to come up with creative ideas, which often are simply
lifted from other companies in other industries. Keep an
open mind as the bizarre ideas come flying your way.
Dumping cold water on things at too early a stage sends a
clear signal that you're really not sincere in appreciating
real creativity.

Let's take a look at three companies that teach us valuable lessons in this area.

# NUCOR

A classic example of creative plagiarism that completely revolutionized an entire industry comes from Nucor. If you go back to the
1960s, the giant integrated steel mills such as U.S. Steel, Bethlehem
Steel, Republic Steel, and Armco Steel dominated the U.S. steel
market. Their total market value at that time was $55 billion, and
these companies looked absolutely invincible.

## Japan's Approach

There's an interesting story from U.S. Steel that took place in 1966.[11]
A guy named Ken Burns worked for U.S. Steel, and he was described
as a very ambitious financial wizard. In early 1966, he told his management that he was going to spend his vacation visiting several
Japanese steel mills. He cited the fact that those mills were suppos-

edly some of the finest in the world, and surely U.S. Steel could learn some new things from them. His idea was met with cold stares and obvious disapproval.

Burns decided to go to Japan anyway. He was very impressed by what he saw. Probably the most significant items were the new high-tech furnaces and the very efficient continuous process of making the steel and immediately casting it into the shapes and sizes that customers wanted. The Japanese skipped the steps of first forming ingots, then eventually melting down those ingots and forming steel for the customer. Burns was confident that with the streamlined flow in those facilities and the new furnaces, huge improvements in efficiency could be made at U.S. Steel.

Burns went back to Pittsburgh, talked at length of his experiences in Japan, and got basically nowhere. He was told that the Japanese were of no concern, since they had a very small share of the U.S. business, and if they ever became a force, strong lobbying in Washington, D.C., could restrict their ability to import their foreign steel. That kind of legacy thinking existed in all of the major integrated steel mills in the 1960s.

While what happened to Ken Burns has never been reported, his ideas represented a giant opportunity that was seized in 1968 by a small company called Nuclear Corporation of America in Charlotte, North Carolina. This company later changed its name to Nucor.

## Nucor: The Minimill Concept

Nucor developed its business model by cleverly plagiarizing on a number of fronts. In several industries, nonunion manufacturing plants seemed to work well. Also, the scrap steel business was becoming very significant and seemed to offer the opportunity to provide raw materials for a steel mill rather than relying on the complicated process of starting with iron ore.

In the area of furnaces, there were a whole lot of bright ideas out there. The one that Nucor jumped on was electric arc furnaces. These were smaller units, but they could handle the task of making steel with no problem. They did not have the throughput of the giant furnaces of the integrated steel mills, but that could be an

> *Dumping cold water on things at too early a stage sends a clear signal that you're really not sincere in appreciating real creativity.*

advantage because the capital investment required for these furnaces was very small, and you could place them in local facilities to serve a relatively small geographical area and operate very efficiently. Another practice that Nucor wanted to exploit was leasing industrial facilities at bargain rates from someone who had outgrown a particular facility or was going out of business.

Nucor put all of these ideas together and created the minimill concept. Its first mill was in Darlington, South Carolina, in 1968. Rather than smelting iron ore and using big furnaces, Nucor collected inexpensive scrap, primarily crushed automobiles, and melted it in electric arc furnaces. As the company began expanding, it continued to use only nonunion manufacturing facilities located in rural areas. This generated labor savings in the 30 to 40 percent range compared to the urban production environments in which most of the integrated steel operators were located. Each of the Nucor facilities was designed to serve roughly the three or four states that were adjacent to the facility. Nucor made steel in small quantities very economically. It began by making reinforcing bars, called rebar, used in concrete construction and steel joists used in home construction.

The integrated steel mills looked at this activity and concluded that they hadn't been making any money in rebar. That is no surprise, given their expensive cost structure. They decided to let the minimills have that business, which was highly profitable for the lean Nucor. Leveraging its success, Nucor and other minimills then began to branch out into rolled steel and continued to grow very significantly.

## Nucor: The Results

By the mid-1980s, minimills were growing at a compound annual rate of 15 percent, while the big integrated steel mills were declining by 9 percent a year. By the mid-1990s, the combined market value of all of the big integrated steel mills was in the neighborhood of $13 billion, down from the $55 billion of the glory days in the 1960s. Their employment, which had peaked at 450,000 in the 1970s, was down to 135,000. By 1994, the market value of just one of the minimills, namely Nucor, was $5.0 billion, while U.S. Steel stood at $4.1 billion.

Nucor has continued to expand its business, exploiting the business model that it constructed through creative plagiarism. In 2005, it reported sales of $12.7 billion and net income of $1.3 billion, and it was the largest U.S. steel producer.[12] In the fall of 2006, its market value was $17 billion and its stock price was at an all-time high of $54 a share, double what it had been just two years earlier.

Nucor is an amazing story. It borrowed practices from many different industries and melded them together into a new business model that revolutionized the structure of the steel industry. There's equally good learning from looking at the behavior of the big integrated steel mills. They basically watched all of this go on and did nothing. It's a classic case of being captured by legacy practices and believing that the way to make steel was the way they had made it for decades. These legacy practices brought the majority of the large integrated steel mills from being at the top of American industry in the 1960s into bankruptcy by the late 1990s, and it is a classic case of success being followed by failure.

## WAL-MART

Back in the late 1980s, when Procter & Gamble was working very closely with Wal-Mart, I was exposed to Sam Walton in several meetings. I was impressed with how he spoke at length about his experiences of visiting Marks & Spencer stores in London and studying their logistics practices. He told one story of asking a clerk who was working in the cut flowers area how Marks & Spencer stores always seemed to have such fresh-looking merchandise. He asked the clerk if he could go to the back room to see what kind of replenishment practices were in place. He wanted to know where Marks & Spencer's suppliers were located, how often they delivered fresh flowers, and what the ordering process was. Here was a guy who was already operating an incredibly successful business, but he was deeply curious about better ways to do logistics. Logistics is the heart of Wal-Mart's business, and Sam looked under every rock for bright, new ideas on how to do things better than current Wal-Mart practices.

# TOYOTA

Honda was first to the market with an electric car, and it really wasn't all that successful. The car had good acceleration, which surprised customers, and it was a very comfortable vehicle, but it was highly limited by the battery life, and that was a huge consumer negative. In fact, you couldn't drive the car more than about 125 to 150 miles before it had to be plugged in to be recharged.

Toyota took full advantage of all this learning and creatively plagiarized as it developed the Prius. It knew that the design had to incorporate a very convenient way to constantly recharge the battery with no inconvenience to the owner of the car, and that it should kill the project if it couldn't solve that problem. The hybrid approach that it subsequently developed and went with represents leveraging the learning from the Honda experience and a lot of engineering creativity. All along the way, there were many skeptics who viewed electric cars as a total failure because of Honda's experience. That didn't stop Toyota from barging ahead, continuing to work on the problem, and coming up with a creative way to solve it.

Studying and reapplying what works, as Toyota did with the development of its hybrid car and as we saw with Nucor and Sam Walton, is the hallmark of companies that are capable of sustaining success.

It is tough to constantly have to recognize that your currently successful business model may be on the verge of being outdated. There is no time to bask in glory; you need to get to work on its replacement.

### PART II

# TRAP #2
# PRIDE:
# ALLOWING YOUR PRODUCTS TO BECOME OUTDATED

**Great products** are all about unique, distinctive capabilities that are constantly updated and kept fresh. Unfortunately, there are plenty of examples of very successful products that have been left alone and allowed to drift into mediocrity because their custodians became frozen in the practices that they believed were the secret of their success. That pride in the victories of the past prevented them from keeping up with the demands of the marketplace. Left unchanged, these legacy practices and thinking typically lead to the product's downfall.

The Oldsmobile automobile in the United States is a good example of this.[1] The first Oldsmobile, made by the Olds Motor Vehicle Company, went on sale in 1897. The company was purchased by General Motors in 1908. For the next 60 years, Oldsmobile was the clear innovator in the auto industry. In 1901, it was the first car to have a speedometer. In 1926, it was the first car to use chrome plating around the radiator. In 1932, it was the first car to offer an automatic choke. In 1940, it was first on the market with an automatic transmission. In 1949, Olds launched its "rocket engine," the first mass-produced V-8 engine. In 1963, it was the first to offer a turbocharged engine.

From the 1950s through the 1970s, Oldsmobile had a very distinctive image built around innovation and its "rocket" engines. The styling of the Olds was unique. It featured a wide, "open maw" grill, suggestive of jet propulsion. Throughout much of this period, Olds used twin pod-styled taillights, again as a nod to its "rocket" theme.

This constant flow of fresh ideas paid off. By the late 1970s, the Oldsmobile Cutlass was the nation's number one selling model. In

*This slow, painful slide into irrelevance happens when management succumbs to those three basic human tendencies: loss of urgency, a proud and protective attitude, and an entitlement mentality.*

the mid-1980s, Oldsmobile was selling over 1 million cars per year, making it the number three brand behind Chevrolet and Ford.[2]

By the early 1990s, however, Oldsmobile was in trouble, because it had turned its back on its innovative tradition. It had failed to keep the design fresh and contemporary, and it didn't provide any new and exciting features that were unique to Oldsmobile. In fact, for efficiency reasons, it was getting very hard to tell the difference between a Chevrolet, a Buick, a Pontiac, and an Oldsmobile. They looked remarkably similar, and, in many cases, they shared the same chassis and drive train.

Bob Garfield of *Advertising Age* summarized the situation in 1992 when he wrote the following: "The Oldsmobile division of GM lacks imagination, distinctiveness and focus. Oldsmobile has no real niche in the automotive world. Their effort to position Oldsmobile as the GM division with 'intelligent engineering' fails because other GM cars have the same technological advances. Oldsmobile is left as a car that appeals only to the older generation and may be doomed as a separate brand."[3]

Oldsmobile never was able to shake itself out of those doldrums, and in fact, as Bob Garfield predicted in 1992, Oldsmobile was removed from the marketplace in 2003.

This type of slow, painful slide into irrelevance happens to successful products when their management succumbs to those three basic human tendencies: loss of urgency, a proud and protective attitude, and an entitlement mentality. These three tendencies brought down the 1-million-car-per-year Oldsmobile franchise.

So what are the ways to avoid these problems with your products and services? That is what the next three chapters are focused on.

# 7

# UNIQUENESS: AN ABSOLUTE ESSENTIAL

There's probably nothing more important in the business world than creating unique and distinctive products. Attention-grabbing, up-to-date features signal to the customer that the product is not only keeping up with current trends but setting the pace. When you are the first in a particular business category to provide a fresh, new capability that excites and attracts customers, you become the leader who sets the tone for the entire category.

With each product, there should be a steady stream of rejuvenations that create excitement because they are attractive, distinctive, and of high interest to the customer. Besides Oldsmobile, there are some tremendous examples in the automobile business that demonstrate the importance of distinctiveness. Let's review another auto company that seems to have a knack for creating unique and exciting cars.

## CHRYSLER

Back in 1996, Chrysler was clearly at the top of its game. It had achieved that status by bringing out some very distinctive and successful automobile lines. It invented the minivan, which was an instant success. It took Jeep and generated a new version of the Grand Cherokee that basically created the sport utility vehicle category. Both the minivan and the Grand Cherokee were successful because each was so distinctive. These were very unusual and unique automobiles at the time, and they became so popular that virtually every automobile manufacturer had to jump in and attempt to compete with them.

During this period, Chrysler was also riding on the success of the stylish Dodge Intrepid, Chrysler Concorde, and Eagle Vision. These were very unique-looking family sedans for their time, and they caught on quickly.

These distinctive models were driving Chrysler to tremendous financial and marketplace success. In the five-year period from 1991 to 1996, Chrysler's share of the U.S. automobile market went from 12.2 percent to 15.9 percent. Its revenue in 1996 was $60 billion, which was twice the level of 1991.[1] But this prosperity would soon come to a crashing halt.

## Chrysler: The Merger

In 1998, Chrysler merged with Daimler-Benz to form Daimler-Chrysler AG. It looked like a fantastic marriage. Chrysler had been making moderately priced cars and light trucks; Daimler had been making Mercedes luxury cars and heavy trucks. Chrysler was strong in North America and weak in western Europe; Daimler was just the reverse. Chrysler was good at design and product development, while Daimler excelled in engineering and technology. While Daimler-Benz was actually buying Chrysler for $38 billion, the two companies positioned the move as a merger.[2]

The next three years were very tough for Chrysler. After several years of exceptionally strong car and truck sales, demand for Chrysler's high-margin minivans and SUVs was cooling off, primarily because the competition was catching up and Chrysler was standing still. While losing its momentum in developing distinctive cars, Chrysler also was spending huge amounts of money on staffing and sloppy practices, and the organization was becoming quite fragmented. For example, it was passing up opportunities for economies of scale by allowing each of the different car units to line up its own component suppliers. To demonstrate this point, the windshield wipers on the Jeep and the Dodge Durango were basically the same, but the two car units bought them from different suppliers. The different car units also had different suppliers of corrosion protection materials used in the simple piece of rolled steel that reinforced the plastic bumper surfaces.[3]

*A former Chrysler executive said it very clearly: "We hired too damn many people." At the same time, the company was making financial forecasts that really had no basis in fact.*

During this period, the fragmentation was causing the company to add large numbers of people. A former executive at the time said it very clearly: "We hired too damn many people."[4] At the same time, the company was making financial forecasts that really had no basis in fact. It was telling the press that its market share would go to 20 percent by the year 2000, which was far above the company's historical levels. In commenting on this period, Dieter Zetsche made the famous quote that we included earlier in this book: "If you are very successful, you start thinking you can walk on water."

## Chrysler: New Leadership

All of this excess coupled with the absence of any distinctive new vehicles led to incredible financial trauma. For perspective, in the second half of the year 2000, Chrysler lost $1.8 billion and spent $5 billion in capital. When Dieter Zetsche took over as CEO during this period, he found lots of complicated financial projections but no thorough analysis of the company's strengths and weaknesses. He quickly moved into action, cutting 26,000 jobs, which was 20 percent of the workforce, and reducing the cost of parts by 15 percent. He also closed six assembly plants. This cost-cutting drive was led by

> *The biggest embarrassment during 2003 was that Chrysler's U.S. market share had declined to 13 percent and that the company had lost its 53-year position as America's number three car maker to Toyota.*

Wolfgang Bernhard, whom Zetsche had hired as his chief operating officer.

But the most important task, which Zetsche took on himself, was to get the excitement back into Chrysler cars and trucks. The company's strength over the years had been coming out with very distinctive new models that caught the attention of the public and were immediately successful.

Getting all these costs out of the system and coming up with brilliant new automobiles obviously took some time. By 2003, Chrysler was still struggling while it worked on the fundamentals. This was a tense time for the company because Zetsche was clearly pointing the organization in the right direction, but the fruits of his labors were yet to be seen. Arguments galore popped up in the press about the big mistake that Daimler-Benz had made by buying Chrysler. The market value of DaimlerChrysler declined to $38 billion in mid-2003, a far cry from the Daimler-Benz market cap of $47 billion just prior to the acquisition of Chrysler. The biggest embarrassment during 2003 was that Chrysler's U.S. market share had declined to 13 percent and that the company had lost its 53-year position as America's number three car maker to Toyota.[5] By the end of 2003, the company had generated operating losses of more than $4.5 billion over the past three years, and it really needed a shot in the arm.[6]

### Chrysler: A Very Distinctive New Car

Zetsche's plan began to take hold in the spring of 2004 with the introduction of the new Chrysler 300 sedan. Its hulking look, with small side windows and a massive egg-crate chrome grill, caused *Car and Driver* magazine to describe it this way: "This mobster in a pinstripe may just save the franchise."[7] Obviously, Chrysler had struck a nerve with its new 300 sedan. *BusinessWeek* writer Kathleen Kerwin wrote: "It has been a long time since an American sedan turned heads the way the 2005 Chrysler 300 does. Parking attendants give it pride of place; at a mall, it is a magnet for admiring men. It's clearly a guy thing. But even I, not enthralled at having to drive this behemoth, had so much fun with it I hated to give back the key."[8]

What made this car so exciting to drive was the incorporation of a Mercedes-derived independent suspension and the proven Benz five-speed automatic transmission. This caused the car to shift very smoothly, ride well, and handle spectacularly.

Another really distinctive aspect of the new Chrysler 300 was its pricing.[9] There was a basic model, with a 2.7-liter, V-6 engine, listed at $23,595. Antilock brakes and extra stability control were optional on this version. For $33,000, the customer could get the high-end 300C model, which was equipped with a 340-horsepower, 5.7-liter Hemi V-8. This engine was named for the rounded, or hemispherical, shape of the combustion chamber, and the design came from the legendary engine in Richard Petty's Hemi-powered Dodge Charger, which won 27 Nascar events. You could also add textured leather seats and brushed metal details inside the car; with these, the price would approach $40,000. The car won an enormous number of awards. It was *Motor Trend's* Car of the Year, and it even got very positive reception from the Ford lovers at www.BlueOvalNews. com, which was the official Web site for Ford fans. At that Web site, 46 percent of visitors rated the 300C as "excellent." As noted in *BusinessWeek*, Wes Brown of the auto consultant firm of Iceology said, "It makes the majority of vehicles on the road look like blobs."[10]

## Chrysler: The Hemi Engine

With the launch of the Chrysler 300, it became very clear, very quickly, that the Hemi engine was something very special to consumers. Chrysler ran some fabulous advertising to hype the Hemi engine. The TV commercials showed two stereotyped "hicks." Zetsche referred to them as "dumb and dumber." The one guy, who was obviously the owner of the truck, is basking in glory while the

*The thing that is impressive about Chrysler is that it usually ends up doing what automobile companies should do: it produces some spectacular vehicles that customers get very excited about, such as the Chrysler 300 sedan and the Hemi engine.*

other one walks up and makes the famous statement, "That thing got a Hemi?" Naturally, the owner acknowledges that it does, and the two of them start drooling over the car. As noted by Neal Boudette, the phrase "that thing got a Hemi?" became a popular part of the auto-industry vocabulary.[11]

While the Chrysler Hemi engine had been around for years, it had been used sparingly. While the Hemi added $10,000 to the price of a Chrysler 300, it clearly was a huge part of the incredible popularity of that model. Curiously, the Hemi was built at a low-wage Mexican facility, and it actually cost 5 to 10 percent less to manufacture than a modern dual overhead cam V-8. The Hemi had a single camshaft, while the traditional dual overhead cam V-8 had four camshafts.[12] Obviously the Hemi was a real profit generator.

Another really attractive aspect of the Hemi engine was its efficiency during highway driving. To help fuel consumption, the company developed a system that automatically shut off four of the eight cylinders in the Hemi when the car was cruising on the highway.[13] This feature, called *cylinder deactivation,* enabled the car to achieve 25 miles per gallon in highway driving.

In addition to the Chrysler 300 and the Hemi engine, Chrysler was also successful with its other 2004 introductions, which included the Dodge Magnum sports wagon and updated versions of the Dodge Caravan and Chrysler Town & Country minivans.[14]

By spring 2005, Chrysler was in high gear. The company began to offer the Hemi in a variety of other different Chrysler models, and Dieter Zetsche acknowledged that the Hemi was "one of the building blocks of the turnaround of this company." Besides the big success of the Chrysler 300 and the Hemi, about one-half of the Dodge Magnums, Dodge Ram trucks, and Dodge Durango SUVs sold by Chrysler were also fitted with a Hemi, thus driving Chrysler's financial results to very positive levels. Interestingly, at the same time, GM and Ford were in serious trouble. Standard & Poor's rated both companies' bonds as junk, and many of their suppliers were going bankrupt.

## Chrysler: The Results

The secret to Chrysler's significant turnaround, driven by CEO Dieter Zetsche, was summarized well in the *Wall Street Journal* when it said, "Mr. Zetsche pushed engineers working on new cars to give each model features customers can't get elsewhere, additions for which they might pay extra."[15] Clearly Dieter Zetsche understands the need for distinctiveness.

The financial payoff from all of this was huge. DaimlerChrysler AG posted an operating profit of $1.9 billion in 2004, compared with a loss of $685 million for 2003.

In mid-2005, Dieter Zetsche was named CEO of Daimler-Chrysler, so he added to his Chrysler responsibilities a Mercedes business that was losing money. By mid-2006, Mercedes was returning to profitability, but high gas prices were hurting Chrysler's SUV and truck business. Unfortunately, Chrysler didn't adjust production accordingly. With no unique new models or innovations that created excitement to counterbalance the problems, in the fall of 2006, Chrysler experienced a $1.5 billion quarterly loss. This was causing the press to revisit the question of the value of the Daimler and Chrysler merger.

But stepping back, Chrysler has truly been on a roller coaster over the last 20 years. Whenever it tastes success, it seems to go into a mode where it believes it will be successful from then on, and it gets sloppy with its production practices, hires too many people, and shuts down the innovation. This is a classic situation of legacy practices taking over once some degree of success or stability is achieved. The thing that is impressive about Chrysler is that it usually ends up doing what automobile companies should do: it produces some spectacular vehicles that customers get very excited about, such as the Chrysler 300 sedan and the Hemi engine, and it gains real momentum because of its distinctive entries.

The lesson from this Chrysler story is very clear. Consumers are fascinated by new, unique products, but organizations tend to lose their drive to constantly develop such offerings once they achieve some degree of success.

# 8

## MAKE
### WELL-ANALYZED
## BIG BETS

Every organization should be focusing on evolving its products and services to the point where it is clearly leading its industry. The goal should be to have products superior to those of the competition. It's that kind of leadership that typically generates market share growth and industry-leading profit margins.

To do this, there are some fairly straightforward steps to pursue.

1. **Figure out the next big thing.** Based on an in-depth analysis of your industry and its recent trends, the technologies that underpin the industry, and the activities of your competitors, you should be in a position to outline what kind of bets it might take to launch you into the leadership position in your field. This analysis should not be a part-time task for the people who are responsible for the current offerings. It requires some degree of distance from the going business so that the evaluator's thoughts are not influenced by the everyday concerns of the current business.

**2. Be realistic.** You need to be realistic about assessing the future of your successful businesses and evaluating the key trends that may suggest that your current products and services will become generic. Even worse, your current offerings may become outdated and be clearly inferior to alternatives that may emerge in the marketplace. Once you have a successful business or service, there is a big risk that your pride will compromise your ability to really think realistically.

**3. Be thorough.** Every angle of the industry must be inspected with regard to its potential and its vulnerability. You need to cover all bases as you think through an alternative strategy and gauge how successful it may or may not be.

**4. Allocate top talent.** It's vitally important that you assign your very best people to the tough task of figuring out how to get ahead in your particular world. This also demonstrates to the organization the priority you give to the task of moving forward rather than basking in current glory.

**5. Watch out for skeptics and critics.** You need to listen to everyone's ideas about what to do to aggressively attack the future. But you also need to be particularly sensitive to the fact that a lot of people associated with the going practices will come up with a variety of reasons why change will probably be very risky. What they don't dwell on is the fact that *not* changing would probably be even more risky. We will see in this chapter how Verizon's Ivan Seidenberg handled his critics.

**6. Ignore prior yardsticks.** The measures you are currently using to gauge the success of your particular product or service may no longer be the relevant ones in the new world that you may be able to create. Hence, it's important to carefully analyze how to evaluate things in the future.

**7. Be flexible.** You will need a great deal of flexibility to determine the plan that will put you ahead. Expect to change constantly with regard to what you are going to pursue and how you are going to pursue it. Incorporating learning on the fly is an incredibly valuable skill. Additionally, it encourages people to get moving and start making things happen, with the expectation that they won't have it perfect, but they can certainly make course corrections on the way.

Let's take a detailed look at two companies that represent good examples of making well-analyzed big bets.

# VERIZON

One company that is certainly facing this dilemma of making a big bet is Verizon Communications. Here is the setting. Both telephone companies and cable operators are realizing that as all media become digitized, the particular wire into the home that they control could be the source of virtually all of the digital services in that home. Specifically, that one wire could provide telephone service, television service, pay TV services of all types, Internet service, and a variety of other things. Consequently, if you are a telephone vendor such as Verizon, it is critical to judge the speed with which this will happen and to assess how you can seize this opportunity and become the leader in this business.

## Verizon: The Big Bet

During the Consumer Electronics Show in January of 2004, Ivan Seidenberg, the CEO of Verizon, described Verizon's big bet to everyone in the industry. He outlined his company's plans to spend between $10 and $20 billion to replace the century-old copper wire telephone lines to homes with up-to-date fiber. This would create an information highway for commerce, entertainment, education, health care, and much more, right into the living room. As noted in *Fortune,* Seidenberg described it as the "all broadband, all the time, lifestyle," adding that the industry was "at the beginning of a communications revolution."[1]

The reason why Verizon had to move quickly and try to set the pace in this area was the fact that cable companies were beginning to realize that telephone calls could be made over the broadband capabilities that they were providing to homes. There was a flurry of new Internet telephone services such as Vonage and Skype that provided, in many cases, free phone calls to anywhere in the world for any length of time.[2] All you had to be was a subscriber to a particular company's broadband service.

Given the competitive landscape, it was clear to Verizon that now was the time to make the big bet. In recent years, cable giant Comcast had been spending tens of millions of dollars to upgrade its infrastructure to provide its customers with not only robust TV offerings, but also high-speed Internet connections and emerging free telephone services. One big advantage that Verizon had over the cable companies was the fact that the customer service reputation of cable companies has been suspect for years. Verizon also knew that if it put fiber all the way to the home, its "pipes" to the home would be a lot bigger than those of the cable operators and consequently could provide much better capabilities to that particular household.

### Verizon: A Multifaceted Plan

Verizon has been very thorough in its pursuit of this big bet. For example, the company has launched a major government relations effort to convince the U.S. government that Verizon should not have to go through the very difficult and time-consuming process of applying for municipal franchise agreements in each and every community in which it plans to launch its new service. Current regulations indicate that the company would have to do that, and it knew that getting over that hurdle was a necessity in order to really execute with speed.

Verizon also realized that it needed to be extremely thorough in creating a set of media opportunities for its customers. That meant that it needed television programming expertise, and that's what it went out and got. It hired Terry Denson, an experienced executive in the video programming area, and charged him with developing the television service that Verizon would offer.[3] It was critically important to ramp up capabilities in this area quickly. If Verizon was going to compete with the cable companies, it had to be every bit as good, if not better, in its offerings to households. Given that this was a completely new area for Verizon, it was critical to get top talent put against the task. That's what Verizon did.

## Verizon: Criticism Comes with the Territory

Verizon's big bet has critics and skeptics galore. CEO Seidenberg has a great attitude toward these kinds of comments. He was quoted as saying, "In the early stages of anything new, management shouldn't be particularly bothered by investors who are skeptical about the strategy. Most investors only understand that which has already been done. They never really like things that haven't been done before. That's why Christopher Columbus had so much trouble getting financing."[4] What Seidenberg was reacting to was some of the short-sighted mutual fund investors on Wall Street, who were frightened by Verizon's spending between $10 and $20 billion on an effort that looked like it defied financial gravity for a phone company to achieve. Another financial analyst named Scott Cleland was quoted as saying, "Nobody in their right mind wants to take fiber from the curb to the home. It's a huge cost with zero benefit. You simply don't need that much speed attached to the house."[5]

When Verizon announced its plan, people in the financial community immediately went to work calculating what they believed the return on capital would be for such an outrageously expensive project. Given that most of the analyses were quite alarming, forecasting that payback wouldn't occur for over a decade, harsh criticism was launched at Verizon. What Verizon was betting on here was that the game would change. It wasn't exactly clear what might be possible in the future. On the other hand, one thing that was very clear was the fact that the game was going to change very significantly. Digital convergence was going to become a reality; it was only a matter of when.

Both management and investors require patience during periods of making big bets, as evidenced by Verizon's stock price, which

> *"Most investors . . . never really like things that haven't been done before. That's why Christopher Columbus had so much trouble getting financing."*
>
> —Ivan Seidenberg

has been bouncing around in the $30 to $40 per share range in the 2003–2006 period, waiting to see how the big bet will pay off.

This wasn't the first time that Verizon and CEO Seidenberg had made a big bet.[6] People had looked at the company's $52 billion acquisition of GTE in 1998 with great skepticism, but it turned out to be a brilliant move. Verizon was also criticized by financial analysts when it announced that it was going to spend $4 billion to create the highest-quality wireless network. It has paid off handsomely. Wireless now accounts for about a third of Verizon's total revenues, and, as noted by Roger Entner, then at Yankee Group, "By far and away, Verizon Wireless is the quality leader in the wireless market."[7]

## MICROSOFT

In the world of making big bets, few can match the size of the wager Microsoft is making with its marketing of the Xbox. The first version of this product was launched in 2001, and by 2005, just prior to the launch of the second version, called Xbox 360, the company had accumulated losses in the $5 billion range, but it had sold 20 million units and over 170 million games in the process.[8] Back in 2001, when the Xbox was first launched, nobody was more aware of just how big a bet this was than I, since, as chief operating officer, I had the Microsoft finance organization reporting to me!

As Scott Woolley of *Forbes* magazine put it, "It is a breathtakingly bold gamble."[9] On the other hand, Matt Rosoff of the Web site Directions on Microsoft had the following view of the effort: "Microsoft mainly got into these businesses as a defensive measure. They were concerned that Sony PlayStation was going to usurp what Microsoft sees as the PC's rightful place as the home hub, the gateway to the outside world."[10]

## Microsoft: The Rationale

The notion of the "home digital hub" is clearly the long-term driver of the Xbox effort.[11] This is Microsoft looking into the future and clearly forecasting that there will be convergence of a variety of digital capabilities in the home that will require a centralized control mechanism to sort it all out. While game machines are a good place to start, the new Xbox 360 design also includes lots of capabilities to manage digital photos and digital video. It enables users to share broadcast video. Also, it can become the household's music center, not only storing music but making it available to a variety of users in the household. It also has the ability to be the coordinating device in managing telephony capabilities, Internet connectivity, chat sessions and messaging.[12]

The Xbox 360 also has the ability to interface easily with a whole variety of attachments, such as digital cameras, MP3 players for digitized music, and video camera capabilities to enable families and friends to videoconference.

The supplier of these digital hubs for the home will be in a very powerful position to coordinate the variety of capabilities just spelled out. It will also be in a strong position to set the standards used by the providers of these services that will want to be recognized by the particular digital hub. This will give the supplier of that hub a real leg up in becoming an integral and necessary device in individual households.[13]

The launch of the Xbox in 2001 and now the Xbox 360 in 2005 clearly demonstrates Microsoft's view of the basic technology trends in the home and where key opportunities may lie. This is exactly the kind of thinking that needs to accompany such big bets. While Microsoft has been immensely successful in providing software for desktop and server computers, the Xbox demonstrates a sensible advance into a new direction that Microsoft hopes is completely consistent with how people's habits will evolve over time.[14]

## Microsoft: Assigning Top Talent to the Effort

Earlier we mentioned the importance of allocating top talent to the big bets. Microsoft certainly did that with the Xbox. It picked two of

> *When management constantly meddles with projects, often the assumption is that management wants to make the key decisions. So the leader of the project tends to wait to be told what to do. That's a real recipe for disaster.*

its seasoned all-stars to run the effort. Robbie Bach came from a sales and marketing background and distinguished himself by helping Microsoft Excel and Microsoft Word become industry standards in their respective areas. J. P. Allard is the Xbox designer and comes from a strong background in software technology at Microsoft. The whole company immediately knew that this was an important effort because of the two individuals who were put in the two key Xbox jobs when the effort was first launched back in 2001.

Another important element of this project was the fact that Bach and Allard were totally empowered. The two were clearly given all the responsibility they needed to make this thing a success. There was no meddling from the top. For example, in October of 2003, Bach and Allard got together with Bill Gates, the chief software architect of Microsoft, and Steve Ballmer, the CEO, and hashed out the basic design of the next Xbox. After the meeting, they went away and carefully distilled all of the details of the plan into a three-page summary, which they worked out with Gates and Ballmer. Once agreement had been achieved, it was up to Bach and Allard to make it happen. To make a project successful, the people in charge need to know that making it happen is their responsibility. When management constantly meddles with projects, often the assumption is that management wants to make the key decisions, and so the leader of the project tends to sit back and wait to be told what to do. That's a real recipe for disaster.

Even though Microsoft has accumulated losses in the $5 billion range to date, the new Xbox 360, launched in 2005, will continue to lose money—an estimated $100 or more for every box. On the other hand, Microsoft is confident that eventually homes will need a device that handles all of the various digital services they will be using, and it is confident enough in that future to make what is, by any standard, a gigantic bet.

Big bets are essential in order to achieve the kind of market leadership that companies want. While the lesson from Verizon and Microsoft Xbox shows how important well-analyzed big bets are, it is also important to realize that once top management places its bet, all the legacy thinking that exists in an organization will favor the status quo and will work to slow down efforts to reconfigure the business for the future.

# 9

# CONTINUALLY REVITALIZE YOUR CORE PRODUCTS AND CAPITALIZE ON INFLECTION POINTS

Once one of your products is out in the marketplace and enjoying some success, the tendency will be to leave it alone, and to start doing some new and very different things. That's when legacy practices take over and start to build defenses against change. This further drives the organization in various random directions, while leaving its core products alone. You need to take the following kind of steps to avoid losing focus on your core products:

1. **Always be improving your core products.** Whether it is a product or a service that you are selling, you need to constantly put creative people to the task of making it better. I was absolutely blown away when I joined Procter & Gamble's R&D division and learned of the large number of chemists and chemical engineers who were working solely on improving the chemical formulations for getting dirt out of clothes. The target was to make the company's current for-

mulations obsolete. For your core products, the goal is always better, cheaper, and category superiority. That is job number one.

**2. Never end up in a parity situation.** There's nothing worse than being caught in an industry where all of the products are basically the same and competition boils down to a slugfest around price. Creativity needs to be applied to your core products and services on a regular basis to make sure that they have unique capabilities and advantages that your competition is not providing.

**3. Don't spread your efforts too thin.** A real deathblow to innovation in your core products is to have your focus get too fragmented by too many other projects. This happens all the time in organizations, and lack of focus usually leads to mediocrity. It's OK to do some other things, but don't ever take your eye off your primary task of improving your core products.

Let's take a look at a company that was riding a wave of success, causing it to dive into too many new and unproductive areas. Fortunately, a new leader saw the problem; the company regrouped and refocused on its core efforts, and it was rewarded handsomely.

# TEXAS INSTRUMENTS

In 1995, Texas Instruments was truly at the top of its game. Its big losses in the early 1990s were behind it, and it was regularly beating Wall Street's estimates. It was the leading manufacturer of high-volume memory chips as well as technologically advanced proprietary chips.[1]

## Texas Instruments: Diluting Its Efforts

In the mid-1990s, Texas Instruments was launching numerous efforts to get into a variety of new businesses. This diluted its focus on its main chip business, but it was shielded by its overall success. The company was spending an enormous amount of time probing possible product initiatives in military electronics, notebook computers, and printers.[2] In doing so, it was short-changing one product area that was absolutely core to its business, namely digital signal processing (DSP) chips. A DSP chip performs high-speed computations on information, and these chips are used in a variety of products, such as disk drives, modems, and cellular phones.

When Tom Engibous became CEO of Texas Instruments in mid-1996, he realized that the company was suffering from a serious lack of focus. Tom knew that to really perform, Texas Instruments simply had to figure out what its core products were and then focus on those products and constantly improve them until it was the leader in each of these particular fields.

## Texas Instruments: The Cleanup

During the period between his appointment as CEO in 1996 and late 1999, Engibous sold off 14 businesses and focused primarily on two areas: digital signal processors and analog chips.[3] These were two of the semiconductor industry's fastest-growing segments, and they were the two core product areas of Texas Instruments.

As noted earlier, a digital signal processor from Texas Instruments can be programmed to do a variety of things. For instance, with a digital camera, DSPs allow the camera to have virtually no shot-to-shot delays. They are also the tool that enables you to produce extremely high-quality pictures. In laser printers, DSPs reduce the time it takes to print a page. In tiny digital speakers, DSPs mimic a wide range of tweeters and woofers, and can create unique sounds.

The genius of the Texas Instrument DSP is the fact that it is programmable via software, so that the same chip can do a multitude of things; all it needs is different software. That is to say, the DSP in a cell phone can be the same chip as the DSP in a digital camera. The only thing that differentiates the two is that they are programmed to do different tasks.

Texas Instruments' other core area, which was quite different from DSPs but very complementary, was analog chips. These chips take measurable physical entities such as sound, pressure, or temperature and convert them to the digital ones and zeros of computer language.

As one example of just how focused TI became on keeping its core DSP business vital, it worked to train as many engineers as possible how to program its DSP chip. Specifically, it provided engineering professors at more than 900 universities with assistance in teaching students how to program the software for a Texas Instruments DSP.[4] Several thousand students each year take courses in which they are trained to program these chips. This is a unique approach to making sure that the company's core product line of DSP chips remains vital and healthy in the future.

In a *Fortune* article in 1999, Doug Rasor, TI's head of emerging DSP businesses, said, "We really do believe DSP's will show up in all kinds of places that are hard to predict. So we are trying to cast the widest net possible."[5] Texas Instruments was doing good business with its DSPs in a broad variety of applications, such as Internet audio, digital cameras, printers, Internet telephony, digital speakers, handheld information appliances, electric motor controls, and wireless networking equipment.

The financial rewards from this cleanup between 1996 and 1999 were huge. The stock price went from $8 a share to $60 a share in those three years.

## Texas Instruments: Tough Times

The bursting of the Internet bubble in the year 2000 hurt TI badly, but not as badly as many other companies with which it competed. Its highly preferred products continued to be used by its customers; it was just that its customers' businesses were soft. Most importantly, during this period, Texas Instruments maintained its research and development investment, cut any fat that it saw in its organization, and improved its manufacturing processes.

In late 2002, Tom Engibous did an interview with *BusinessWeek* in which he was asked about his dedication to his core product line, given the brutal nature of the markets during the bursting of the Internet bubble.[6] His response was, "The foremost thing that we are

> *For your core products, the goal is always better, cheaper, and category superiority.*

doing during this downturn is we are not slowing our R&D investment. Meanwhile, a number of our competitors have had to make significant cuts in their R&D budgets. I believe that if we invest in certain areas, such as wireless, broadband, high performance analog products, and high performance digital signal processing products, we will be paid back handsomely over the next two to five years."

By the end of 2003, Texas Instruments was beginning to really shake off the bursting of the Internet bubble and get rolling. In the latter part of 2003, its revenues were growing 13 percent per year, and its profits were increasing 23 percent per year.[7] Analysts were predicting continued growth for Texas Instruments, given that its two core product lines, digital signal processors and analog processors, had become so important in such a broad variety of products, such as PCs, cell phones, digital cameras, MP3 players, and auto navigation systems. That growth prediction became reality, and by the fall of 2006, TI's stock was at $33 per share, double the $16 a share level of early 2003.

When you step back, what Tom Engibous did at Texas Instruments was fairly simple. He focused very tightly on two core product areas, digital signal processors and analog processors, relentlessly looked for new applications for those products, and worked closely with a broad set of segments of the consumer electronics industry in making sure that it was TI's DSPs that were going into these companies' products. Training all those engineers on how to program TI's DSP chips, keeping the focus on staying at the leading edge of DSP technology, and continually fostering new customer applications in emerging consumer electronics categories has been a powerful strategy for Texas Instruments. It also provides a good lesson on the value of constant focus on improving and expanding your core products.

For successful organizations to remain on top, it is critical that they beat their competitors in seizing important marketplace and technology inflection points and trends that can clearly make a difference in their industry. You see this over and over again when established companies get embarrassed by some newcomer emerging with bright new ideas that capitalize on important trends. Here are some tips that can help to make sure that your organization doesn't miss those key opportunities:

1. **The people who are responsible for the current business are typically not adequately sensitive to future trends.** These individuals are busy running today's business, and, most importantly, they have probably developed a set of legacy practices that they have relied on heavily over the years to get to their current level of success. Consequently, they are very wedded to those practices. Their ability to imagine a business model based on a technology or a trend that could wipe them out is greatly compromised.

2. **Organize to create objective assessments of future trends.** It's imperative to have individuals in the organization whose only responsibility is analyzing where the world is going and understanding what that means for the current business. It's important that the managers of these folks make it clear that this group must start with a clean sheet of paper and not make any compromising decisions about what it thinks management wants. The group's members have to know that their job is to seek the truth about what will be coming in the future, regardless of what this says about the current business or the thinking of the people currently running the organization. You need smart, strong-willed people to do this well.

3. **Inflection points come in many forms, so you need a broad perspective.** For example, tax structures can be important. We are seeing dramatic change in the timber business as a result of the advantaged tax situation of real estate investment

> trusts (REITs). The REIT organizational structure has significant advantages over your classical wood products and timber company. In the area of raw materials, an obvious example is the sudden increase in the cost of oil and gas, which may make certain approaches prohibitively expensive or open the door for other opportunities. Technology can bring about all kinds of changes in thinking. A good example here is digital photography and what it has done to the film business in recent years.

Taking action when you begin to sense an inflection point is coming often requires some serious risk taking. It is often difficult to forecast the future with adequate certainty, so you need to use some judgment. Here is a good example of that.

## TOYOTA

As I mentioned in Chapter 3, "Legacy Thinking and Behavior Can Be Avoided," the Toyota Prius has been an incredible success, and it represents an interesting example of a company seeing and understanding key trends and taking early action. Jeffrey Liker describes the emergence of the Prius in *The Toyota Way*.[8] The book goes back to 1993, when Toyota Chairman Eiji Toyoda selected Executive Vice President of R&D Yoshiro Kimbara to lead a small group of upstream engineers and charged them with developing a car for the twenty-first century. The members of that group developed a belief that there would be ever-increasing pressure on gas and oil prices, and they proposed a small, fuel-efficient car for the time when gasoline would be multiples of its current price. They fundamentally believed that the eventual emergence of China and India as industrial powers would put tremendous pressure on the global oil supply. In addition, their bet was that in some countries, minimum thresholds of gasoline consumption per car would be legislated for environmental reasons. These were risky judgments, but the group members were confident that these inflection points would occur; they just didn't know when.

## Toyota: Organizing the Effort

These concerns were taken to the Toyota top management team, which decided to organize to see whether the opportunity was real. It assigned as lead engineer a strong performer by the name of Satoshi Ogiso, who was 32 years old. His job was to develop an objective assessment of whether this looked like a good opportunity and, if so, to recommend that a team be pulled together around a design that would put Toyota way ahead if these trends became a reality.

*Taking action when you begin to sense an inflection point is coming may often require some serious risk taking.*

As they say, the rest is history. Ogiso came back to the management team after a few months and convinced them that the inflection point and the related opportunity were going to emerge in the years to come. Ogiso believed that Toyota had technology that could utilize electricity to power a car, but the battery would be replenished when needed through the use of a small gasoline engine in the same vehicle, so that the battery did not have to be plugged in at night; a critical issue that we mentioned in Chapter 3.

At this juncture a chief engineer was named, Takeshi Uchiyamada. The role of chief engineer is a very powerful one at Toyota. This person is completely responsible for making the effort a success from all perspectives: design, engineering, cost, and performance. The chief engineer recommended that a small group of highly talented Toyota professionals be pulled out of their current responsibilities and assigned to the Prius project to confirm the design. The Toyota management agreed, and off the group went to develop the Prius. As we saw in Chapter 3, it emerged as a huge success.

This is a great story that really underscores the key points we mentioned earlier. Toyota anticipated a key inflection point, namely, the increasing cost of a key raw material, gasoline. Realizing that the current structure of the organization would probably not do the idea justice, it assigned top talent to the project in order to gauge its potential impact and then subsequently staffed the effort with really strong individuals. It really is a classic case of running your current business well and, separately, anticipating an important trend and staffing it with good people to make sure it gets properly checked out.

# ENCANA

Another example of jumping on important trends early comes from the EnCana Corporation. This company was formed in 2002 through the merger of Alberta Energy Company and PanCanadian Energy Corp. Since the year 2000, this organization has been investing in thousands of acres of land in Canada that it believed were rich in hard-to-extract gas and oil. Basically, it was betting that the price of oil would continue to rise and that eventually it would get to the point where it would be economical to incur the high cost of getting gas and oil from hard-to-process heavy crude, bitumen, and oil sand. This effort was under the direction of Gwyn Morgan, a petroleum engineer who had worked for Alberta Energy and then joined EnCana with the merger.

An enormous amount of land in Canada was amassed by this Calgary-based company. Given the upswing in oil and gas prices over the last several years, EnCana has taken full advantage of its somewhat speculative land purchases to become the largest natural gas producer in North America, surpassing both Exxon Mobil Corporation and BP PLC.

Roger Biemans, the president of EnCana at the time, described the situation very succinctly: "We're not discovering new resources, but finding a way to commercially exploit resources that were considered uneconomical."[9] Basically, gas that was easy to harvest has long since been harvested by traditional drilling techniques. EnCana based its bet on the fact that there are many smaller pockets of gas and oil captured in dense geological formations that require rock to be fractured and the gas to be pressured out.

In preparation for taking advantage of this opportunity, EnCana developed a variety of new approaches to get at hard-to-harvest oil and gas. For example, it has well-drilling procedures that drill down and then go out sideways at various depths, creating a structure that basically looks like the roots of a tree.

Not only did EnCana prepare well for this inflection point with its well-drilling procedures but the scale of its effort is unmatched. The company acquired an enormous amount of land. Specifically, En-Cana owns 40 million acres of land in North America that runs from as far north as the Canadian North-west Territories all the way down to Texas. Also, it has more active wells than any other company in North America. Specifically, it has about 5,000 wells, and this helps it achieve unique economies of scale.

*EnCana acquired an enormous amount of land. It's a great example of thinking about the future and organizing to play a leadership role in it.*

EnCana has been rewarded financially for its foresightedness. Since 2002, its annual revenues have almost tripled, moving from $5.9 billion to $17 billion in 2006. EnCana's profit margin is 18 percent, which is far higher than that of most energy companies. Its net income of $5.3 billion is six times higher than the 2002 level. As a result, EnCana's share price has gone from $15 in 2002 to about $50 in the fall of 2006.

Legacy practices in the oil and gas industry would have caused most people to think EnCana was crazy to accumulate all those oil and gas fields that had already been explored by legacy technology and found to be uneconomical to pursue any further. EnCana's point of view was that some day that trend would turn in its favor. It's a great example of thinking about the future and organizing to play a leadership role in it.

These examples from Texas Instruments, Toyota, and EnCana demonstrate the need to continually search for ways to improve and refresh your products. Don't let pride in your past successes get in the way. You must constantly be on the lookout for new technologies and major structural changes in the market that are important inflection points. They represent big opportunities for your products.

### PART III

# TRAP #3

# BOREDOM:
# CLINGING TO YOUR ONCE-SUCCESSFUL BRANDING AFTER IT BECOMES STALE AND DULL

**The business world** is filled with examples of once-exciting brands that became dull, old, and stale. This often happens because less focus is placed on the brand once it is successful. The folks running those brands assume that they have found the magic formula, and it is now time to sit back and reap the benefits. Usually that mindset also leads to a slowing of the flow of product excitement and to sloppy marketing and sales execution. People are confident that their success will be enduring, and they start diluting their efforts with a variety of distractions.

The fast-food company McDonald's is a good case study here. In 2002, McDonald's was in bad shape. *Fortune* ran an article by David Stires titled "Fallen Arches: McDonald's has had six straight earnings disappointments. Its stock is down 42%. And we can't even remember the jingle! What happened?"[1] Yes, that was the title of the article! Cory Hughes of Loeffler Ketchum Mountjoy, an advertising firm in Charlotte, North Carolina, put it this way: "They were the Great American Meal. And they have gone from being the Great American Meal to being the leader in fast food. From a brand perspective, that is a big drop."[2]

The basic problem, as explained in the *Fortune* article, was that not only were people no longer able to recite the McDonald's theme but, more important, "Customers were complaining about slow service, rude employees, and cardboard-tasting food."[3] Even worse, McDonald's was tardy in reflecting the move to healthier foods. Articles were being written daily about the high fat content and calorie count of its famous burgers. The company's problems in this area were magnified by the comedy/editorial movie released at that time called *Super Size Me*, which featured a guy who decides to eat every meal *only* at McDonald's for 30 days, always goes the super size route in making his selections, and ends up with health problems.[4]

McDonald's stock price took an appropriate hit, going from $50 a share in 2000 down to $12 in March 2003.[5] At that time, a new CEO was named to clean up the problems and get the company back on track. McDonald's had let all the elements of its marketing mix slide into disarray: the strategy/theme, the lack of acknowledgement of the current food trends, and poor execution at store level. I will tell you more about the McDonald's story a little later.

The kinds of problems that McDonald's experienced are all too common. Marketing and brand building is not a deep science, but it does require doing the fundamentals well, and doing them well all the time. It is all about creating an exciting identity for a product or service based on distinctive positioning and/or unique features of the product itself. It's the uniqueness and distinctiveness that can consistently generate trial of the product by new users and consistent reuse of the product. You then have to constantly refresh things and beware of industry trends and try to get out in front of them. Here are some important elements to keep in mind as you work to avoid the trap of leaving successful brands just the way they are because they have been successful!

# 10

## BE CLEAR AND CONCISE, BUT MOST OF ALL BE DISTINCTIVE

It is startling to see how many products in the marketplace are struggling as a result of a severe case of lack of identity. In these cases, you have no clear idea of what the brand stands for. The hard part of marketing is having the discipline to always know precisely what you are trying to make the brand stand for.

Let's take a look at how one company tackles this ongoing challenge.

### PROCTER & GAMBLE

I worked at Procter & Gamble for 26 years, but I never stopped being impressed by the clarity of P&G's brand strategy statements. It guards those statements religiously and uses them as guidelines in virtually every aspect of marketing and product development. The P&G brand strategy statement contains three sentences. The first sentence explains what the benefit of the product is to the user. The second sentence is the reason why a user could believe that the product

> *When I was the senior vice president of marketing at P&G, the benefit statement for Tide was "the superior cleaning detergent." That was it.*

could deliver that benefit. Third, there is a sentence that describes the character of the brand. That is, if the brand were a person, how would you describe that person's personality? Of the three statements, only the second, the reason why a user could believe that the product could deliver the benefit, is optional. You must have the first, the customer benefit, and the third, the character statement.

What's important about these statements is that they are the road map for virtually all decisions related to the product, package (or whatever is used to deliver the product or service to the user), and advertising. The advertising should be consistent with the character statement and should clearly convey the benefit of that product and the reason why a user could believe in it, if there is a reason why for that product. The package/delivery mechanism should capture the character of the brand while, if possible, aiding in the communication of the benefit. The product should deliver the benefit consistent with this brand strategy.

## P&G: Detergents

To give you a couple of examples, when I was the senior vice president of marketing at P&G in the early 1990s, the benefit statement for Tide detergent was "the superior cleaning detergent." That was it. One simple sentence, but it said a lot. It meant that R&D always had to be supplying superior cleaning capabilities for Tide. It's interesting that today, 15 years later, the Tide benefit is "fabric cleaning and care at its best." Basically, the benefit is still superior cleaning, but it has been modified to ensure superior fabric care as well. Consequently, Tide offers a safe bleach additive version, a fresh fragrance version, and a fabric conditioning version—all with Tide's superior cleaning.

At that time, Oxydol detergent was "the superior whitening detergent." Brilliantly white shirts would be shown in the advertising, and the product contained blue speckles that would signify to the user that there was a reason why Oxydol was superior. And it was—on whites.

There was solid product chemistry to back up the benefit claims for each of these products. However, in most laundry situations, consumers had a tough time seeing the difference because their clothes weren't that dirty. What's important is the message that the consumer takes from the advertising and from product usage over the long haul. That's the goal of the brand strategy statement. The key to all of this is to nail down specifically what you want the brand to stand for and then relentlessly carry out what that statement says in all the details related to the product, the package, and the advertising.

## P&G: Crest Toothpaste

Naturally, it's important to keep the brand contemporary over time, and the brand strategy statement needs to change as the benefits you provide to the consumer change and the marketing environment changes. Just as an example, in the 1960s and 1970s, Crest toothpaste focused exclusively on its superior cavity protection with its famous fluoride. When that attribute became generic, P&G started to launch new flavors and packages to appeal to the broad interest of consumers in using pumps rather than tubes or brushing with a gel rather than a paste product. New chemistry related to tartar control emerged in the 1980s, and a tartar control version was launched. Next came gum health, and you saw a flurry of products featuring gum health benefits. In recent years, tooth whitening has become important. As all of this innovation emerged, and fluoride and cavity protection became generic, Crest broadened its benefit statement along the lines of "superior oral care for your family."

Procter & Gamble viewed these statements as sacred. To demonstrate what I mean, I can recall being part of the Crest brand group when we launched a kids flavor back in the early 1980s. The proposal

> *The key to all of this is to nail down specifically what you want the brand to stand for and then relentlessly carry out what that statement says in all the details related to the product, the package, and the advertising.*

had been floated to the top management a few years before I joined the brand group, and the CEO had penciled a note in the upper right corner of the proposal that said, "Suspend this until I retire." He reminded us that Crest was an immensely successful product and that it was all about cavity protection, not frivolous flavor offerings.

Two years later, with a new CEO on board, the brand group dusted off the old proposal, and it was my job to make the argument more convincing. We assembled an arsenal of market research data that clearly said that mothers wanted a fluoride toothpaste like Crest, but they also wanted flavors that kids liked, thus making it easier to get them to brush. The research also confirmed that mothers were making purchase decisions based on the acceptability of the flavors to their kids. We also had solid data that demonstrated that certain flavors, plus the gel form, uniquely appealed to children.

We sent our proposal to the new management, and, after a few grueling sessions combing through the consumer data, we got approval to roll out a kids flavor for Crest. We had finally convinced management that the data were clearly saying that cavity protection was still important but flavor was also important. In the marketplace, the second Crest flavor was a big success. It was marketed along the lines of your getting all the great cavity protection of Crest with a flavor your kids will love. The total Crest brand achieved a meaningful market share gain. It's an interesting example of the amount of tender loving care that should go into the brand strategy.

# McDONALD'S

Let's go back to our McDonald's story. In 2003, the company tackled its big problems by developing a clear and concise brand strategy focused on turning customers of McDonald's into lovers of McDonald's.[1] That was the strategy: to turn "likers" into "lovers." The company focused all aspects of its operations to deliver on that theme. The new advertising campaign carried the tagline "I'm loving it," and the advertising was tailored to the company's various target audiences. For a particular demographic group, it showed people with that set of demographics celebrating the great experience at McDonald's. It overhauled its menu, included a number of healthy food alternatives, and, most of all, launched a major effort to have the service in the stores really cause customers to love the experience. The happy ending to this McDonald's story is that the changes led to an abrupt and significant turnaround. In the second half of 2004, McDonald's posted same-store sales gains of over 10 percent, a performance that the company had not achieved for 30 years.

Along with the need to have a clear and concise statement of what you want the brand to be, there is one more key need: distinctiveness. If your brand is to be successful and remain successful, it has to stand out and clearly bring something distinctive and fresh to the customer. Sometimes these elements are physical attributes. An example is the high quality that is built into Lexus automobiles. Lexus consistently, year after year, wins quality awards by such significant margins that its quality clearly is a distinct advantage for the brand.

Over the decades, Tide detergent, which is called Ariel in many countries outside the United States, has been able to constantly put on the market the very best cleaning detergent. In the case of Tide, it's important to note that its superior formula gets upgraded on a regular basis as the chemists develop improved approaches. For example, the formula originally contained phosphates as a key cleaning ingredient. Environmental issues caused phosphates to be suspect, and new formulas that were phosphate-free emerged. Enzymes were then added to these products to make them more effective.

Then came safe bleach additives that further extended the superior performance of Tide; then cold-water formulas.

Sometimes the distinctive aspects of a brand are emotional. A great example of this is CoverGirl cosmetics, which became enormously successful by using top fashion models to create the aura that consumers are pampering themselves by using the same great products that the high-fashion models who grace the covers of fashion magazines use. While other cosmetics companies, such as Revlon, had used fashion models, when CoverGirl was founded in 1961, it built its entire franchise on the concept of using the products that cover girls use. In fact, the very name it selected, Cover-Girl, is the brand strategy.

Sometimes, brands have both physical and emotional distinctiveness. You would put Porsche in that category. It's well known for being right at the top with regard to sports car performance while also having an aura of being *the* thoroughbred sports car.

## HARLEY-DAVIDSON

A great example of really understanding distinctiveness and freshness is Harley-Davidson. In 1985, that company was in big trouble. Its motorcycles were of poor quality, and that was commonly known. The most severe problem was one of constant oil leaks. For the previous 10 years, the business had been in a tailspin, and by the mid-1980s, the company was very close to bankruptcy.[2] Fortunately, Jeff Bleustein stepped in as the engineering vice president during this decline and finally conquered the quality issues. He is generally viewed as the guy who put an end to the chronic oil leaks.

From that point on, Harley-Davidson became an incredible success story, primarily because of its fantastic branding. It basically built a motorcycle cult. It attacked the building of this brand from many angles, but the core element in all its products and marketing was the distinctive Harley attitude of individualism, freedom, and rebellion.

From a product standpoint, the deep, throaty sounds created by a Harley-Davidson motorcycle are very distinctive. It sounds big and mean, and the bike itself is clearly a no-nonsense instrument. It has all the functional niceties that you would expect, but it is usually done up in black and chrome and has a distinct Harley-Davidson look. With the newest Fat Boy bike, which starts at $18,500, many Harley's are sold to the upscale crowd, but you can still buy a Harley for $6,500. Having a broad price range is important to Bleustein, who points out that "we work hard to keep it a brand for the people."[3]

From a positioning standpoint, the attitude portrayed by Harley-Davidson owners is one of being somewhat of an outlaw, bad-boy biker, seeking free-spirited adventure. As James Speros of *Advertising Age* put it, "Buy a Harley and you're not just buying a finely made machine or a mode of transportation; you are buying into a way of living, a mystique cultivated over the company's long history."[4]

## Harley-Davidson: A Broad Marketing Attack

Harley-Davidson tackles the marketing task in a very multifaceted manner. For example, there are 600 Harley Owners Group (H.O.G.) chapters throughout the United States. Each of these chapters has hundreds of members who are proud owners of Harley-Davidson motorcycles. These chapters organize motorcycle trips, beer blasts, and a whole variety of other social activities, all focused around the sense of rugged individualism that the Harley-Davidson motorcycle represents.

While Harley-Davidson owners are often viewed as hard-core ruffians with big tattoos and bad tempers, what's surprising is that the average salary of the Harley-Davidson customer today is $78,000 per year.[5] That individual is typically riding on a $16,000 motorcycle, which is the average cost of Harley's biggest motorcycle, a Cruiser.

Harley is great at creating celebration events within the Harley-Davidson culture. For example, at the company's 100th Anniversary celebration in August of 2003, more than 250,000 people from all over the world descended on Milwaukee, Wisconsin, to celebrate this birthday.[6] Given there are over 880,000 members of the various H.O.G. chapters worldwide, this was an amazing turnout and shows the incredible strength this brand has with its customers.[7]

Harley also launches a variety of other marketing activities that are continually bombarding its customers with ways to get further involved with the brand. For example, there is a broad variety of clothing and accessories available to these bikers, and the company keeps its customers fully aware of special events such as bike rallies and other get-togethers that they may wish to take advantage of. It licenses the Harley brand to other products as well. For example, there's even a Barbie biker doll and a chrome Visa credit card with Harley-Davidson branding.[8]

### Harley-Davidson: Fresh but Consistent Ideas

While it's clear that Harley-Davidson understands distinctiveness and works hard to retain its "bad-boy" image, it also knows the importance of creating freshness in its products. This has recently led to the introduction of the Harley V-Rod, which is a high-powered, sleek-looking motorcycle known for its outstanding performance. It's also launching a set of new sport bikes to compete with the Japanese motorcycles, which are quite popular with younger motorcycle riders.

All this brilliant marketing is focused on Harley's distinctive image, which Jeff Bleustein, who has been the CEO of Harley for a number of years, really understands. He has been quoted as saying, "You always need to keep a little bit of the bad in the brand."[9]

For the past 20 years, Harley has racked up an incredible record of earnings and sales growth. As a result, shares of Harley-Davidson, which were worth $0.39 as late as 1987, soared to more than $63 by the fall of 2006. Harley's distinctiveness has created quite a ride for its shareholders.

These examples from P&G, McDonald's, and Harley-Davidson provide a very simple lesson: be clear about what your brand stands for, and then create distinctiveness and maintain distinctiveness. It sounds simple, but we all know how tough it is to do.

# 11

## FOCUS
## RELENTLESSLY
## ON DETAILS
## AND EXECUTION

O nce you have a clear and concise brand strategy that is distinctive, you face the tough job of executing that strategy with excellence in the marketplace. This is not the most glamorous part of marketing, but high-quality execution is critical to really bringing the brand to life.

All elements of the marketing have to be consistent with the benefit and the character of the brand. This includes the package, the attitude of your sales personnel and customer service personnel, all the various types of ads you use, and the product use experience itself.

Here is an excellent example of a company that does all of these things really well.

## STARBUCKS

This company is an excellent example of superb brand execution. Many of us experience it every day. Starbucks has a very clear picture of what it wants to be in the consumer's mind, and it works endlessly to have every aspect of the consumer experience line up with that objective.

## Starbucks: The Beginning

In 1983, Howard Schultz was on a trip to Italy and visited an Italian coffee bar in Milan. While he was enjoying his latte, he also began to think about the same concept of a coffee bar for America. Upon returning to Seattle, he couldn't get the idea of a coffee bar out of his head. When a six-store coffee company that sold coffee, filters, coffeemakers, and coffeepots went up for sale in 1987, Schultz raised $4 million and bought out the owners.[1] By the way, the original owners of the small Starbucks chain had chosen the name "Starbucks" because they thought words beginning with ST were very memorable, not because they thought fondly of the first mate in *Moby Dick*, named Starbuck.

Nine years later, in 1996, a financial analyst for Piper Jaffray saw the future fairly clearly when he said, "It won't be anything terribly enlightening if I say we think they will become one of the biggest consumer brands, not just domestically but internationally. They pay a lot of attention to detail, and everything the consumer touches drips with quality."[2]

## Starbucks: What Is It?

When you first walk into a Starbucks store, it's fairly obvious as you look around that you're not going to get an ordinary cup of coffee. The fixtures are postmodern trendy, the surroundings invite friendly conversation, and there's this incredible aroma of roasted Arabica coffee beans throughout.[3] In a recent review of Starbucks, Diane Brady of *BusinessWeek* summed up Starbucks well when she said, "What people really crave is the hip, relaxed ambiance, the music, even the baristas who remember the regular's favorite concoctions."

When Brady interviewed a Starbucks customer by the name of Amy Berkman who was sipping her daily Chai latte at a Starbucks outlet, she found out that Amy was there because that is where she hangs out with her friends. Berkman doesn't like coffee; she likes the experience of being at Starbucks. Over the years, Howard Schultz has summarized this thinking very succinctly when he's asked what Starbucks is all about. He says, "The product is the experience." Starbucks is not just in the coffee business; it is, most importantly, creating an emotional experience.[4]

### Starbucks: Thorough Training

In a *Fortune* magazine article in 1996, Jennifer Reese discussed how disciplined Starbucks was in protecting that experience that Howard Schultz refers to.[5] She mentioned a woman by the name of Kim Sigelman who was managing a Starbucks in Emory, California. To demonstrate the degree to which the baristas are trained to protect the consistency of the Starbucks experience, Sigelman explained in that *Fortune* article what it meant to her with the following quote: "At first I felt the dress code was an affront to my personal being. But I took some time to evaluate where I wanted to be and realized there were sacrifices I'd need to make." The story goes on to say that this caused her to confront the difficult decision of removing her tongue stud because it didn't conform to the dress code and covering up her four tattoos during work. She said, "It's people like my parents who spend $300 for an espresso machine at Starbucks, and they don't want to see my tattoos; I can understand that." Starbucks baristas are thoroughly trained in protecting that unique Starbucks experience.

Next, to ensure a positive experience with the product, the company puts enormous effort into training seminars that teach its employees how to be a Starbucks barista. "Brewing the perfect cup" is a key class that all "partners," which is what employees are called, attend during their first six weeks of employment. Starbucks runs these classes back to back, given the number of stores it is opening. Participants have to read sections of material out loud to the other students in order to really get them to sink in. They learn how to remind customers to purchase beans weekly, to understand that their tap water may be unsatisfactory for making coffee, and to remind

> *Starbucks is constantly looking for new ways to create excitement.*

customers never to let coffee sit on a hot plate for more than 20 minutes. Concerning the water, the manual states, "You wouldn't want to make coffee with unpleasant tasting water anymore than you'd want to make a milkshake from sour milk."

It's in these training courses that baristas also learn about some of the new products and the ways to make them. As Starbucks launches new products such as the Frappuccino, it's vitally important that these products be executed with high quality, and thus there is no substitute for high-quality training of each barista.

Not only is it important for the baristas to be up-to-date on the products but they also need to be trained in treating customers in a positive and enthusiastic way. In fact, Starbucks stresses the importance of projecting a sense of teamwork to customers through the interactions with fellow employees in the store. These are significant topics in the training of a barista, and they are all focused on the goal of customers achieving a consistent Starbucks experience.

### Starbucks: The Products and Stores

Starbucks also works very hard to make sure that it is staying contemporary and providing new excitement for its customers, all within the context of its very well defined brand. First, there's the coffee. The company is constantly searching throughout the world, literally, to find the very best coffee beans. It works hard at developing relationships with coffee-bean growers in a broad variety of countries to make sure that it is being offered the very best coffee beans. If a particular grower simply isn't keeping up with the quality thresholds that Starbucks has, it cuts that grower off. In commenting on this incredible drive to get the very best coffee beans, Howard Schultz says, "We're zealots and we are proud of it."[6]

Starbucks is constantly looking for new ways to create excitement and makes sure it is not resting on its laurels. Its launch of the Frappuccino, a frozen coffee drink, in the mid-1990s sent summer sales through the roof, and the Frappuccino has been a raging success ever since. To capitalize on that success, Starbucks started bottling a version for sale in supermarkets. It also worked with the ice cream manufacturer Dreyer's and launched one of the nation's top-selling coffee ice creams. In addition, it made a deal with United Airlines so that United customers can enjoy the rich taste of Starbucks coffee while dreaming of the ambiance of the Starbucks experience, even though they are on a commercial airline!

Concerning the stores themselves, Schultz long ago refused to ever franchise the Starbucks stores. He simply wouldn't trust anyone else with the Starbucks customer experience. In a 1992 *Fortune* article, he stated, "All this vertical integration is based on asking ourselves, what do we have to do to obtain the best product and the best atmosphere for our customers? The answer is, we have to do everything ourselves."[7]

## Starbucks: Protecting the Brand

So how do Howard Schultz and his team keep that consistent Starbucks experience while constantly refreshing the product line? In a *Fortune* magazine article in 2005, CEO Jim Donald stressed the importance of protecting the experience by indicating, "Our success comes down to the way we connect with our customers, our communities, our farms—with each other. We just had a four day leadership conference. The theme was Human Connection. We didn't once talk about sales and profits. We talked about how we continue to grow and how we connect. You know, Howard has always said that we're not in the coffee business, serving people; we are in the people business, serving coffee."[8]

Back in 2003, Schultz indicated, "We want to become one of the most respected and recognized brands in the world . . . like Coke." Well, if Starbucks continues to guard that unique experience while constantly creating excitement at the store level through well-trained baristas and new product and service ideas, its recent trends, which are phenomenal, will probably continue. A typical customer stops by his or her favorite Starbucks an average of 18 times a month. No American retailer has a higher frequency of customer visits. Sales

> *To create a really solid reputation for a particular brand, it is vitally important that the image and the visuals be absolutely consistent and true to the single image that you are working to create.*

have climbed an average of almost 20 percent a year since the company went public. Starbucks is the essence of keeping the core of a brand very strong while constantly worrying about how you are interacting with your customers and what kinds of new ideas you are putting out there to make sure you don't rest on your laurels and simply sit back and enjoy your success.

Starbucks does a great job of using all the elements of marketing and the product experience to reinforce and drive home its image. To create a really solid reputation for a particular brand, it is vitally important that the image and the visuals be absolutely consistent and true to the single image that you are working to create. Frequent exposure of consumers to a consistent image is the secret to creating a clear identity for a brand and product. The graphics for the brand name and logo should always be the same, no matter where they appear, and the "tone" used to convey information about the product needs to be absolutely consistent across all marketing elements. Starbucks does all of these things very well.

Getting the branding details right every time and executing with precision every time is the secret to building a significant franchise. Starbucks teaches us valuable lessons here every day, day after day.

# 12

## STAY
## RELEVANT

A leadership brand is not going to remain a leadership brand unless it not only keeps up with key marketplace trends but leads them.

As we discussed earlier, McDonald's had a lot of problems in 2002, but one that clearly represented a critical vulnerability was the fact that McDonald's lagged the trend toward healthy foods. In health-food articles in the press, the company was constantly referred to as the provider of the most fat and calories per dollar. In November of 2002, McDonald's hired Kay Napier from Procter & Gamble as a marketing executive, and she quickly and bluntly told her management, "Women don't feel good about going to McDonald's." She was told that McDonald's had tried salads three times and had failed each time. She was not satisfied, and she pushed until all agreed to try it again.[1]

The twist that Napier added in this fourth attempt to sell salads at McDonald's was that she was determined to make sure that the product delivered on the promise of getting a *great* salad at McDonald's. She refused to go the cheap route. The company's new salad offering included 16 types of lettuce. The dressings were from Paul Newman's dressing line, and that helped increase the overall quality image of the offering.

*Get out in front of key industry trends, or face the distinct prospect of losing relevance and getting hurt badly.*

By the end of 2003, McDonald's had sold over 150 million of those salads, and this was helping to turn around its very nasty business problem. Equally as important, other parts of McDonald's were catching on to the importance of participating in the healthy food trend rather than bucking it. Specifically, the company launched an all-white-meat Chicken McNuggets offering for Happy Meals for kids, and an immediate business gain of 15 percent kicked in.[2] It also launched other healthy items, such as Chicken Selects, a whole chicken breast filet, and these offerings beat its expectations.

The learning from this example is obvious: get out in front of key industry trends, or face the distinct prospect of losing relevance and getting hurt badly.

Relevance is particularly important as companies attempt to market their brands to new demographic groups or in different geographical areas. It's important to be very sensitive to the following issues that affect relevance:

1. **Understand the local culture and acceptable practices.** When a marketer decides to launch a brand in a new geographical area, inadequate sensitivity to local customs often emerges as an issue. In some countries, your current packaging graphics could mean something that you don't expect. The tone of your advertising could be unacceptable in that culture, and the media tools you use in the countries where you are successful may not be the right way to launch your marketing efforts in a new country. It behooves you to thoroughly understand the local culture and local consumers and to get hard data on habits and practices in the new area.

**2. When evaluating the risks of changing some elements of your successful marketing mix, err on the side of reflecting local culture.** Quite often there's a real hesitancy to change any elements of the marketing mix, such as the packaging, the structure of the advertising, and various characteristics of the product itself. Sometimes local customs suggest that things should be changed, but you worry about breaking away from the approaches you've used successfully in the past. Those are legitimate issues that should be thoroughly researched, if possible. On the other hand, it's important to judge how much of a turnoff your current practices are to another culture so that you can evaluate those risks properly. If it's a close call, clearly you should err on the side of reflecting the local culture.

These are very tough issues because you have worked hard to understand what is causing your brand to work and what elements of your product have driven its success. Moving into a new geographical area and getting the input you need to change some of that is challenging. The legacy approach will be to protect everything; since the product was successful elsewhere, there should be no reason why it won't be successful in a new area.

## COCA-COLA

This global beverage giant was certainly adamant about protecting its legacy approach to packaging in Germany.[3] Here's the background. In the beginning of 2003, Germany put a law into effect that required the return of nonreusable soda containers to stores for a refund of 0.25 euro (roughly 33 cents). Retailers did not like this law because it required them to accept the return of containers bought at other stores without adequately compensating them for the cost of handling these containers. Basically, the government was attempting to get all soda manufacturers to go to a common reusable container. The hope was that this severe penalty would drive them to that solution.

## Coca-Cola: A Crucial Decision

Naturally, Coke balked at this, since it believed that its distinctively shaped bottle was a key part of its heritage and an integral element of its brand identity. No doubt its thinking was reasonable, but it gave too little thought to the potential ramifications of ignoring this major recycling effort in Germany. The decision turned out to have huge repercussions for Coke. Specifically, the big discount chains in Germany such as Lidl and Plus, which were inundated with more than their fair share of nonreusable soda containers being returned, which they had to pay 0.25 euro for, decided to stop carrying Coca-Cola in their stores. Instead, they put all of their marketing muscle behind their store brands, which were packaged in the common reusable containers. They took a public stance, refusing to stock Coke until Coke was delivered in the standard reusable container. This was a way for them to be relieved of their obligation of paying for nonstandard containers.

By mid-2003, Coke relented and adopted the reusable container, but its problems were not over. The big discount chains were very slow to restock Coke, and its relationship with these huge and important customers was seriously damaged. When they eventually did restock Coke, they gave it very unsatisfactory shelf space.

## Coca-Cola: The Business Implications

The position taken by Coke and the problems that resulted had severe business implications. While Coca-Cola's share of cola sales in Germany was 62 percent at the beginning of 2003, one year later that had decreased to 55 percent. Coca-Cola as a company took a $374 million charge for its Europe, Middle East, and Africa unit in 2004, and it cited this German problem as the major source of its weakness. Coca-Cola's sales in Europe continued to decline and were off 12 percent in the first quarter of 2005. In reporting on those first-quarter results, Coca-Cola's CEO Neville Isdell indicated, "Germany will continue to be a challenge for the balance of the year."

Stepping back, what Coke basically did was misread the pain that the retail trade was feeling as a result of the government's decision to drive out nonstandard containers. To make matters worse, its key competitor Pepsi-Co reacted quickly to the new German legislation and delivered its products in the acceptable bottles, and its market share increased from 11 percent in 2003 to 15 percent in 2004.[4]

Those kinds of calls are really tough, since you want to protect the elements of your brand that you know have made you successful and brought you notoriety in the past. On the other hand, you've got to be objective about what the marketplace is saying and adjust accordingly.

> *Protect the elements of your brand that you know have made you successful in the past. On the other hand, you've got to be objective about what the marketplace is saying and adjust accordingly.*

## PROCTER & GAMBLE

Another example of this need to consider local practices involves Procter & Gamble and its business in Japan. Throughout the 1970s and 1980s, Procter & Gamble had a very difficult time in Japan. It lost hundreds of millions of dollars. Brands that had been immensely successful in numerous countries were taken to Japan by Procter & Gamble but simply never took off. The advertising agencies that Procter & Gamble used in Japan were primarily Japanese subsidiaries of the big global ad agencies that P&G used elsewhere. While these agencies hired Japanese creatives and art directors, their management was often from America or Europe, and, most importantly, the headquarters staff at Procter & Gamble worked hard to globalize all aspects of the company's brands whenever possible. That meant that if you had a successful advertising campaign that had built a brand in many countries, that campaign would be your starting point in any new country to which you took that brand.

In Japan, here's what that meant for Head & Shoulders advertising: you show people with dandruff flakes and the social unacceptability of that, and then you make Head & Shoulders the hero by curing the problem, leading to a happy user. That's often re-ferred to as problem-solution advertising, and Procter & Gamble was the master of it. In laundry commercials, you would show two previously dirty garments, one of which was cleaned using the P&G detergent while the other was cleaned using a competitive deter-gent, and then demonstrate visually how the P&G product was clearly superior in its cleaning ability. Additionally, as in virtually all other countries, Procter & Gamble did not run advertising about its company (i.e., P&G) in Japan. All the advertising was for individual brands; none was for the P&G company name.

## Procter & Gamble: Tough Lessons

Procter & Gamble's frustration over its lack of success in Japan be-came great enough that P&G decided to talk to some pure Japan-ese advertising agencies to get their viewpoints on the company's lack of success. The folks that provided some of the best insight were from the Dentsu advertising agency in Japan. This is a pure Japan-ese ad agency, and it is generally regarded as one of the best Japanese ad agencies in handling Japanese brands. After P&G got to know these folks a bit, the Dentsu management finally got up enough nerve to explain to P&G that the Japanese culture and the Japanese television viewer considered much of its advertising to be insulting. They delicately explained that the Japanese really don't like to see problem situations, and they don't like to see individuals portrayed in such negative situations. Also, they stressed that Japanese con-sumers want to know about the company that produces these prod-ucts. In most countries, Procter & Gamble was proud of the fact that its company name had a very low profile and all the notoriety was associated with the brands. It turns out that in Japan, that thinking is wrong.

These were humbling lessons for the Procter & Gamble market-ing folks, but they had to face reality, and many years of failure in the country caused them to be a lot more receptive.

So what did the company do? It started using pure Japanese agencies to a far greater extent, and those agencies made advertis-ing that celebrated the products and the good things that they did for consumers, showing only positive things in the advertising. Also, Procter & Gamble began to advertise its company name and explain to the Japanese public who Procter & Gamble was and what its corporate values were.

Some of these changes in marketing approaches, coupled with Procter & Gamble finally figuring out the complicated distribution system in the consumer products business in Japan, caused the company at long last to start to experience genuine success in that country.

When you step back, Procter & Gamble was simply following its legacy practices from country to country. It became overconfident enough that it failed to do the basic homework when it got to Japan. It didn't really probe to understand local customs the way it should have. It didn't work hard enough to ensure that its practices would be relevant and acceptable to the local culture and habits.

Lots of companies have made big mistakes by ignoring local cultures as they attempt to globalize their offerings. What causes this to happen is the legacy practices that emerge around products and brands as they achieve some degree of success. The thinking is that the company should freeze everything just as it is and go with these practices worldwide, cashing in within every country. Unfortunately, things just aren't that simple. Once again, if you think you have it all figured out, beware.

### PART IV

# TRAP #4
# COMPLEXITY: IGNORING YOUR BUSINESS PROCESSES AS THEY BECOME CUMBERSOME AND COMPLICATED

**As successful** organizations grow, they often fall into the trap of hiring too many people, which makes the organization more complicated. They then reorganize into smaller groups to get as much clarity of responsibility as possible, but this often leads to unproductive fragmentation of processes that should be carried out organization-wide. These smaller groups' rationale is that they've been doing well, and so they deserve to manage their own affairs.

Before long, these groups decide that they are different enough from the rest of the company to need their own information technology systems and their own human resources personnel and practices. They work to break off from any corporate manufacturing activities and then develop their own product supply and logistics processes and their own manufacturing plants. Naturally, when a segment of an organization is trying to operate independently, it needs its own financial staff and financial processes that reflect the nuances of that particular part of the company. You get the picture. Things fragment into fiefdoms, and each of those fiefdoms constantly works to remain as independent as possible. That's simply human nature.

This kind of fragmentation makes instituting changes in key processes very hard. Determining organization-wide information becomes very hard, and implementing a new approach in an area like finance or human resources becomes very complicated, since the various fragments are all off doing their own thing.

I recently did some consulting with the management of a $10 billion company that supplies a variety of materials to the automobile industry. The reason I was brought in was that the company was having profitability problems. When I probed for detailed data on headcount for each of the company's divisions and each of its staff areas, such as finance, manufacturing, information technology, and human resources, the management said they could tell me how many people were in the corporate groups, but that it would take a significant effort to figure out, for example, how many HR people there were throughout the company in the various divisions. I asked why, and they told me that each group had its own information systems and that the systems weren't linked together. So, without significant effort, it was not possible to generate such a report.

After spending two days with this organization and realizing how hard it was to figure out how the various areas like information technology and human resources were really structured and what the related expenses were, I suggested that the managers needed to face up to the fact that they didn't know much about their cost structure and that they needed to take a couple of months and put a finance team on the task of figuring out what and where their costs really were. For example, we agreed they would isolate headcount by division and by functional area, such as finance and IT. They said this exercise would take two or three months, since all that information existed within the units, but not centrally, and the units had their own approaches to defining such measures and had built their own unique databases.

When I had my second visit with that company three months later, it had just finished the ugly task of pulling together all the data. The management team was shocked when it saw the numbers. For example, there were 1,250 human resources people throughout the company. Previously, all the managers had known was that they had about 60 HR professionals in the corporate group. Benchmarking with other auto-parts suppliers in the industry of roughly the same size suggested that they should have had about 300 HR people at most.

Each of the divisions had gone off and built its own set of practices for managing people and doing performance appraisals. Each division had its own people databases to keep track of benefits and salary plans. In the finance area, each division had developed its own chart of accounts, and each had hired a fair number of financial analysts to monitor the new measurers developed to capture the nuances of its activities relative to what was going on in the rest of the company. Put another way, the company's fundamental business processes for running the organization were completely broken down and fragmented, and introducing any organization-wide change was extremely difficult.

As organizations age and as they experience success, these kinds of difficulties with the core processes that the organization uses to run its business emerge all the time. There is case after case of companies that eventually run into profitability problems because they don't tackle these things on an ongoing basis and they don't have strong leadership to keep these processes lean and crisp.

Now let's look at some tips as to what you should do to avoid this trap, while also looking in detail at some examples that shed important light on the source and the nature of these kinds of problems.

# 13

## DON'T WAIT FOR THE CRISIS

**W**hy is it so hard to constantly push for improvement in the processes that help run the organization? The reason is that change is very hard for individuals to accept. They are admitting that they are not as good as they would like to be. That's a tough thing for humans to acknowledge. Managers are often reluctant to push the people in charge of a particular process for fear that they will insult them because things seem to be running OK for the time being.

The price you pay for waiting and allowing a process to become out of date can be enormous. Eventually, you end up in a crisis mode, trying to fix things just to catch up without any notion of actually trying to get ahead of your competition. In addition, by tackling these things when they are running fairly well, you have more of an opportunity to experiment with different approaches, since you are not "under the gun" to fix the problem now.

## SCHNEIDER NATIONAL

Schneider National is a trucking company that serves customers such as Wal-Mart and Lowe's, and it provides a very robust example of letting things slide but then putting together a series of steps to ensure, on an ongoing basis, that processes are constantly improved.

Founded in 1935, Schneider is a privately held trucking company with headquarters in Green Bay, Wisconsin. It consistently grew, and by the late 1990s it had become the largest trucking company in the United States. You may have seen some of its large orange trucks and trailers out there on U.S. interstate highways.

> *Change is very hard for individuals to accept. They are admitting that they are not as good as they would like to be. That's a tough thing for humans to acknowledge.*

In the year 2000, Schneider's growth began to really sag. Yes, the economy was softening, but the company was hurting far more than it should have been as a result of the declining economy. Both its productivity and its return on capital were declining.[1]

One thing that was causing Schneider's problems was the fact that during the 1990s, a tremendous amount of trucking capacity had come online in the country. With the slowing economy, this led to significant overcapacity, and consequently, customers began to be able to look at many trucking companies and select those that were providing the best service and value.

During the 1980s and 1990s, when Schneider had been growing very fast, its services were in extremely high demand because the trucking industry was not very well developed. Hence, there was not a great deal of focus on what its service looked like from a customer's perspective. For example, it was taking Schneider 30 to 45 days to get back to a customer after that customer submitted a request for proposal (RFP).[2] Since business had always come Schneider's way without much effort on the company's part, preparing and delivering responses to a customer's request for a specific set of services was quite low on its priority list. In 2000, the overcapacity in the industry and the slow economy changed all this.

Michael Hammer described in the *Harvard Management Update* how Schneider National put some operational principles in place to make sure that this kind of thing didn't happen again, while also fixing the immediate problems, such as the slow response to customers when they wanted Schneider to bid for their business via an RFP.[3] Here are the six steps Schneider took to put a set of procedures in place on an ongoing basis so that it didn't have these kinds of problems again.

1. **Process focus.** Schneider developed an enterprise process model that described how the business works. It then dissected that model into its component processes and committed itself to constantly perfecting each one of them. Examples of these processes are (a) responding to RFPs, (b) acquiring new business, (c) receiving orders and fulfilling them, and (d) developing a specific transportation plan for a specific order. Developing this thorough model of how the company should operate was a turning point in understanding how it could keep paying attention to these areas on an ongoing basis.

2. **Process owners.** Each of the processes outlined in the enterprise process model was assigned a particular process owner, who was a senior executive empowered to make whatever changes were needed to keep that process superior to the competition. This kind of focused responsibility makes it absolutely clear what the expectations are for that individual.

    It's important to note the emphasis on *one* individual being responsible. Too often, organizations form ad hoc committees, put them in charge of improving a process, and then dismantle the committees. Having a key person responsible for making sure that a particular process is innovative and industry leading on an ongoing basis greatly improves your chances of not waking up some morning and realizing that your legacy processes have driven you to mediocrity.

3. **Managerial engagement.** The senior managers in an organization must completely bless this approach of having process

owners and the expectation that things will be constantly changing and improving. The management of an organization has to provide strong leadership by setting expectations that things will be constantly improving. Think Toyota.

> *Have a key person responsible for making sure that a particular process is innovative. This greatly improves your chances of not being driven to mediocrity by your processes.*

4. **Full-time design teams.** When potential improvements in a particular process are spotted, people need to be assigned to the task of achieving those improvements, and they need to be working on this full time. Too many organizations make the mistake of having several employees spend part of their time doing process improvement work. What the management is basically telling these people is that process improvement is secondary to their current responsibilities. The results typically reflect that kind of second priority. Projects languish, and in most cases, nothing of significance happens.

5. **Building buy-in.** Changing processes can be a very bruising exercise for employees. Their instincts are not to change, and the group that brings in fresh ideas is often looked upon as the villain. To counter this, the design team needs to fully engage those whose work will be affected. It needs to get people's ideas and work to enroll them in the cause to make significant improvement.

6. **Bias for action.** Both the design team and the process owner need to operate with a mindset that says that 80 percent is good enough. In the case of Schneider, the design team adopted a principle of "70 percent and go."[4] This means that when the team developed an improvement, even

> though it hadn't achieved perfection, it implemented what it had and modified it on the fly. Importantly, when you do that, you tend to learn a lot during the implementation that can make things far better than if you had waited around trying to get the change to a higher level of perfection before you implement it.

Schneider National used this six-step approach to jar its business out of its tailspin and to get a tight focus on satisfying customers. The effort was highly successful. The response time for those RFPs that we referred to earlier, which had been 30 to 45 days, was cut down to 1 to 2 days. Schneider reported that this had a major impact on its customers, and the percentage of bids that Schneider won increased by 70 percent, which led to a sales increase of hundreds of millions of dollars per year for Schneider.

It is clear that Schneider National should not have waited for the crisis of an economic slowdown to occur before doing these things. On the other hand, it is also clear that successful organizations have a tendency to hire too many people, which generates complexity and all kinds of duplicate efforts in areas such as human resources and information technology, which should be consistent companywide. You end up with processes that are complicated, disjointed, and typically require a lot of concurrence across numerous groups to get companywide changes made.

Also, with time, processes tend to get more and more out of date as the people in charge of those legacy systems fight to retain them in the form with which they are familiar. When acquisitions occur or new products are launched, typically new systems are added to the mix, and people build bridges to old systems. Before long, you've got a crisis. You've got incredible complexity, high costs compared to your competition, and no standard way to carry out the normal processes required to run the organization.

These kinds of problems typically emerge in the areas of information technology, procurement, human resources practices, manufacturing practices, and financial reporting. The legacy people who have been managing the legacy processes do a good job of protecting these processes, and the organization tends to add all kinds of complicating features to them. The concept of driving standards and simplicity becomes very difficult. Legacy personnel take the attitude that they, and the processes they are protecting, are critical to the everyday execution of the business. This attitude makes them almost impenetrable to their management. When any challenges emerge, the individuals responsible for these processes often hide behind their prior success and raise all kinds of objections to changing things that have previously been successful or are viewed as critical to running the business on a day-to-day basis.

The six steps we just outlined should enable the organization to avoid this type of crisis. But a strong focus on continually achieving simplicity, efficiency, and standards is required. Let's take a look at a major bank that required such focus and leadership to clean up its crisis.

## BANK ONE

In early 2000, Jamie Dimon became the CEO of Bank One. When he joined the organization, it was in rough shape. In 1998, Bank One had merged with First Chicago NBD.[5] Bank One was primarily a retail bank in the Midwest and Southwest, and First Chicago was primarily a corporate bank that made loans to medium-sized manufacturers. While it looked as if the two banks complemented each other well, a classic problem occurred with this merger—no one was really in charge. Dave Donovan, head of human resources at Bank One and a veteran of First Chicago, said, "The two camps would argue for months over whether retail or corporate should get the big resources, which people from which former bank should run the businesses, and everything else."[6]

These merger problems had a big impact on Bank One's financial results. The bank had twice missed its earnings expectations by very significant margins. The primary problems were in the First USA credit card division, which saw its income fall from $303 million in the first quarter of 1999 to $70 million in the first quarter of 2000. This huge drop of 77 percent, plus other problems at the bank, had caused the stock to hit a 52-week low of $24 in February 2000, down about 50 percent since June of 1999.[7]

## Bank One: The Drive for Simplicity

Jamie Dimon had proven himself a real wizard in cleaning up messy mergers during his many years of experience at Smith Barney and Citigroup. Undoubtedly, Bank One was the biggest mess he had faced yet. There was a devastating lack of simplicity and organization-wide standards. For example, there were 87 different bank charters and seven different deposit systems.[8] The company had three clearing networks and five wire transfer platforms. All of these various systems needed maintenance, and since each was different, they required different personnel and/or technical skills to support them. The company was spending 16 percent of its noninterest expenses on computer systems, compared to the industry benchmark of 10 percent.[9]

So what did Jamie do? While rolling out some exciting new banking products, he overhauled the bank's major systems, which had been acquired over the years, into one single computer system with standard procedures by which all employees interacted with it. For example, he was faced with a variety of data systems in the investment banking area. He unified all of them into one system.[10]

Jamie sent some very concrete signals to the organization that he was running the show and that he intended to massively clean up the messy processes at Bank One. To publicly reinforce his intentions, when he joined the company, he bought two million shares of the stock and explained clearly to Wall Street, and to his employees, that he expected to make big money on that investment. Jamie made an incredible statement when he bought that stock for $28 a share. He said: "I don't know if the stock was worth $35 or $20; $20 is more likely. I just thought I should eat my own home cooking." Shawn Tully of *Fortune* magazine said in 2002, "Dimon is a back to basics, in the trenches manager who cares little for grand five year plans or big mission statements."[11] In fact, Dimon made the statement, "I'd rather have a first rate execution and a second rate strategy anytime than a brilliant idea with mediocre management."

## Bank One:
## The People Cleanup

> *"Excuse me. This is reality. Deal with it!"*
> —Jamie Dimon

To help him drive for the efficiencies that he knew he could achieve, he also cleaned house with respect to talent. Shortly after coming on board, he named Salomon Smith Barney CFO Charles Scharf as Bank One's new CFO, and he lured Bill Campbell, co-CEO of Citigroup's Global Consumer Group, to be a technology consultant. That was just the beginning. During his first 24 months, he replaced 12 of his top 13 managers; 7 of these 12 were outsiders, and 5 were picked from the Bank One ranks. Most of the outsiders were individuals that Jamie had worked with in his past life. Scharf put it well when asked about why he joined Dimon: "It wasn't really a choice. I'm just following the best leader I've ever seen."[12]

One key ingredient in driving for simplicity and efficiency is the ability to deal with reality. This is a major strength of Jamie Dimon's. As discussed by Patricia Sellers in a *Fortune* article in 2002, Jamie dealt with a very sensitive problem at Bank One very quickly.[13] Specifically, he didn't believe that his folks were telling it straight with regard to just how bad the credit losses could be during a recession. When he got some pushback, his comment was, "Excuse me. This is reality. Deal with it!" As the economy tightened, although this was not officially called a recession, Jamie's instincts proved correct; the bank's credit losses increased by $1.5 billion.

In pursuing simplicity and efficiency, you need to have clear and nonoverlapping responsibilities for your people, and you should make minimum use of big committees or task forces. Jamie sure exhibited these characteristics when he shrank the board of directors of Bank One from 20 people down to 11 and focused them on important questions such as, "What are the things that could blow up the company?" and "What are the moves we could make to really generate significant improvement and results?"

## *Bank One: The Results*

All of this drive for efficiency and effectiveness had a huge impact on Bank One's costs. In two short years, Jamie decreased expenses at the company by 17 percent, which was equivalent to $1.8 billion.[14] The company reported a $544 million loss just prior to his arrival. Once all of the major efficiency moves were completed, earnings skyrocketed. For perspective, three years after Jamie arrived, the fiscal year earnings were a record $3.5 billion. In 2003, Bank One achieved a net increase of 434,000 new checking accounts, compared with only 4,000 the year before. Credit card sales leaped 83 percent, and home equity loans increased 29 percent.[15]

What is interesting here is that in January 2004, Jamie Dimon orchestrated a $58 billion sale of Bank One to JPMorgan Chase, and that represented a 14 percent premium for the Bank One shareholders. In the deal, it was agreed that in 2006, Jamie would succeed William Harrison and become the CEO of the new bank that emerged from this merger. Put another way, Jamie Dimon got to start all over again doing what he does extremely well: deliver first-class financial results by focusing on achieving lightning-quick business processes. By fall 2006, it was clear that he was off to a fast start. JPMorgan Chase has already completed a very challenging move to one credit card system, lowering the bank's cost of processing statements by 38 percent, and Jamie was in the midst of reducing the number of global data centers from 80 to 30 by 2008.

The lesson from Banc One's aggressiveness in tackling its problems and Schneider's procrastination is clear. Don't wait for a crisis to streamline the organization. Start attacking complexity now.

# 14

## DEMAND
## NEW APPROACHES
## TO "PROVEN"
## PROCESSES

rocesses can take on a life of their own. For example, once a manufacturing line is up and running and the appropriate bells and whistles have been added, it develops a momentum of its own that resists change. This also happens with computer systems, for example, the intricate sets of computer programs that handle a company's vital functions such as ordering, shipping, and billing procedures and financial management systems.

What typically happens is that once these things are well established and the organization achieves some degree of stability and/or success, the procedures and systems tend to be viewed as so extremely mission-critical that it would be risky to fiddle with them. Also, the people who support these processes on an ongoing basis are often left in place because they end up having deep expertise on how to keep these things running well.

With time, two problems set in. First, the people who support these systems year after year tend to get out of date with respect to new technologies or new approaches to the kind of process they are managing. Their objective is to execute with excellence, and they feel deep pride when they achieve that excellence. No doubt such reliable daily execution is an accomplishment, but it also eventually represents a missed opportunity to take advantage of new things.

Second, the people supporting these processes, over time, become so associated with them that subconsciously they worry about what would happen to them if they were asked to do something else within the organization. They know deep down that they have lost touch with the technology trends because they have put all of their energies into operating with excellence day to day. Consequently, they get very defensive about any kind of change. They know they face the risk that if there is a change, they will be moved out of their job, and what would happen then? They fear the unknown and become more and more protective of what they do.

So what do you do to avoid these kinds of problems? First, you need to rotate people through assignments so that they don't fall into this trap. Yes, it does require some extra training when you move new people into these slots, but the payoff is huge with respect to the curiosity that new employees bring and the fresh perspective that often leads to real innovation.

Second, you need to be clear that you are looking for significant improvement in these processes, and you need to spell out what measures will be used. Management has to be incredibly vigilant to prod these groups to make sure that processes continuously improve over time and don't fall into the trap of becoming legacy processes that are a burden to the organization.

# PROCTER & GAMBLE

P&G provides a great example of a company that took a "proven" process that had served the company well for decades and made important modifications in order to generate big improvements. The example concerns its market research activity.

## P&G: The Proven Process

For decades, Procter & Gamble's market research organization was viewed as having a terrific array of consumer research tools for measuring the potential of product opportunities, qualifying them in the marketplace, and then reading their performance once the product was launched.

*You need to rotate people through assignments so they don't stagnate.*

For example, if you take a product such as Tide Liquid, which was introduced by P&G in 1984, the company had verified technically that the formula cleaned better than the leader in the liquid detergent category at that time, which happened to be Wisk. P&G had given the Tide Liquid product in a plain bottle to a group of consumers, and it had given the competitive product in a plain bottle to another representative sample, and it had confirmed that the cleaning capabilities of the new formula were superior to those of the competitor. Such blind product tests were an institution at Procter & Gamble.

For a particular category, such as detergents or antiperspirants, the P&G brands that participated in that category would regularly field usage and attitude studies and habits and practices studies. These market research tools helped the company understand thoroughly how people were using the products and what their attitudes toward the various products were. It also did focus groups, where it would hear about the pluses and minuses of its current offerings. It would also conduct one-on-one interviews with people in an interview room, where they would talk about their experiences with the product.

P&G was well aware of the risks of qualitative research, such as focus groups and one-on-ones. In such research, you are trusting people to tell you how they did things when they were back in their homes instead of directly observing them to get the full picture of just how they interacted with the product and how satisfied they were during its use.

No one can quarrel with the results that Procter & Gamble achieved for decades using its arsenal of "proven" market research methodologies. On the other hand, when A. G. Lafley became CEO in 2000, he recognized that P&G was going to have to crank up its innovation dramatically in order to meet the revenue and profit goals the company had established.

## P&G: A New Twist

Lafley and his management team instituted a very important new approach to their "proven" market research practices.[1] Specifically, they went out of their way to cut their reliance on traditional quantitative studies, such as habits and practices studies, and qualitative tools, such as focus groups. They demanded that their product development and marketing people get out into the field and actually observe individuals using Procter & Gamble products and other related products in their homes. Their mode of operation switched to one of regularly making appointments to visit homes and watching the way people washed their clothes, cleaned their floors, and changed their babies' diapers. As consumers went about these tasks, the P&G observer would ask them about their likes and dislikes.

About the same time, a whole new generation of innovation consultants that focused on what is called *microinnovation* was emerging. In thinking about developing and designing products, these organizations constantly preach the need to connect with customers' emotions and to understand clearly how they are feeling and how satisfied they are as they use the products in a particular category.

In commenting on Procter & Gamble, Patrick Whitney, director of the Institute of Design at Illinois Institute of Technology said, "P&G had the best chemical engineering and marketing operations in the country. It didn't care about the user experience. While that is a slight exaggeration in that I'm sure the individuals at Procter & Gamble did care about the user's experience, they weren't serious enough about it to spend time in the homes watching people do the tasks for the particular category they were responsible for." Whitney concluded his comments by saying, "It had to create new products, and to do that, P&G had to get closer to the consumer."[2]

In the August 1, 2005, issue of *BusinessWeek*, Bruce Nussbaum describes in considerable detail how Procter & Gamble and General Electric innovate and generate new products. He noted: "What is the methodology of the new design strategy that Lafley, [Jeffrey] Immelt, and others are adopting? The basics are simple. They start with observation—going out and directly seeing customers shop at malls, families eating at restaurants or patients being treated in hospitals."[3]

In order to really institutionalize a change in a "proven" practice such as the market research process used for decades at Procter & Gamble, the leader needs to constantly reinforce the need for the change. A. G. Lafley certainly

> *Holding up the picture of what the future will look like goes a long way toward making sure that people achieve it.*

does that. It was reported recently that on a field trip to South America, he ended up in the laundry area of a home, where he was observing how things were being done and learning about some of the hurdles that Procter & Gamble could potentially help that consumer overcome. Making sure the story of his visit to this South American laundry room got out to the rest of the troops was a great way to make sure they understood that there was an important new step in their "proven" practice.

Let's look at another way you can make it clear that you want new approaches; namely, reorganizing. When an organization structure stays the same for years and years, and the focus of that structure is to simply carry out today's current business model using today's current business processes, the organization can get very set in its ways, and that is a prescription for legacy thinking and legacy practices. When employees see an organization configured around change in a way that clearly indicates that generating improvement is important, they get the picture very quickly.

Here are a few tips that I have found useful over the years in signaling to the members of the organization what is expected and what will be rewarded:

1. **Organize around new approaches.** Pulling people out of their current responsibilities and forming an organization that is focused on generating significant improvement is a

powerful tool. It tells the organization that you are going to do things differently in the future. It also gives you the focus you need to make the important changes.

2. **Put your best people in the operations that are focused on change.** Staffing decisions send a very clear signal about the culture of the organization. Employees know who the best and the brightest are, and when you take those kinds of people and give them key responsibilities, it's quite clear what the organization values.

3. **Be clear about what success looks like.** The leader of a group needs to describe clearly to the group, over and over again, how things should operate in the future. Holding up the picture of what the future will look like goes a long way toward making sure that people achieve it.

Let's take a look at a global giant that offers us a superb example of reorganizing to generate significant improvement.

# SAMSUNG

Ten years ago, Samsung was known primarily as a maker of inexpensive black and white TVs.[4] It really wasn't a significant player in the consumer electronics business, an arena that was dominated by Sony. That has totally changed. It has taken Samsung less than a decade to become the world's most profitable and most dominant consumer electronics company, taking over that position from Sony. Specifically, in 2006 it was reported that Samsung was ahead of Sony in three key areas. Samsung's annual revenue was $78 billion, versus $67 billion for Sony; Samsung's profits were $10.3 billion, versus $1.5 billion for Sony; and Samsung's market capitalization was $96 billion, versus $39 billion for Sony.[5]

Much of Samsung's success is due to its creation of a new process for generating new products. It consists of an organization called the value innovation program.[6] Within Samsung, it is simply referred to as the VIP. It is a stand-alone organization that is focused on the process of generating leading-edge projects and getting them to the marketplace much faster than any of Samsung's competitors.

This VIP organization is the brainchild of Jong-Yong Yun, the CEO of Samsung. The VIP center of Samsung is a five-story building within the company's massive complex encompassing large factories and two office towers. It's located in Suwon, South Korea, which is where Samsung Electronics was founded in 1969.

> *At Samsung headquarters, 40 dormitory rooms are available for employees when in the midst of a project to enable them to keep their focus.*

The VIP facility houses large training rooms and has three floors of workrooms for the various teams focused on specific projects. The top floor has about 40 dormitory rooms, each containing two beds, a shower, a small desk, and a chair. There are some small kitchens that are shared by several units on the fifth floor as well. In the basement are billiard and Ping-Pong tables, a gym, and a sauna.

The purpose of the rooms on the top floor is not to have the project people move in permanently. Instead, the rooms give them a place to sleep when they are in the midst of a project and they don't want their concentration broken by going home and getting involved with other things.

Samsung is a strong believer in being first to the market. It knows that if competitive products arrive soon after it puts its products on the market, the whole category will quickly become generic, and there will be very little opportunity for good profits. Thus, it puts tremendous pressure on the project teams to create extremely exciting things that will have a big impact in the marketplace and be tough for competitors to duplicate quickly. Samsung's engineers are charged with reducing complexity very early in the design cycle of their products and building in lower manufacturing costs, and thus higher profit margins.

With the VIP center and the product development process that it represents, Samsung makes it very clear to the organization what

> *One reason why processes sometimes get neglected is the assumption that they are less important than the company's sales, marketing, and finance activities. But processes can be your reason for winning.*

it wants to see happen. By putting its very best people in there and charging them with generating industry-leading products that get to the market very quickly, it lets everyone in the organization understand what behavior is desired.

Stepping back from these specific examples, one reason why processes sometimes get neglected is that there is an assumption that these processes are of secondary importance compared to the company's sales, marketing, and finance activities. No doubt processes can sometimes just keep you in the game. But there are other times when they actually can be your reason for winning, your core strategic advantage. For example, with Toyota, we saw that its kaizen continuous improvement process was clearly its competitive edge over time, and it is the most important core competency of that organization. Another company that has a process that is its strategic advantage is Wal-Mart. No one is better than that organization with respect to logistics.

There are also many processes that an organization carries out that are important in order for it to be in the game but that are not necessarily strategic. An example of this would be an airline's online customer capabilities. While some Web sites and online ordering processes are better than others in the airline industry, they really don't stick out as a competitive advantage for any airline.

Some companies have processes that differentiate them from and give them superiority over their competitors. No matter what your situation is, each process should be evaluated regularly to make sure it is up to date and to determine whether new approaches or new technology could enable it to become a competitive advantage in your industry. Unfortunately, what happens in many cases is that core processes become entrenched legacy practices, leading to a real lack of agility when change is really important in order to remain competitive.

Here is a description of one company that is totally focused on its logistics process; in fact, this process has been the company's reason for being.

# DELL

In 21 short years, Dell grew from a dorm-room operation to America's most admired company in 2005, as rated by *Fortune* magazine.[7] The key driver of this sensational story is the fine-tuned logistics process that Dell has unrelentingly focused on throughout its history. Specifically, it sells its products only through direct-to-consumer initiatives. Individuals can place orders using mail, phone, or the Internet. By 2005, Dell had ridden this logistics advantage to the number one position in the United States in desktop PCs, notebook PCs, servers, profits, growth rate, and profit margins.

The Dell formula is fairly simple. It sells things related to the computer industry that are of high volume and can fit into its direct sales logistics model. The company is clearly the world's most efficient assembler and distributor of Wintel technology. By Wintel we mean machines that run Microsoft Windows software and have Intel or AMD microprocessors.[8]

## Dell: Its Advantage

The key difference between Dell and other PC providers is the fact that every single Dell machine is made for a specific order. Its competitors produce large quantities of their products based on a sales forecast and place them in inventory. The advantages of the Dell approach, if you can pull it off, are enormous. As Andy Serwer of *Fortune* magazine indicated in his March 2005 article, Dell typically carries only 4 days of inventory, while IBM has 20 days and Hewlitt-Packard (HP) has 28 days.[9] These statistics show the huge difference in the amount of capital needed by Dell and its competitors. Dell asks its suppliers to place their warehouse inventories as close to the Dell factories as possible. When you visit a Dell plant, you can see supplies of components being unloaded from trucks right onto the assembly line. The similarity between this company and Wal-Mart is amazing. Both dominate their industries via superior logistics.

Not needing to have legions of salespeople who call on retailers and encourage them to push Dell machines is a gigantic advantage. With all Dell machines being made to order and delivered directly to the customer, Dell can sell its products at a lower price. Also, Dell typically gets paid by the customer weeks before it has to pay its suppliers.[10] That is definitely a Sam Walton approach. Sam always said that he would rather run his business on other people's money than use his own precious capital.

### Dell: The Culture

To keep Dell's direct-to-consumer approach absolutely in the forefront in his industry, Michael Dell has created a culture of paranoia about maintaining its excellence in logistics, and this has had a gigantic payoff. While highly successful, the leaders of this company are extremely humble and constantly worried about the future. For example, when Michael Dell was told by *Fortune* magazine that his company was being named America's Most Admired in 2005, his reaction was, "I know my mom would be proud, but I certainly don't feel like we are the most admired company." He then added, "Well, that's really nice, thank you very much. I'm humbled by that but we've got a lot of work to do."[11]

This paranoid attitude is what caused Dell in early 1994 to be very concerned about the fast-emerging Internet and very interested in how it could turn the Internet to its advantage. With lightning speed, Michael Dell and his crew developed an exciting Web site and launched Dell.com in June 1994. The Web site was crammed with valuable technical support information as well as price lists, intricate details of all the products, and clear menus telling customers how to place their order with Dell and how to track that order online. The Internet is a dream tool for someone who views logistics as the source of advantage in an industry. Consequently, it's not surprising that Dell emerged quickly as a leader in this area. Michael Dell himself was receiving hundreds of requests per month to give speeches on how Dell was using the Internet to its advantage.[12]

## Dell: The Marketplace Results

As mentioned before, Dell was not only the revenue giant in the PC industry in the United States and worldwide but also the profit leader. For perspective, in 2004, Dell's gross margin of 18 percent was actually lower than IBM's and HP's. The reason is that Dell tends to sell lower-margin machines. On the other hand, when you look at net margin, you see Dell at 6 percent while its competitors are close to 1 percent.[13] The reason is the incredible advantage that Dell has in operating expenses, since its direct sales model generates huge advantages in sales and administrative costs. Put another way, Dell skips the middleman, but its competitors have to pay for that middleman, which creates the need for big sales organizations and large amounts of inventory. This results in high costs and variability in its competitors' business. For perspective, in 2004, Dell was doing $900,000 of sales per employee, while the number two in the industry, HP, was generating $540,000 per employee.

Not surprisingly, a lot of PC manufacturers have fallen by the wayside. For example, while IBM basically invented the PC business, it was extremely frustrated by its results and sold its PC division to the Chinese firm Lenovo. Gateway was put into a severe tailspin by Dell and has never recovered. Compaq weathered the Dell storm fairly well until the Internet hit, and then Dell's advantage became so huge that the company also went into a tailspin and wisely sold out to Hewlett-Packard. While the merger of Compaq and Hewlett-Packard temporarily gave it the number one position in PCs in the United States, Dell clearly had the merged company in its sights and overcame it to become number one in the United States. As one analyst put it, the HP-Compaq merger gave Dell a "bigger butt to kick."

Believe it or not, when Dell started in the PC business, Commodore was the industry leader, with a 27 percent market share.

Tandy, Atari, Packard Bell, and Kaypro were also players that faded fast once Dell got into high gear.

Many people criticize Dell because of its small R&D budget. On the other hand, it has done a marvelous job of keeping its products close to the leading edge of technology and focusing only on high-volume categories that fit with its logistics expertise.

It is interesting to note that Dell's business softened significantly in 2006. The primary reason is that its primary competitor, HP, has finally woken up and is moving aggressively to get its costs down.[14] For example, HP eliminated its central sales group, cut over 30,000 jobs, and hired fresh executive talent from Siemens, Palm, and Dell. HP is also reducing the number of data centers that service its business from 85 to 6.[15] All of this is putting enormous price pressure on Dell, causing it to miss several revenue projections in late 2005 and 2006.[16] Even the Most Admired Company can't stand still. In fact, it slipped to number eight on *Fortune*'s Most Admired list in 2006, and after that list was announced, the company suffered additional problems involving a massive laptop battery recall and a decline in its service ratings. In early 2007, Michael Dell stepped back into the CEO role (which he had given up in 2004) to get the company back on track. Superior, lightning-quick logistics has served Dell well for two decades, but the world constantly evolves and improves.

In conclusion, people rarely focus on the business processes once a company enjoys success. The assumption is that things will continue to operate well, as they have in the past. But often the business processes that helped the company achieve its success typically get out of date and overly complex and often emerge as a big impediment to continued success. Our case studies here from Jamie Dimon at Bank One, Michael Dell at Dell and others clearly demonstrate that you need to constantly consolidate and reexamine the core processes that run the organization, or you risk slipping into the trap of complexity.

### PART V

# TRAP #5
# BLOAT:
# RATIONALIZING YOUR LOSS OF SPEED AND AGILITY

**Successful** organizations that were once agile and fast-moving typically tend to reward themselves with more manpower. These extra folks tend to make the business more fragmented, which complicates and slows down decision making. It also leads to slow reaction times to changes in the marketplace, and to a defensive attitude, with many of the groups buried deep in the organization fearing that change would cause them to lose some of their responsibilities and turf.

This diffusion of responsibilities and overly complicated organizational structure result in decisions being debated at length. Unique ideas get watered down because consensus-oriented decision making tends to take over.

A chemical company in the northeast with revenue of roughly $7 billion per year found its business in sad shape in early 2003. It tried to analyze why its costs were so high and why the place had become so complex. As it did a thorough analysis, it uncovered incredible fragmentation throughout the organization. But the information systems mess was probably the worst example.

In the summer of 2003, when the company finally got an accurate count of all the information systems that were being supported by the various arms of the IT organization, the number was quite startling. There were 2,400 separate information systems that required support personnel on an ongoing basis. But more importantly, the company needed people who had some degree of familiarity with each of these systems, so that when it wanted to change them, it had the capacity to do so. This was generating mind-bending complexity and huge costs. The company calculated that it was spending 7.1

> *Customers were tired of dealing with so many different procedures from the same company. And when customers demanded information or assistance that cut across the divisions, the company found it very hard to respond.*

percent of its revenue on IT. The benchmark in its industry was 3.0 to 3.5 percent.

The reason for this problem was the company's divisional structure. Each division had become an isolated unit, or silo, with its own sales organization, manufacturing group, finance group, information technology organization, and human resources personnel. Each of these fragmented components had developed its own information systems to help it run its part of the business. There was no commonality or standards across the organization. More important, this was causing huge problems for customers, since some of those customers bought chemicals from more than one of the divisions. Customers were tired of dealing with so many different procedures from the same company. And when customers demanded information or assistance that cut across the divisions, the company found it very hard to respond.

There were two reasons for this slowness and lack of agility. First, the processes within the various divisions were not designed to work together or to record things in a consistent manner. Second, the company resolved cross-division issues through meetings and consensus, since there was no functional authority in areas such as sales, manufacturing, and logistics that could quickly make a decision on an issue.

The trap of bloat, fragmentation, and consensus decision making leads to loss of agility, which can hurt you badly as you struggle to create new ways to serve the customer or to get out in front of an important product trend quickly. Now let's look at some ways to avoid this trap or to get out of it if you have been captured by it.

# 15

## ARE YOU PARALYZED BY YOUR CURRENT **BUSINESS PRACTICES?**

The people responsible for the various aspects of a business that has been successful typically become very proud and protective of what they do. While there are exceptions, these people tend to be incapable of effectively developing and launching improvements or new processes that would move the organization forward. Too often, they are simply too wedded to the past. What is really problematic is that if the issue of changing things in their area comes up, they will want to take control of any such effort. That is because they fear that they will end up the loser if someone else gets involved and attempts to change things in a way that may make them obsolete.

In addition, if you assign the task of designing and developing the future to the owners of current business processes or products while leaving them with their current set of responsibilities, the future always tends to be a distant second priority.

Current owners will be fearful of change. They will always give it a low priority if they are assigned to bring it about. The lesson is clear: put fresh, talented people on important change projects, and give them the independence they need to think creatively.

# KODAK

Finding a way to get serious momentum to develop a completely new business model or an important new initiative can be very hard. Kodak provides a rich example. In Chapter 2, "Why Does This Happen?" we briefly mentioned the lack of urgency at Kodak with respect to digital photography during the second half of the 1990s. Let's go into the details and see what we learn.

## Kodak: The Mid-1990s

Kodak was one of America's leading companies in the 1980s and early 1990s. It generated impressive financial results, it was the clear leader globally in photographic film and processing, and it earned awards such as placing in the top 10 on *Fortune's* list of most admired companies. Unfortunately, by 1997, Kodak's business was in very bad shape. Operating earnings were falling very significantly, it was losing significant market share to Fuji in a bloody price war on film, and its costs were out of sight as a result of a tradition of no layoffs. George Fisher, who had been CEO for four years, finally had to face the music and make some dramatic changes at Kodak. In the fall of 1997, he announced the elimination of 20,000 Kodak jobs, which sent a shock wave through the company. While short-term market analysts worried about the film business, the longer-term thinkers were concerned about Kodak's lack of focus on digital photography. Although it was putting a lot of R&D money into digital, it was clearly lagging behind many Japanese companies.

As Linda Grant of *Fortune* magazine stated at the time, "Fisher moved too slowly."[1] This was a company whose core business was under attack, and it was clearly having trouble accepting that fact. While its excessive cost structure was killing its film business, the technology that would eventually be its core business, digital photography, was not getting the proper focus and attention. It was lost in the hassles of the current business crisis. The film crisis was the result of Kodak's not adjusting to the new streamlined staffing and low pricing structure required in the new competitive environment that Fuji had generated.

## Kodak: 1999

Given all this turmoil, it wasn't surprising that in June of 1999, Kodak suddenly announced that CEO George Fisher would be stepping down. The timing was a surprise; most people had expected Fisher to work through the end of his contract, which was January 1, 2001. He was replaced by a Kodak insider, Dan Carp.

The problems that led to Fisher's exit were the same as those that had been discussed in 1997. *BusinessWeek* wrote in 1999 that "Fisher waited too long to tackle Kodak's bloated costs" and "Kodak's long-term future is still not clear."[2] Its film had lost its distinctiveness compared to the aggressive Fuji product, and Kodak was treating digital as a second priority. Both film and digital needed to be tackled with gusto and hard-driving leadership. In retrospect, aggressive people should have been put in charge of the digital effort and given the freedom to maximize its impact.

By 1999, Kodak's stock price had dropped to $69 per share, compared with $90 in 1997. As *BusinessWeek* put it, "Despite its lustrous brand name, Kodak was trading at a multiple of just 14 times expected 1999 earnings, according to First Call Corporation, a huge discount to the 25 multiple accorded to the Dow Jones Industrial Average."[3] Kodak's slow reaction to Fuji and to digital photography had caused Wall Street to lose confidence in its future earning power.

## Kodak: 2002

Amazingly, three years later, in 2002, the same core problems at Kodak were being discussed. As noted by Andy Serwer of *Fortune,* "Despite all of Kodak's best efforts, this grand old American brand could very well go the way of Wang. Which is to say, the company may be hanging around for years, but for all intents and purposes, it'll just be twisting slowly in the wind."[4]

The problems in 2002 were no different from the problems that Kodak had been grappling with in the mid-1990s: Fuji kept chipping away at Kodak's very profitable film business, and the digital image revolution was taking place. Kodak was putting some good ideas in the marketplace with respect to digital photography, but it was clear that it was one of many. In addition, it was also clear that digital would be a far less profitable business than Kodak's traditional film business. As noted in *Fortune,* one knowledgeable Wall Street source described Kodak as "entrenched, in-bred, and unresponsive."[5]

In 2002 there was growing concern that Kodak was continually underestimating the speed with which the marketplace would move from film to digital. Kodak was absolutely shocked when the final figures for 2001 came in and showed that digital camera sales had climbed 30 percent. The financial implications of the company's not having tackled its core problems aggressively were immense. The stock price had moved from the $69 level in 1999 down to $27 in early 2002. The company's revenues, which had been at roughly $19 billion per year in the early 1990s, were down at the $13 billion level.

### Kodak: 2003

In late 2003, the situation was becoming quite dire. CEO Dan Carp launched a major effort to overhaul Kodak. He told investors that Kodak would be cutting its dividend by 72 percent in order to put $3 billion into digital photography. He described digital photography as the key hope for putting Kodak back on a growth track. The reaction to this announcement was quite negative. For example, Bill Symonds of *BusinessWeek* wrote, "Problem is, after years of disappointments, investors have little faith in the ability of Carp and his management team to deliver."[6] Carp's announcement caused a quick 14 percent drop in Kodak's stock price, and shareholders were enraged. Jim Mackey, a business consultant, said, "Investors have lost confidence that Kodak knows what to do with the money."

The problem was that this bad dream had been going on for many years. Symonds summarized the situation by saying, "The problem isn't that Carp has the wrong vision—but that he waited until the sky was falling to embrace it. Kodak stumbled in its efforts to build a digital consumer business. It has taken a scatter shot approach to digital photo processing, placing bets on everything from online kiosks to minilabs used by retailers to print photos. By contrast, arch rival Fuji Photo Film Company started sooner, has better technology, and focused more on minilabs, which are expected to dominate the processing market."

During this period, Dan Carp made the amazing statements we cited in Chapter 2: "I saw my first digital camera at Kodak 20 years ago . . . I knew right then that this company was going to transform itself."[7] Dan Carp was making that statement in late 2003, when the company had basically been run over by its competition for the past 10 years. It took Carp and the troops far too long to recognize the power of the digital technology trend, and once they did, they attacked it piecemeal. Even more important, the film business wasn't managed well during the interim. As mentioned earlier, management should have been slashing costs dramatically for the previous decade in order to make sure that Fuji did not gain one single share point, while launching a superaggressive independent effort behind digital that had as its goal to dominate the market as film went the way of the buggy whip.

### Kodak: 2005

Consistent with Kodak's prior behavior, by 2005 not much had changed. As *The Economist* noted: "Back in 2003, Mr. Carp assumed that the film industry would decline by some 10 percent a year in America and by 6 percent worldwide. In fact, it is likely to shrink by 30 percent this year in America and by 20 percent worldwide. The world, it seems, is changing faster than Kodak can."[8]

Given all these problems, it was not surprising that in May 2005, Dan Carp resigned as CEO. There is no doubt that he could describe the nature of the problems at Kodak during his five-year reign, but the company wasn't able to mobilize quickly and get in front of those problems. In the first quarter of 2005, Dan Carp had again announced "disappointing" financial results. Kodak had

*Kodak couldn't act with decisiveness and agility, and it couldn't do two things at the same time—namely, manage film while aggressively launching digital.*

generated a net loss based on yet further restructuring charges, and revenue had declined 3 percent, following the long-term trend that Kodak had been seeing for years.[9]

Dan Carp was replaced as CEO by Antonio Perez in 2005. Perez had spent most of his career at Hewlett-Packard. It didn't take Perez long to figure out what was going on. He immediately stated publicly that the continued steep decline in film sales would require the company to do a lot more restructuring than had previously been announced. He was reflecting the fact that Kodak's worldwide film sales had fallen 31 percent versus a year ago. It had previously forecasted a drop of 20 percent. The restructuring he announced was very dramatic, with a goal of laying off about 24,000 workers, or one-third of Kodak's workforce.[10] More important, digital finally got the focus it had deserved for 10 years.

If you step back and look at the almost 10-year history we've just described, there is one common theme throughout the period: Kodak couldn't act with decisiveness and agility, and it couldn't do two things at the same time—namely, manage film while aggressively launching digital. Its focus was exclusively on film for too long, and in the film business, it lacked the agility to properly fight Fuji. It's a sobering lesson on the importance of protecting your existing business while also tackling new opportunities, even if they do end up cannibalizing your existing business. You have to be agile and fleet of foot on both fronts and then let the consumer decide what direction the industry will go in.

Another vulnerability that arises when you are paralyzed by your current business practices relates to moving your existing business into new environments. Specifically, when faced with taking an existing business into a new geographical area or tackling a new business category, most successful organizations simply reapply legacy practices that have led to success and stability in the past. They tend to get wedded to their existing practices in virtually all areas, such as the marketing positioning of the products, advertising, sales approaches, information technology practices, financial analysis tools, and so on. The notion of "if it ain't broke, don't fix it" is often relied upon, without checking whether it's broke or not, or whether it's about to be broke.

Here are two important points to keep in mind as you move fast in placing your products or services into new geographical areas or new business categories.

1. **Use fresh talent to develop plans for new areas.** When you enter a new market or a new geographical area, all the standard practices you have used in the past should be suspect. Current practices need to be probed in depth by people who do not have a vested interest in simply continuing the status quo.

2. **Determine the differences in the new environment and what changes are needed because of them.** Often success causes individuals to view any differences in a new marketplace as unimportant nuances. The theory is that you'll stick with the basics that you've learned well and that have led to past success. No stone should be left unturned in this area. All differences that emerge must be thoroughly investigated and evaluated in the context of whether they warrant modifications to your current practices.

Let's review an example of a company that seems to do these things very well.

## CITIGROUP

This global financial services powerhouse is a good example of an organization that has performed well by being very agile as it expanded its business from country to country.

The subject of geographical expansion is critically important to Citigroup. This is because about 60 percent of its net income comes from North America. Unfortunately, North America is not a high-growth area for a global bank such as Citigroup, which already has deep penetration in that region.[11] It knows that the high growth rates are outside North America, where it is adding customers at twice their North American rate. Consequently, the bank's real focus is on international markets, and its goal has been clearly stated: it wants half of its earnings coming from international markets by 2009.

## Citigroup: The Challenges

To achieve this goal, Citigroup can't simply reapply its current banking practices in other areas of the world. For example, Bernard Condon of *Forbes* magazine cited the kind of challenges the bank faces in an area such as Brazil.[12] He described a busy street in São Paulo where dozens of salesmen from competing loan shops are pressing flyers into the hands of the passing crowd. The individuals are calling out, "Loans! We make personal loans." That's a far different situation from the one Citigroup faces in cities such as Toronto or Atlanta. It has to be quick on its feet to understand the local practices and adapt to them.

Another key challenge that Citigroup faces in some of these countries is the fact that customers don't trust banks with their hard-earned cash. Also, in many of these countries, people have never used credit cards and have never taken out a bank loan to buy something like a TV or an automobile. The marketing has got to reflect these cultural realities if it is to enable people to understand how a bank can make their lives easier.

A further obstacle in some of these countries, such as Russia, is the primitive legal structure. In many cases, there is no deposit insurance program, and there are no credit bureaus. Citigroup employees are working with local governments to get such activities authorized and to get lending laws changed so that credit card interest can be accrued in a way that's both acceptable to government authorities and understandable and appealing to consumers.

Clever marketing approaches are needed. For example, Citigroup often exploits its connections on the corporate banking side as it enters a country. It will work with the multinational firms that do business in that country to get them interested in providing Citigroup services to their employees in that country.

The sales challenge for Citigroup in these countries is quite unusual. Often the bank has to meet with an individual three or four times before it can persuade that person to believe that his or her money will be safe in a Citigroup bank. Also, it needs to assure its customers that they can withdraw their money at any time, and it needs to have devices such as ATM machines, online capabilities, and branch offices that make it clear to potential customers that their money can be available to them virtually immediately if they need it.

## Citigroup: Learning, Agility, and Results

Citigroup salespeople in these countries need to be trained thoroughly in how to learn about the culture, the ideal ways to interact with customers, how to describe the bank's current offerings so that they are understandable, and how to develop relationships that will attract customers and make them loyal to the bank. Its flexibility is paying off. For example, in India, its strong focus on learning how small and medium-size enterprises operate has enabled it to acquire over 20,000 customers borrowing $500,000 to $1 million, making its India operation one of its fastest-growing corporate banking efforts.

The thing that is impressive about this story is how Citigroup, which had a well-developed approach that had led to success in North America, has worked tirelessly to reflect each country's unique characteristics and move fast. Its agility is critical to its success, and that is often very hard to achieve in an organization that has enjoyed long-standing success. It's a great example of doing things right with respect to staying agile and pursuing clear goals.

# 16

## ASSIGN TOP TALENT TO THE TOUGH ISSUES AND GET OUT OF THEIR WAY

Volumes have been written on the importance of getting the right people in the right job. Different organizations go about this in different ways, but once these people are on board, you need to get them excited about what they can achieve, and then delegate responsibilities to them and see what they can do. Let's take a look at how some organizations go about hiring new employees and delegating responsibility to them.

### PROCTER & GAMBLE

During my 26 years at Procter & Gamble, I learned to appreciate the process it used to consistently get the absolutely very best marketing and business management talent available. The way it went about this was unique. While it followed the same procedures in most countries, I'll describe the process in a U.S. context. P&G

would hire roughly 150 of the very best students from the very top universities who were interested in marketing and place them in its brand management organization. It consisted of many brand groups, with each having three to five people. Each brand group was assigned a single brand, and it was the group's role to make that brand grow significantly in the marketplace.

These brand groups were incredibly exciting places to be. The most experienced member of each brand group was the brand manager, who had, on average, three to five years' experience with the company. The group was managing a brand that had revenue anywhere from $200 million to $1 billion. Importantly, all changes related to that brand would originate from the brand group. It coordinated with product development to figure out what was the best way to improve the product, it was in charge of the package and keeping it contemporary, and it developed the marketing plans and got approval from management to execute them. It was a very exciting and inspiring opportunity for these young people. The job of pointing out opportunities to make these brands grow was completely the responsibility of the brand group.

*One lesson I learned from both P&G and Microsoft, is that once you get great people on board and have them fired up, the worst thing you can do is to encumber them with bureaucratic processes, committees, task forces, clearance processes, and other busywork that simply gums up the work.*

What was most important here was that all 200 of these folks knew at the outset that every year roughly one-third of them would be let go. These personnel decisions were based on business results and estimated long-term potential. It was an up-or-out system that started with the very best talent coming off the campuses. What

P&G was doing was continually distilling that talent pool until some incredible businesspeople had been clearly identified and, through a variety of experiences, made capable of running major portions of the company.

Having personally worked in the P&G brand management environment for several years, I can tell you that it was very stimulating. In fact, it was quite liberating to know that the only thing that counted was results. It was very clear what you needed to do: come up with bright ideas that worked in the marketplace. Also, the place had such a fabulous reputation for its on-the-job general management training that there was no fear of getting fired. Headhunters would be all over you with superb job opportunities. Basically, the place really was all about hiring great people and getting out of their way.

# MICROSOFT

During my almost seven years as chief operating officer of Microsoft, I saw a very different hiring process that was also quite effective, particularly in the technology industry. Microsoft was looking for individuals who had an incredible passion for the computer industry and, most importantly, were superintelligent. The company trained its employees to interview candidates for passion and intelligence. It would seek out candidates from top schools and from other companies. The emphasis was on IQ, and these recruiters were taught a variety of questions to use in probing for such intelligence. By IQ I am implying deep quantitative thinking skills, which, coupled with passion, are ideal for tackling technology and business problems.

For example, a candidate would be asked to estimate the number of gas stations in the United States. What was important was to see what kind of steps this candidate would come up with on the spot to make a reasonable estimate of that number. You weren't after a "correct" answer; you were interested in the speed and creativity with which the candidate could put together a reasonable process for making a somewhat reasonable estimate. I often tell people that I believe the core competence of Microsoft, in my opinion, is recruiting. It recruits for incredible enthusiasm and raw intelligence, and the list stops there. You could be quite "unusual," but as long as you were incredibly enthusiastic and remarkably intelligent, you would fit in well at Microsoft.

During the period while I was at Microsoft, from 1994 to 2001, the company was growing very rapidly, 25 to 30 percent per year. Headcount was kept very tight, and consequently, the idea of delegating responsibility was an absolute necessity to run the place. Capabilities such as the Internet were just beginning to emerge, and Microsoft was battling strong competitors such as WordPerfect and Lotus 1-2-3. The task was clear: we needed a better product than those competitors, and we needed a lot of innovation in order to get ahead of important technology trends. Given the lean staffing, you had no alternative but to delegate and count on people to make it happen.

One lesson I learned over the years from both P&G and Microsoft, as well as from the consulting I have done since, is that once you get great people on board and have them fired up to achieve marvelous things, the worst thing you can do is to encumber them with bureaucratic processes, committees, task forces, clearance processes, and other busywork that simply gums up the work. Greatness is all about distinctiveness and uniqueness, and the way to get that is to have great people who are really excited about making a huge difference. Committees and bureaucratic processes chip away at uniqueness and make things satisfactory to everyone but exciting to no one.

# NIKE

Let's take a close look at another company that has done very well over the years in an industry that requires speed and agility.

## Nike: The Beginning

In 1964, Phil Knight launched a small shoe business with his old track coach, Bill Bowerman. They imported relatively inexpensive,

> *Knight's model was very simple: find excellent people who care passionately about the product, and get out of their way.*

but very high quality running shoes from Japan made by Onitsuka Tiger. Knight literally sold these shoes out of the back of his car at high school track meets. However, he and Bowerman were worried that Tiger would look for a more established distributor, so they thought they should invent their own brand and get into the business.

They moved fast. They selected the name Nike because it was the name of the Greek goddess of victory. They paid a local student in Portland $35 to develop a logo: a simple swoosh (which is now identified with the Nike name throughout the world). Even in those very early days, Phil Knight was looking for passionate people. Daniel Roth of *Fortune* magazine described some of the early meetings of the team: "Nike's early management meetings were rowdy, drunken affairs known internally as 'buttfaces.' When fights broke out among his men—and they were mostly men—Knight would rarely interrupt. He liked to see the passion."[1]

### Nike: Delegation

Knight was also known for being totally hands-off about direction. For example, when he started up Nike's business in Europe, he told his sales folks to "sell shoes." He knew that he had hired really good people, and he needed to let them run (no pun intended).

As an example of the independence that he gave his people, it's interesting to look at how the famous waffle-sole shoe came into existence. Its inventor was Knight's partner Bowerman. He personally recounts, "I was looking at my wife's waffle iron, and I thought it looked like a pretty good traction device."[2] He did some experimenting by pouring a liquid rubber compound into his wife's waffle iron. This led to Nike's launch of the waffle shoe in 1970, and it was perfectly timed because the United States was beginning to turn jogging into the national pastime. Part of the reason why was a book called *Jogging*, which was launched in 1967 by none other than Bill Bowerman.

Bowerman had been Knight's track coach at Oregon. Phil Knight absolutely adored Bowerman because Bowerman truly knew how to inspire people. Looking back at those track days at Oregon, Knight said, "Bowerman really did get into your head that you could be the best in the world." Phil Knight became an absolute student of that capability, and to him, Bill Bowerman was his absolute inspiration. In fact, the road that leads to the Nike empire in Oregon is called Bowerman Drive.

Knight's model was very simple: find excellent people who care passionately about the product, and get out of their way. He certainly did that with the initial team that launched the company. Bowerman designed the shoes, and Jeff Johnson managed the marketing. Bowerman was the driver of the famous waffle-sole shoe, and Johnson was the guy who paid $35 for the swoosh.

There are many stories about Knight and his complete delegation of duties and dislike for complex structures. Mark Parker, who was co-president of the Nike brand, said that in formal presentations, when people are plowing through PowerPoint slides, Knight "sort of checks out."[3] Another story about Parker and Knight refers to a visit they made to the famous Wal-Mart Saturday morning meeting. Lee Scott, the CEO of Wal-Mart, was running through the standard kind of business review with numbers galore and directives galore, and the story is that Parker turned to Knight and said, "It's a little different here." Knight responded: "You are damn right."

What is interesting about Knight is that he's really not a people person. As Roth of *Fortune* says, "He manages to do three things better than just about anyone in the business: hire good people, shuffle them around, and inspire them."[4] In the spring of 1983, Phil Knight decided to take an extended personal trip through China. He designated employee Bob Woodell as the president, and off he went to China. Unfortunately for Woodell, the jogging craze in the United States started to cool off, but aerobics was red hot. Woodell kept the focus on running and basketball. Reebok saw the trend and jumped all over it.

## Nike: Decisive People Moves

Knight quickly realized that he needed to get the right people in the right jobs quickly, and he returned in the fall of 1984 to reenergize the company. The late 1980s were rough as Phil Knight worked to get the ship back on course. He reported to shareholders in 1988 that "all of our Vice Presidents listed in the 1981 annual report have left." His job was to rebuild the company with a hand-selected new team, using his usual simplistic approach of going after great people with lots of passion for the product.

The early and mid-1990s saw Nike achieve incredible results. By mid-1996, it was selling $6.5 billion of sneakers, apparel, and sports equipment per year, with annual profits of just over $550 million. That's a profit margin of 8.5 percent, which is incredible, given that a lot of people believe that items such as sneakers, apparel, and sports equipment are commodities.

By mid-1997, Nike's market share of U.S. footwear was over 40 percent, and Nike was clearly on top of its game. Once again, as happened back in 1983, Phil Knight seemed bored and was spending less time at the company. If you read articles about Nike during this period, it's not clear what Knight was doing with his time, but he was often seen attending sporting events. Basically, the company was being run by Tom Clarke, a product developer who was named president in 1994. Repeating history, just as it had done the first time Phil Knight checked out, Nike's business began to soften. The high-end sneaker market in the United States went into a downturn, and Nike got hit with some incredibly negative publicity. It was accused of producing its shoes in Asian "sweatshops."

By 1999, Phil Knight was back in the saddle at Nike, and Clark was moved to a different job within the company. As reported in the press, "Knight did what he does best: find and motivate talented people, let them do their own thing. He brought in outsiders, stars like Mindy Grossman of Ralph Lauren to run apparel, Don Blair from Pepsi to be the CFO and Mary Kate Buckley from Disney to head up new ventures."[5]

Phil Knight was very astute in spotting key trends, not just in the world of athletic shoes and apparel but also in what was going on in the world around him. For example, when the Internet began to emerge, Knight's intuition said that it was important, but remember, he's not a detail guy. So what did he do? He brought in an impressive list of Internet industry executives to educate his employees about the web.[6] He kicked off the sessions by saying, "I don't understand all this stuff, but it's incredibly important, and we are going to get ahead of it." Knight put good people on the task, and before long, Nike.com was a major contributor to the company.

> *Put great people in key jobs, inspire them to go for fabulous dreams, and then get out of their way.*

## Nike: Inspiration

Knight was famous for hiring great people. He would point them in a certain direction and leave it entirely up to them to figure out what to do, but he would also make sure they knew that he expected great things. One story from former Vice President of Global Marketing Liz Dolan demonstrates how Knight came upon this approach. Knight told Dolan, "Once during college he had asked Bowerman for some advice on improving his running times. Bowerman replied: triple your speed." Dolan then explained, "That's the kind of advice you get from Phil." She elaborated: "He is less likely to sit down and break it down for you. He believes you can figure it out . . . he focuses more on talking to you one-on-one to get the best out of you rather than setting corporate strategy per se."[7]

In 1999, when he returned from his second "sabbatical," Knight called a rare all-employee meeting. They all met in Nike's Bo Jackson Fitness Center, and 1,500 people listened to Knight tell them that they had been down before but that they had always come back. He stressed that it was now time for them to "elevate their game."[8] At the end of this presentation, he apologized for his absence, and he started to choke up. Clearly all 1,500 people in that audience understood that it was their job to go out and truly make his dream of elevating their game a reality because they knew that he genuinely cared so much for them and for the company. Former General Manger Andrew Black said, "I'll never forget that speech." He went on to explain, "He inspired you to such a level that you just knew you wanted to do more for him than you were doing before. He challenged all of us to really get focused. He's the kind of leader— you can hear a pin drop when he speaks. He had the whole place giving him a standing ovation for quite awhile when he finished."

For the next several years, Nike did what it does best, and by the end of fiscal year 2004, it was back on top. From 2000 to 2004, revenue grew from $9.5 billion to nearly $14 billion. The company's market share of branded athletic footwear grew back to 40 percent, and the next biggest was Reebok at 13 percent.

Between 2000 and 2004, Nike stock price grew from $40 per share to $87. It has continued to make progress, reaching $100 in late 2006. An investor who had bet $1,000 on Nike and its waffle-sole shoe and $35 swoosh when it went public back in 1980 would now be holding $73,000.

There are lots of ways to run an organization, but it's very clear that one way to constantly chase out legacy practices is to put great people in key jobs, inspire them to go for fabulous dreams, and then get out of their way. Phil Knight was clearly world class in this regard. His people love him because they know that he cares deeply about seeing the group succeed, and he deeply trusts them to make it happen.

# 17

## THE KEY
### TO SPEED AND AGILITY
## IS LEADERSHIP

You simply must get the right people in the key jobs if you are to move organizations along smartly to tackle the future. Those individuals can't have a consensus mentality; they have to be real leaders who enjoy taking some risks and quickly modifying things on the fly as they learn new facts in their pursuit of setting the trends.

Let's take a look at an example of a fairly successful business that was starting to weaken but where a strong leader took charge and started making some tough decisions to get things back on track.

## HEWLETT-PACKARD

Hewlett-Packard has been immensely successful in the printer business. It has had more than a 50 percent market share of that fast-growing business for the last two decades, and by 2005, its revenues were in the range of $24 billion per year.

Printers represented 73 percent of HP's $2.4 billion in earnings in fiscal 2004, even though they represented less than a third of Hewlett-Packard's $80 billion in sales for that fiscal year. It's very easy to get set in your ways when those kinds of numbers are being posted regularly.

## HP: The Challenges

By 2005, there were clear signals that HP was dragging its feet in the printer industry. Dell had launched printers that went head-to-head against HP's offerings. HP's market share of the U.S. printer business had fallen to 47 percent in 2004, and printer prices were dropping. As a result, its operating margins were dropping, and revenue growth was slowing a bit every year and was expected to come in at about 5.7 percent for 2005.

Besides Dell as a competitor, the real concern was a host of cartridge refillers that were going after HP's incredibly lucrative ink sales. All of these competitive forces caused Marco Boer, an information technology consultant, to assess the situation as follows: "They are getting whacked from all sides."[1]

Clear evidence of the slowing occurred in the first quarter of 2005. HP's printer division saw revenue grow only at 5 percent, compared to the 11 percent growth that had occurred a year earlier. Importantly, profit margins fell to 13.8 percent, from 15.6 percent a year earlier.

For the first time in years, HP was clearly under attack. Besides Dell, HP was seeing strong competition from Epson, Canon, and Lexmark. All of these competitors had rolled out redesigned products at cut-rate prices in 2004. These competitors, plus the ink refillers charging prices that were 20 to 50 percent less than HP's, were the source of HP's difficulties.

## HP: A Leader Emerges

Clearly HP should have anticipated these kinds of activities and gotten out in front of them with some fresh new products and services. It finally began to do that, led by Vyomesh "VJ" Joshi, HP's executive vice president running the printer operation. In December of 2004, VJ organized a three-day meeting with his top managers.

He went over the *Harvard Business Review* paper called "Darwin and the Demon," which is a description of the perils that businesses face when they fail to adapt to new conditions.

> *It is important to cut your losses and move on when things aren't working. That requires real leadership.*

In 2004, VJ also made his concerns clear by issuing a 48-page white paper that stated, "History is against us."[2] He then went on to explain, "Extraordinary businesses always become complacent and don't do the tough things to make themselves healthy. It was clear that we needed to change."

While HP shouldn't have waited around for weak market share and weak margins to tell it that it was not attacking the future fast enough, at least one of its key leaders saw the need and grabbed the issue and ran with it.

One of the first steps that VJ took was to launch a major cost-cutting effort in order to generate funds that could be used for growth initiatives. He launched a voluntary severance program in the United States that eliminated 1,900 jobs. For some of the units within the printer division, this resulted in a departure rate as high as 25 percent. Another bold step was to move the assembly of inkjet cartridges from in-house HP facilities to low-cost contract manufactures in Malaysia. Not only did this save a lot of money; it sent a clear signal on what was important for the employees of HP to focus on—namely, the future.

Joshi also led the charge in shifting HP's investments away from the basic product line to the areas of high potential growth, such as digital photography and digital publishing. He also launched efforts to build revenue streams from services, such as online photo printing sites and licensing HP's printer technology.

As it worked to attack the future, HP developed some very unusual and high-potential technology referred to as "page-wide arrays."[3] This technology would use thousands of nozzles to print an entire page at once, as opposed to having a single cartridge that moves across the page. This is the kind of thing that the leader in an industry should be tackling with gusto, and at long last HP had started to do that kind of thing.

In order to keep the organization lean and focused on the future, VJ also led the charge to discontinue activities that had been going on for years but ended up having marginal impact. For example, there had been a multiyear effort to get into the corporate copier business. The business had never really materialized, and VJ put an end to it. There was also a major project focused on developing products for the health-care sector. It was also killed. All of this made the organization leaner and more focused on developing a continuous stream of industry-leading products, something that a successful organization should be constantly working to achieve.

Stepping back, while it took some rude financial results to wake up HP in the printer area, it seems that it had gotten the message, and now the only question is whether or not it waited too long to tackle things and gave its competitors too big a jump on matching and eventually exceeding the offerings that had made HP's printer business successful.

Concerning speed, agility, and leadership, one other area we should cover is the importance of cutting your losses and moving on when things aren't working. That requires real leadership. Let's look at this problem in detail.

Once an organization approves a project and it gets rolling, it's often very difficult to stop it or change its direction. For an organization to really remain agile, it needs to be fully capable of constantly looking over what it does and judging which things should be eliminated and which things should be more fully supported in the future. Shutting down a project or a service is very difficult for three reasons:

1. **People get protective.** The individuals who are working on the project, as well as the management that agreed to the project, have a vested interest in making it successful. Over time, the notion of eliminating "their baby" becomes a real

problem. The reason is fear. For those working on the project, they fear what would happen to them if the effort were eliminated. For the management that agreed to the effort, the tendency is to continue because it fears embarrassment. Shutting down a project is often viewed as a negative, and everyone involved worries about carrying a stigma of failure. For these reasons, it can be extremely difficult to get an organization to stop an effort.

2. **Lack of objectivity.** The people who are working hard to make a project successful are basically advocates of that effort. You want it that way. On the other hand, people often lose their objectivity when they are put in an advocacy position. This results in the effort's being looked at through rose-colored glasses. Problems that exist are worked on, but the fundamental question of eliminating the effort entirely is rarely put on the table.

3. **Low priority.** When a project is started, the going business of the organization typically has first priority, and the careful nurturing of the new project gets second priority. Consequently, there is no sense of urgency to constantly evaluate whether the effort ought to be stopped or not. This typically leads to shallow analysis of what is really going on, and that results in poor decision making with regard to the future of the effort.

Let's take a look at a major corporation that had troubles in this area but whose strong leadership eventually emerged and dealt with them.

## INTEL

This corporate giant provides us with a robust example of an organization that really struggled with some new projects and a lack of leadership. During the latter part of the 1980s and all of the 1990s, Intel dominated the silicon chip microprocessor business and,

> *Leadership, focus, and talent are the key components for keeping your organization fast and agile.*

along with Microsoft, really established the PC business as a giant industry. In the late 1990s, however, Intel was a victim of the Internet hype. It was particularly vulnerable because it was riding a wave of huge success and had a lot of cash. It launched several efforts to move beyond personal computers and into markets such as communications, information appliances, and Internet services.[4] Specifically, it began making chips for networking gear, for cell phones, and for handheld computers, and it launched efforts to market its own hardware in the form of network servers, Web surfing devices, and routers to guide data over networks. It also attempted to build a services business, with Intel running e-commerce operations for other organizations.

In 1999, Intel paid $2.2 billion to acquire Level One Communications, a maker of chips for broadband devices.[5] In fact, in 1999 and 2000 alone, Intel spent more than $8.7 billion on 28 different acquisitions.

The majority of these efforts got off to a very slow start, but because of the overall success that Intel was having, these new projects probably didn't get the scrutiny that they should have had in order to judge, on an ongoing basis, what should be shut down and what should be viewed as significant future profit contributors.

### Intel: The Bubble Bursts

Reality came crashing down on Intel in the latter part of 2001.[6] The Internet bubble had burst, and PC sales were declining compared with a year earlier, something that simply had never happened before. In 2001, Intel's revenues dropped 21 percent, which was a traumatic event for a company that was used to double-digit revenue growth. In fact, in the 1980s and 1990s, revenue grew at an average annual rate of 21 percent as Intel chips rode the tremendous growth in the PC market.

One of the biggest projects that Intel had difficulties killing was its Web-hosting venture. It is estimated that Intel put $2 billion into this business, which never really materialized.[7] In September 2001, when Web-hosting leader Exodus Communications filed for bankruptcy, Intel took the position that it was sticking with its Web-hosting venture, even though most analysts reported that Intel's data centers were virtually empty.

## Intel: The Cleanup Begins

Given its late 2001 financial disappointments, Intel finally faced the music and began to kill some things. It closed down a service for broadcasting shareholders' meetings and training sessions over the Web. It closed down the iCat, an e-commerce and hosting service for small and midsize businesses. It also phased out its information appliance business, which was working on small devices to access information on the Web.

In 2005, Intel named a new CEO, Paul Otellini. He was an Intel veteran, and he jumped into the new job very quickly. He announced broadly that the strategy for diversifying beyond microprocessors was going to be put aside; instead, Intel would push its microprocessors into new markets.[8] Basically, Otellini was getting back to the basics of what Intel does well: microprocessors. He focused the entire organization on four end markets: enterprise companies, the home, mobile devices, and chips for health care. In each of these four areas, Otellini charged the organization with figuring out how its microprocessors can be most productively exploited and launching products and services that are focused on customer needs instead of performance statistics for a particular chip. He also took that opportunity to kill whatever projects remained from the company's efforts in the late 1990s to broaden its impact.

The Internet had lulled Intel into a mode of operation that involved simply increasing the speed of the Pentium chip each year while launching several new projects, almost as experiments, into the marketplace. It's surprising that this mode of operation continued for such a long time. While the company's stock price was in the $70 range during the year 2000, it was down to $25 per share by the end of 2001 and was still at that level when Paul Otellini took over in 2005. By the fall of 2006, the price was in the $20 to $25 range, and Intel was clearly finding it difficult to recapture the momentum of its glory days.

There are great lessons in this Intel story. Once projects get started you need to question their existence regularly. Otherwise, you run the risk that they will become entrenched legacy activities. It requires strong and decisive leadership to constantly deal with things that just aren't working. As we can see from all of the companies we discussed in this part, leadership, focus, and talent are the key components for keeping your organization fast and agile.

### PART VI

# TRAP #6
# MEDIOCRITY:
# CONDONING POOR PERFORMANCE AND LETTING YOUR STAR EMPLOYEES LANGUISH

**Many successful** organizations fall into the trap of sloppy personnel management. This is very dangerous, since people are your most important asset. These companies treat all their employees well, but they also treat all their employees about the same. While many companies take pride in this approach, the problem is that the superstars don't get stretched and the poor performers don't get confronted. Typically the performance appraisal system atrophies to the point where it is nearly nonexistent. The organization evolves from a meritocracy to one that is attempting to create a team spirit centered on a successful past.

There are some simple and crisp steps that you need to take to revitalize your talent pool and to create that lean, mean fighting machine. These things are right out of the basic human resources handbook, but it is shocking how seldom they are done with excellence.

1. **Institute a performance appraisal process that is actually used for each and every employee at least annually.** Make sure that there are checks and balances to ensure that everyone gets a high-quality appraisal and that the ratings for people are adequately spread out. Roughly 10 percent of your people should be classified as excellent, and there should be a bottom 10 percent who are clearly classified as doing unsatisfactory work. For those who are not doing well, the ramifications need to be spelled out: if the poor performance continues, they will need to find a new job, either

within the company or outside the company. The middle 80 percent of employees need to be managed according to how they are doing. There are many solid contributors in that group, and they need to be adequately rewarded. Also, there are some emerging superstars, and they need to be given the appropriate attention.

2. **Compensation plans as well as emotional rewards need to vary significantly by performance rating.** Put another way, your strong performers should get significant rewards, and your poor performers should get virtually nothing. Individuals in the middle group need to be compensated appropriately depending on whether they are tending toward the top group or the bottom group. In too many organizations, the salary increases and bonuses are mechanical, and there is not much differentiation between the rewards given to the really strong performers and those given to the weak performers. This is really a demoralizer for your superstars, and it causes your weak performers to really want to hang on because they have such a good deal. Naturally, you don't want either of these things to happen.

3. **Get rid of the deadwood.** You really do need to deal with those weak performers. Everyone in the organization knows who they are and is watching how you are going to deal with them. If you put up with weak performance, it sends a clear signal that people really don't have to work hard to do just fine. Again, it's a major demotivator for your really strong performers.

4. **Fast-track your superstars and rotate your average performers.** Leaving people in a job too long is bad. The superstars need to be stretched. The average performers will become the protectors of the legacy practices they are familiar with. That hurts the organization, and, even more dangerous, the organization begins to believe that those individuals are critical and must be left in their current job because

> they represent a scarce resource that has deep accumulated knowledge. Unfortunately, what they have accumulated are the inflexible legacy practices that these individuals instituted and protected while their skills have atrophied.

You really do want an organization that is anxious to take on the next challenge. Even if you are in the midst of raging success, you need to create an atmosphere that clearly says that you are after the next level of excellence.

In the chapters within this part, we will focus on the key fundamentals that help you avoid the nasty trap of sloppy personnel practices.

# 18

## SET THE BAR HIGH IN SELECTING PEOPLE AND SETTING EXPECTATIONS

First, let's deal with the personnel selection issue. An organization is really penalized when it has people in key jobs who simply aren't capable of meeting the expectations for those jobs. These situations should be dealt with quickly. You need to have very high standards for selecting the new person in order to maximize the impact the organization can have.

When I look back at my almost four decades of experience in industry, my work with various nonprofits over the years, and my long exposure to various educational organizations, I can't tell you how often I have seen managers finally admit it took them too long to remove someone who was not cutting it. You need to help that individual find a better fit for his talent and get a strong new person into the job quickly so that you begin to see the desired results.

The key reason why these decisions take so long is the fact that we are dealing with the performance of human beings, which is not an easy subject for the supervisor and the subordinate to talk about.

Since it is a difficult discussion, the tendency is to delay it. That is the same reason why performance appraisals are often ineffective or don't get done at all.

The task of getting the right people into the right jobs can be made a whole lot easier if you follow four principles:

1. **Articulate clear objectives and delegate clear decision-making responsibilities.** Often people aren't performing well in a particular job because no one has ever clarified what they are supposed to be accomplishing. Also, it's often unclear which decisions they get to make and which decisions require them to seek the concurrence of others. The wise employee will work her boss over very thoroughly to make sure she has ironed out what those objectives are and what kind of decisions she gets to make. When employees have that information, it gives a much better framework for judging, on an ongoing basis, whether you have the right employee in the right job. You can measure performance against those clear objectives, and you can observe whether the individual is making the key decisions crisply.

2. **Select people you are confident can deliver the objectives.** In placing people in jobs, we often compromise, recognizing that while the fit is OK, it is not great. The decision on the "fit" of the individual to the job doesn't require a close match of experience to the task (although that is beneficial); it does require a sense of the individual's innate ability to quickly grasp the needs of the position and take action. If you sense that the fit is not ideal, you should be aware that this usually leads to problems. You should be very stubborn in selecting talent. You need to totally believe that the person can handle the challenges of the job he is being considered for. Taking extra time to get it right pays huge dividends. Don't make compromises by placing people in jobs and hoping that they will overcome your areas of concern. That is a dangerous strategy.

3. **Avoid cronyism.** Managers tend to put people whom they feel comfortable with into jobs. There is some merit to this because the managers have a good understanding of the strengths and weaknesses of these people. But these managers have to understand that they do have a bias in making those decisions. It is incredibly important to be very tough on yourself when placing an individual in a job.

4. **Don't let people meddle who don't have responsibility.** Too often in an organization, when a person is responsible for picking key people for key jobs, other individuals will meddle with that decision. They will attempt to put pressure on that manager to choose someone who will benefit them but who will not necessarily benefit the manager. The person responsible for filling a job needs to have a very clear head with regard to the objectives and the kind of skills that are needed. He or she needs to make very realistic assessments of what candidates will and will not be able to accomplish. Often others have different agendas, and it can really weaken an organization when there is a lot of meddling going on in filling key jobs.

While these kinds of problems occur at all levels of an organization, let's take a look at what has happened at a very high level in a well-known company. I think you'll see some of the kinds of problems we are discussing in getting the right people into the right jobs.

## COCA-COLA

In October 1997, Coca-Cola suffered from the loss of a truly beloved leader, CEO Roberto Goizueta. Goizueta had steered Coca-Cola to enormous financial success with a sustained, 16-year increase in the company's value.[1] Goizueta had been overcome by lung cancer and passed away, leaving Coca-Cola somewhat in shock, since he had been such a magnificent leader of that company.

## Coca-Cola: High-Level Game Playing

In filling a key job such as the CEO of Coca-Cola, or in filling any key job, it is important to make it clear how the selection decision will be made. For a CEO assignment, this is typically done by forming a subcommittee of the board that reviews candidates and sets high standards with respect to making sure that the board gets what it needs. In essence, the subcommittee has to execute all of the steps we just described. What happened at Coca-Cola after Goizueta died was a disaster for that company. As Betsy Morris of *Fortune* magazine put it, "It didn't take long for the feuding to begin."[2]

The two key players here were Douglas Ivester, who was Goizueta's heir apparent, and Don Keough, a longtime Coke executive who had really been the public face of the company during the many years that Goizueta was CEO. While Keough had retired from Coca-Cola and from its board in 1993 for age reasons, he continued to attend all board meetings as an advisor to Goizueta. The board gave the CEO title to Doug Ivester. After that decision, many board members continued to believe that Keough was absolutely critical to the Coca-Cola operation and would regularly seek his input. On the other hand, as Betsy Morris said in her *Fortune* article, "It was well known that Keough and Ivester couldn't stand each other."

It didn't take long for the press to begin to point out the problems that Coca-Cola was having, and it pinned a lot of those problems on Ivester. It was said in *Fortune* magazine that "The biggest problem [about Ivester] was his tin ear. Ivester was high in IQ but terribly short on EQ [Emotional Quotient]. A self-made, stubborn, very shy son of a North Georgia mill worker, he had gotten where he was through brains and hard work. He resented Keough's grandstanding, say people who knew him well, and never fully appreciated the importance of Goizueta's almost daily chats with directors. Before long, head down and full-tilt in a turbulent market, Ivester had alienated European regulators, executives at big customers like Wal-Mart and Disney, and some big bottlers, including Coca-Cola Enterprises."[3]

When Don Keough retired in 1993, he assumed a role at the investment firm Allen & Company, which was run by Herbert Allen,

> *I can't tell you how often I've seen managers finally admit that it took them too long to remove someone who was not cutting it.*

who was also a board member at Coca-Cola. Consequently, Keough's impact on the board through both his very close relationship with Allen and his very active relationship with other board members led to quite a soap opera. Keough would send memos and suggestions to Ivester, but the new CEO tried to keep Keough out of things.[4] As *Fortune* noted, "By shutting out Keough, Ivester made a fatal miscalculation. Making matters worse, Ivester hadn't done much over the years to ingratiate himself with Keough's ally, Herbert Allen, either. In fact, he had done just the opposite."

Given all this infighting, it was not surprising that in December 1999, when Douglas Ivester was on a business trip, he was met at the Chicago airport by Warren Buffett and Herbert Allen and told that the board had lost confidence in him. Ivester agreed to retire.

## Coca-Cola: Another Try

The Coca-Cola board next selected Doug Daft, another Coca-Cola insider, to be the new CEO. Daft had spent most of his career outside the United States. It was a surprise pick, and Daft was described by *Fortune* magazine as being Coke's "accidental" CEO. It went on to explain, "Part of his success in Asia, according to several direct reports, was his consensus-driven style, his knack for diplomacy. He couldn't stomach conflict, though." *Fortune* went on to note that a Coca-Cola executive commented about Daft by saying, "He would run from a fight. He was a nice man, but a terrible pick for a CEO."

Once again, you have to step back and say, why isn't this company following the simple rules that we outlined earlier and naming a committee of the board to do a thorough job of selecting a well-equipped candidate to do this tough job at Coca-Cola? While we are focusing here on the CEO assignment at a major company, the same principles apply to jobs at any level in an organization. You need a strong focus on the basic principles of carefully outlining what the job is and what kinds of objectives you are going to give the individuals, and making an objective assessment of whether the candidate can deliver.

Concerning Doug Daft, the press described him as "a Keough man." *Fortune* magazine noted the following: "Daft sought Keough's imprimatur on big personnel decisions, according to people who knew both men. One of the few times he stood up to Keough was when he named Jack Stahl (an Ivester man) his president and chief operating officer. Keough objected. In an obvious vote of no confidence, Stahl was not named to the board. Before long, Stahl was left out of important meetings, including a key strategy meeting in Wyoming that included all of his direct reports. Stahl then left for Revlon." This caused Daft to get even closer to Keough, realizing his importance in getting things done. Stepping back, it is amazing how strong a role Keough was playing, given that he was simply advising board members after he retired in 1993.

## Coca-Cola: The Impact

All of this meddling and uncertainty at the highest levels of Coca-Cola had a brutally negative impact. The period from 1998 to 2004 was described the following way by Betsy Morris in *Fortune*: "A roiling six years of public blunders and musical chairs in the executive suite, unsettling at any company but especially Coke, where impeccable leadership was always considered critical to maintaining the integrity of its brand and its reputation on Wall Street. Partly as a result, Coke's stock has been trading in the $50 range, well off its high of $88 in 1998."[5]

Stepping back, while Coca-Cola had these difficulties at a very high level, problems of this kind can exist at all levels within an organization. No matter what the setting, when you are faced with filling a position in your organization, you need to carefully define responsibilities, delineate the required skills, and get the very best talent in that job so that success can be achieved. It all sounds so simple, but the human emotions that often emerge from surprising places when you are moving people into important positions can

> *People often don't perform well because no one has ever clarified what they are supposed to be accomplishing.*

really obscure what is really happening.

Now let's deal with the issue of making sure your people know your high expectations. At every level within an organization, employees should understand that they need to execute their current activities with excellence and, equally important, they need to find ways to generate significant improvement in all aspects of their work and the organization's work. There are several valuable ways in which a leader can reinforce such expectations to the troops. Let's review some of the key ones.

1. **Constantly communicate the message.** When you are a manager of a group, you need to be constantly communicating your expectations and underscoring the value you place on getting fresh ideas. Whenever you send out written documents to the group, whenever you talk to the group, whenever you have one-on-one sessions with various members of the group, you need to constantly be reinforcing your high expectations and the fact that you want new ideas and you are counting on folks to generate better ways to do things. This has to be a full-scale attack from all angles. It isn't something you can just mention in a once-a-year State of the Union talk for your organization. It must be constant and consistent for it to really become clear to the organization.

2. **Reward fresh thinking and risk taking.** By reward, I mean not only giving proper financial treatment to those people who are highly effective at improving the organization. I also mean giving these people some public acknowledgement that their work is greatly appreciated. Sometimes that means singling out an individual or a group while talking to the larger group and indicating what that individual or group

has done and why you appreciate it. Once again, managers should look at all the standard vehicles they use to communicate with the troops, and they should think about ways to constantly be sending the signal that this kind of activity is deeply appreciated and that the people who really drive change and improve effectiveness are the ones who are getting the attention.

3. **Put your best people to work to develop new ideas.** Individuals in the organization know who the top performers are. When they see a manager reach for these performers and assign them to develop and implement fresh thinking and to lead change-oriented projects, it sends a very clear signal about what is important in the organization. The individuals themselves will feel highly energized by being given a real challenge, and you tend to get extraordinary performance. There is no finer way to develop people than to throw them into new and somewhat unstructured situations, but be clear about what it is you want to see happen. This is precisely how you develop the future leaders in the organization.

4. **Beware of stifling chains of command.** Too often, organizations have too many layers. At many of those layers are bureaucrats who simply view themselves as gatekeepers. As new ideas emerge, especially when they are different from the way things have been done in the past, all kinds of barriers get put in place. All managers need to constantly be reaching down into their organization to work with the folks who are specifically assigned to an area where action is going to occur. This kind of regular inspection by the manager of how a particular project is going and how the leader of that project is carrying it out sends a critical message to the organization: the delegation of responsibility really means something and people do have the ability to really utilize their talents to the fullest.

# MICROSOFT

There is a great story that came out of Microsoft a few years ago, showing the kind of personal energy to generate improvement we are talking about. It is about the company's need to launch a major effort to strengthen the search capabilities of its MSN Web Service. Google was coming on strong and appeared to be taking over the Web search field. Google was clearly going to be highly profitable because it had found a way to make money from people's Internet searches. It had perfected the ability to place pertinent ads next to the subject matter in which a person was interested.

As reported by Fred Vogelstein of *Fortune*, a Microsoft employee by the name of Chris Payne came forward to confront Microsoft's top management about the need to launch a major effort to catch up with and eventually get ahead of Google in the search engine business.[6] Chris was a recently appointed vice president who was in charge of overseeing a variety of Web products under the banner of MSN. He was given his golden opportunity to make his pitch to Bill Gates and Steve Ballmer, along with several other top managers from Microsoft. I should note that I had retired by this time, so I was not involved in the session. Chris had been making a lot of noise about Microsoft putting inadequate effort into this area, sending e-mails in every direction pointing out the missed opportunity. At Microsoft, it is perfectly legitimate for anybody to e-mail anybody, so Chris made sure he went out of his way to get his message to the very top at Microsoft.

Bill Gates knew that Chris was pointing out a key issue, and so he scheduled a session to allow him to provide his point of view and suggest to the company what it should be doing.

## Microsoft: The Proposal

Chris Payne knew it would be a tough meeting. As Fred Vogelstein reported, "The Chairman never said yes until he had subjected the idea to a withering barrage of questions." Having worked with the company for many years, I know that is exactly how things work at Microsoft. Chris Payne gave his pitch and was pelted from every angle with regard to potential weaknesses in his thinking and in his plans. Up until that point, MSN had been outsourcing its search function to third parties. Payne went into detail on the elegance of the approaches that Google used in its search engine and compared them to the way Microsoft's current offerings on MSN operated. Chris then spelled out the incredible potential of online advertising in a search context.

Chris Payne asked for the order. He indicated that the company should spend $100 million in an 18-month period to build its own search engine, and he outlined how he thought that should be done. He also suggested that Microsoft put its absolute top talent on the effort.

*The very act of Bill Gates and his top folks giving Chris Payne a couple of hours to thoroughly explain his thinking sends a powerful signal throughout the organization. It makes it clear that all employees are expected to come up with ideas to help the company stay competitive.*

When Payne was finished, and all the questions were finally adequately debated, Bill Gates agreed that the effort was needed, and Chris was assigned to lead it. It became known as Project Underdog, and it was staffed as Chris had suggested it should be.

Word of the new effort, which was very high profile because of the success that Google was having, spread throughout Microsoft within hours. Employees saw top performers being pulled from a variety of organizations as Project Underdog was assembled.

## Microsoft: The Culture of Change

This meeting occurred because Microsoft had a culture in which it was fair game to point out the problems and push hard at all levels to make something happen. Not only is that kind of behavior OK at Microsoft, it is expected. The whole culture is basically focused on working to find ways to move ahead of the competition and then to stay ahead of the competition. E-mails that simply pat people on the back for prior successes are strongly discouraged. What is encouraged is pointing out opportunities and creative ways to tackle things. That's the expectation at Microsoft.

The very act of Bill Gates and his top folks giving Chris Payne a couple of hours to thoroughly explain his thinking and recommendations sends a powerful signal throughout the organization. It makes it clear to employees at all levels that the expectation is that they will come up with ideas to help the company stay competitive. In many companies, style and ritual take precedence over the basic ideas. That's a recipe for flat-footedness and mediocrity.

The Coca-Cola and Microsoft stories really underscore the fact that if you're going to avoid the trap of underutilizing your talent, setting the bar high in personnel selection and in defining performance expectations is essential.

# 19

## DON'T BE AFRAID OF BRINGING IN FRESH TALENT

One approach that is used too seldom in experienced, successful organizations is to put fresh talent in key positions. These people are often outsiders to one field but have a solid background of accomplishments in other areas. Fresh talent is especially effective when business practices have become routine and when the organization is falling behind the competition. Here are a few points to keep in mind as you think about your situation and the need to revitalize your group.

**1. Nothing uncovers opportunities quite like a new set of eyes.** When people have been in the same job for a period of time, they become proud of what they are doing and believe that things are running very well. Their ability to come up with creative ways to improve things is very limited. The managers of these folks typically believe that they are doing a very nice job and that there are no problems. On the other hand, longtime employees seldom contemplate what they may be missing. Everyone is enjoying the comfort of the status quo. That's a very dangerous situation.

2. **Moving in fresh talent makes it clear that you are open to change.** Often employees will be surprised when the leader of a group is replaced because the general consensus is that the group is running well and the leader is doing fine. All kinds of concerns about missing the expertise of the person who is being replaced will be raised. That's natural, since the value system that has evolved is one of protecting the status quo. By making the change, you are signaling that you are no longer satisfied with the status quo. Such moves help make it clear that you are looking for bright ideas, not the status quo.

3. **Moving a person into a new position that has big opportunities greatly increases that person's self-confidence.** With increased self-confidence comes a high motivation to be successful and to do something of significance. That is exactly what you want to have happen.

4. **Don't immediately set a timetable for expecting change.** You want the new person to dive into her responsibilities, figure out how to do things better, and then execute. What you don't want to do is assume that you know how long that will take. The fact is, you typically don't. Also, by setting a timetable up front, you are automatically creating constraints that will often limit the scope of change that people consider. You need to delegate the responsibility to the new talent and tell her that you want things to run well and you want bright ideas that will make things significantly better in the future.

5. **Be ready to help remove those who balk.** When you put in a new leader of a group and you see some good ideas emerging, it's important to support those people who are leading

> the change. If it becomes clear that certain individuals are creating major problems in achieving progress, you need to move those folks out to different positions.

Let's review a very positive story that highlights several sound practices in the people area.

## MICROSOFT

When I joined Microsoft in 1994, one of the areas I was responsible for as chief operating officer was procurement. Unfortunately, procurement was very fragmented throughout the company. The largest group of procurement people was in the finance organization. Their primary job was sorting out the mistakes made in generating and handling invoices, tracking down purchase orders, and validating the company's expenditures with various vendors. About 95 percent of this activity was rework, and there was a large staff assigned to do this. By rework we are referring to chasing down prior purchase orders and invoices, confirming the validity of the transaction in question, and finally getting the vendor paid.

The fundamental problem here was that every employee at Microsoft was a purchasing agent. Each had a telephone and a Yellow Pages directory, and when any employee needed something, he called a supplier and had it delivered. The invoice could come to any of a variety of places, and often it would be stuffed into someone's desk drawer. Months later, the vendor would raise the issue of how much Microsoft owed it, and people within the procurement group had to start tracking down the details. Besides finance, there were procurement people in manufacturing, the product groups, information technology, and sales, all of whom were trying to catch up with the randomness.

There was no way the company could track how much money it was spending with a specific supplier, and hence, any possible quantity discounts were being missed because of the disorganized way procurement was being managed—or shall we say not managed—by Microsoft.

The problem was a big embarrassment, and it had to be fixed. Also, we wanted to use Microsoft software in fixing it.

## Microsoft: Picking the Person

In discussing the problem with Mike Brown, who was the chief financial officer of Microsoft at that time, he suggested that we assign the procurement mess to Mike Huber, a relatively young person in the finance organization who was doing a fine job of revising the budget process for Microsoft. Mike had been with the company for only a few years, but it was clear that he had a very good head on his shoulders and that he had excellent people skills and financial skills.

## Microsoft: Defining the Task

We asked Mike to be the head of corporate procurement, and we asked him to pull together a plan that would completely reorganize procurement companywide. We wanted him to use up-to-date technology and build in practices that were foolproof from the standpoint of matching purchase orders with invoices. Also, we wanted the system to have a small number of vendors for each type of equipment or supplies being ordered. That way, we could make annual contracts with these suppliers and get quantity discounts. We made Mike's responsibilities very clear.

Mike Huber dove into the task with incredible enthusiasm. Over the course of a six-week period, he developed a detailed description of how procurement would be reorganized at Microsoft and how the various groups of people dealing with procurement throughout the company would be blended together into one group. The company would then be able to do procurement in a standardized way. He championed a Web-based approach, enabling employees to order supplies through convenient screens on their PCs. The selection of supplies portrayed on the Web-based screens covered all the things that employees typically needed, and electronic ordering enabled employees to get what they needed on a timely basis. At the same time, all of the record keeping such as purchase orders and invoices was handled electronically.

### Microsoft: The Results

The amazing thing was that Mike Huber and his small management team, which was handpicked for the task, were able to develop the plan in just six weeks. At the end of five months, the system was up and running, and by the end of the ninth month, it had been rolled out and was getting rave re-

> *The thing that amazed me about the Microsoft procurement example was that it had taken the company so long to tackle this problem.*

views. Importantly, one year after the effort was launched, Mike Huber and his team were able to decrease the amount of staff doing procurement on a corporatewide basis by about 65 percent. This was primarily because all of the rework had been eliminated. The system automatically matched up invoices and purchase orders, since they were both generated electronically when a request for a purchase was made.

Stepping back, when you have an intelligent person with common sense and good people skills, if you make the objectives very clear and urge that person to be creative, that person can do marvelous things.

The thing that amazed me about the Microsoft procurement example was that it had taken the company so long to tackle this problem. Why didn't the people who were in charge of these efforts and saw most of the staff simply doing rework take the bull by the horns and fix the problem? The reason was that those people who had been executing procurement at Microsoft had basically convinced themselves that a big part of procurement was tracking down lost invoices, original purchase orders, and vendor complaints, and so they just managed it as they always had. It goes back to those basic human tendencies that we talked about in the beginning of the book.

## HARRAH'S ENTERTAINMENT

Another great example of one person having a big impact even though he was not intimately familiar with the area he was assigned to concerns Harrah's casinos. Harrah's was a solidly performing nondistinctive group of casinos in the 1970s and 1980s. Because it basically followed the same legacy business model year after year, the business eventually softened enough so that the board of directors and the CEO realized that they needed to launch a major effort to revitalize Harrah's.

The board of directors concluded that if the company was really going to achieve a major revitalization, it needed to put fresh talent to work on the problem. That is precisely what it did.

## Harrah's Casinos: Fresh Talent

Gary Loveman, a Harvard Business School professor, had been consulting with the company during the early and mid-1990s.[1] His academic specialty was theories on customer service and service economies. Gary brought a unique business approach to the casino business. While at Harvard, he had done a lot of work analyzing the large amounts of data that service companies collect in order to better understand, and hopefully improve, customer service.[2] The Harrah's board liked Gary's quantitative approaches, and he was made chief operating officer in 1999. Most industry professionals considered it to be a very bizarre appointment. The legacy practice in that industry was that casinos needed to be led by individuals who had deep experience in the gambling industry.

## Harrah's Casinos: The Loyalty Card

Harrah's new business model launched by Loveman encouraged every customer entering its casinos to sign up for a Harrah's loyalty card. Every time a customer plays at a table game, such as blackjack, craps, or roulette, or a slot machine, she swipes her card and then is given reward credits as she plays. Players are awarded gold, diamond, or platinum status depending on the amount they gamble and how often they gamble. Reward credits can be redeemed at any Harrah's casino in North America, and there are about 25 such casinos in 13 U.S. states.[3] Reward credits can be used for food, drink, hotel rooms, or shows or for consumer goods from the Harrah's catalog.

Once the casino knows the identity of a player through the swiping of the loyalty card, the casino employees, who are alerted by messages displayed on house monitors, can offer that player enhanced rewards for his loyalty or encourage him to play at times when the casino is typically not busy. Also, if a frequent gambler is losing badly on a particular day, the real-time computer tracking system that records every gambling transaction brings this to the attention of casino management via a computer-generated alert. An employee is then dispatched to offer that customer a free dinner or room in

> *The Harrah's board liked Gary's quantitative approaches, and he was made chief operating officer in 1999. Most industry professionals considered it to be a very bizarre appointment.*

order to lift his spirits and his opinion of Harrah's. Remember, the goal here is customer satisfaction, resulting in loyalty to Harrah's.

On an ongoing basis, Harrah's gets complete information on the annualized value of each player to Harrah's: whether she is a good or a bad blackjack player, whether he bets more when he has had a drink, whether she likes to play for hours on end, or if he is likely to want a reservation in the steak restaurant for dinner. Knowing all these things allows Harrah's to tailor rewards to specific customers in order to increase their loyalty to Harrah's and prevent them from going across the street and gambling at a competitor.

## Harrah's Casinos: The Results

Loveman is going against many legacy practices in the industry. His facilities are not the multibillion-dollar complexes that are getting all the publicity in Las Vegas. He is spending huge amounts of money on technology compared with only modest amounts being spent by the industry in general. For example, total expenditures to date in building the Harrah's Rewards Loyalty Program are in excess of $500 million.[4] The payoff for Harrah's is huge. Since Loveman was named chief operating officer in 1999, then CEO in January

2003, Harrah's stock price has increased dramatically, from $15 in 1999 to $75 in the fall of 2006. The company had more than $7 billion in revenues in 2006 versus $4.1 billion in 2003 as a result of its new business approach and an acquisition. Loveman was voted the best chief executive in the gambling and lodging industry for both 2003 and 2004.

Gary Loveman had the huge advantage of never having participated in the gambling industry prior to his appointment. He truly brought a fresh set of eyes and looked at the industry purely from the standpoint of customer service. When you want to keep your group on the move in a positive direction, it's very clear that putting key people in key jobs can really generate some excitement and some significant forward progress.

# 20

## THE BROADER THE EXPERIENCE, THE BETTER

**M**anagers are often in a situation where one of their employees has been in his current position for several years and is clearly ready for a change that will enrich his skills and perspective. While the manager wants to move the employee to a more challenging job, she believes that the person needs to have sufficiently deep experience in the new area. In such situations, the true need for such depth of experience is vastly overrated. I've seen this situation over and over again in my decades of business experience, and here are my points of view:

1. **Faster learners learn fast.** When you take an individual with good basic intelligence and a fair dose of common sense, it's always surprising how quickly that person can get up to speed when thrown into a new situation. I've always been surprised in a positive way when I've been close to situations where strong performers have been thrown into new roles.

2. **New and different assignments recharge people and stretch them.** When top performers are clearly told that they are

doing very well and that they are being given a new assign-ment in order to stretch them, they feel incredibly ener-gized. These are the kinds of folks who really do want to be stretched, and they will perform accordingly. Also, putting them in charge of the various groups and departments in your organization can really send the message that you en-dorse change and you expect individuals and organiza-tions to evolve over time.

3. **New surroundings lead to new ideas.** There is no doubt that when you throw an individual into a new situation, that per-son is going to view it from a different perspective from that of the person who is very familiar with the content of a job. Consequently, you are apt to get a fair number of new ideas; some of which are naïve and some of which are right on the money. It typically takes no time at all for the unworkable ideas to be exposed, understood, and put aside. On the other hand, the really good ideas can have a big impact.

4. **Broader experience brings mature thinking.** As an individual gets exposed to various parts of an organization, her per-spective gets broader and better aligned with the overall objectives of the organization. This enables her to make decisions for the greater good of the organization rather than for the immediate specific need.

Let's look at three examples.

## eBAY

A great example of stretching people and giving them varied expe-rience comes from eBay. In 2004, Meg Whitman, the CEO of eBay, put Jeff Jordan, the head of eBay's U.S. operations, in charge of Pay-Pal, the electronic payment system that eBay had acquired several years earlier. Matt Bannick, who had been running PayPal, became the head of eBay's international efforts. Bill Cobb, who had been running eBay's international group, took over from Jordan as the head of U.S. operations. When asked why she did it, Whitman responded by saying, "You get so much energy with a new set of challenges."[1] She ought to know. She started her career in brand management at Procter & Gamble, then moved to Bain & Company, then to Disney, Stride Rite, FTD, and Hasbro, and finally to eBay.

# MICROSOFT

Another great example of developing people comes from Microsoft. When I arrived in 1994, there was a very strong and dynamic controller in the finance organization by the name of John Connors. He had originally been with the accounting firm Deloitte & Touche, and he had joined Microsoft to provide financial analysis to the sales organization. After a few years, he moved into the controller role and really excelled at that job for two years. We then had a strong need to get new blood in the information technology organization. The individual in that position was a very experienced chief information officer, but it was simply time for some new thinking. We reached for John Connors and asked him to run the information technology organization. On the surface, that looked like a very risky thing to do, given his lack of information systems experience and his lack of technical depth in any of the areas related to information technology.

## *Microsoft: The Information Technology Experience*

Within two years, Connors had the information technology organization at Microsoft absolutely on a roll. He had thinned out its ranks and developed a clear mission for IT that was twofold: (1) process the ongoing business on a day-to-day basis with industry-leading efficiency and effectiveness, and (2) be a pilot plant for the software developers at Microsoft. At Microsoft, this second objective was viewed as "eating your own dog food." As a result, within two years, not only was IT running extremely well but it was providing a new capability for Microsoft: an in-house customer that would road-test freshly developed software and help find any major bugs.

## Microsoft: The Sales Experience

During the course of John's experience running information technology, it became clear that he did extremely well in making presentations to chief information officers from other companies who were visiting Microsoft in order to learn about Microsoft's capabilities. Hence, the decision was made to move John over to the sales organization, in charge of the segment that dealt with managing very large accounts. This move served to broaden John's perspective on the company and continued to stretch him in new directions.

## Microsoft: The CFO Experience

In the year 2000, we moved John over to become chief financial officer of the company. While he had no direct experience in dealing with Wall Street, we were confident that the training that John had had in such a wide variety of settings would pay off and that he would get off to a fast start. That's precisely what happened, and he had a very successful reign as the CFO at Microsoft.

When you step back, what we are talking about here is classic good management. What was done with John Connors simply makes sense, although at each step, I'm sure you could come up with all kinds of reasons why an imprudent decision was being made.

## Microsoft: The "Key People" Exercise

Microsoft was doing some personnel development of the type I described with John Connors, but we realized at the time that we were not doing nearly enough. This realization led to the development of a "key people" exercise that, over time, simply got better and better at helping the company understand where its key people resided, what their career paths were to date, and what the key jobs were that these people could be placed in so that they could grow and the company could benefit from their typical superb performance.

# PROCTER & GAMBLE

Another example of a company doing a good job of personnel management comes from Procter & Gamble, and it is about me. When I started with Procter & Gamble in 1968, I had a Ph.D. in computer science. My Ph.D. dissertation was all about simulating chemical reactions on a digital computer. You basically write the differential equations that describe the interactions of the chemical compounds, based on the theory of how those interactions take place, and you use the computer to simulate what will occur. Previously at P&G, scientists had built pilot plants, which were test facilities, to see if the chemical reactions performed as expected. In some cases, the pilot plant would catch fire or, on a few occasions, actually blow up. Hence, it's a lot safer, cheaper, and faster to get approximations of what will happen on a digital computer by carefully writing the mathematical equations that describe how the chemistry of the situation should work.

When I joined Procter & Gamble in 1968, it was in the research and development (R&D) division, doing that kind of work with a variety of Ph.D. chemists employed by Procter & Gamble at its massive research center north of Cincinnati.

## P&G: Running Data Centers

After doing chemical reaction simulations for two years, I was asked to run the R&D data center. This was quite a change for me. I'd be managing a small group of people and running an important data center. Naturally, I jumped at the opportunity because I was quite the nerd at that point and really enjoyed computing. After a couple of years, I was asked to transfer from R&D to the corporate information technology organization to be in charge of the regional data centers that were sprinkled throughout the United States in order to help process Procter & Gamble's business each day.

After about two months on the job, it was very clear to me that these regional data centers no longer deserved to exist, since telecommunications capabilities were emerging that would enable salespeople to input orders directly to the central data center rather

> *Naturally, I jumped at the opportunity because I was quite the nerd at that point and really enjoyed computing.*

than performing a middle step and going to a regional data center. Hence, we launched a plan that eliminated all nine of those regional data centers over an 18-month period. Basically, I worked myself out of a job.

I was confident at that time that the company would find something fun for me to do. My management was telling me that things were going well for me from a career standpoint and that the company was very pleased with my work.

As we were closing down the last of the regional data centers, the company decided to have me run the entire corporate data center in Cincinnati that processed the day-to-day P&G business. This was the lifeblood of the company, financially, because all of the bills and all of the revenue flowed through the systems that were running on these mainframe computers. I loved the job. It was like running a small factory. The data center ran three shifts a day, and reliability was the key goal. I had a ball.

### P&G: A Move to Marketing

After two years, I was approached by my management and asked if I would like to go on a one-year broadening assignment to marketing. My first reaction was, "I must have done something really wrong. Those marketing folks are very strange." Management offered me the opportunity to talk with a few individuals in marketing in order to get a feel for what it was all about, and they explained to me that the purpose of the assignment was simply to broaden my outlook on the company. After talking with a few folks in brand management, who came across as surprisingly rational, I indicated to my management that I would take the assignment, as long as they promised to take me back to the information technology world at P&G. Management made that promise, and off I went to brand management.

The year in brand management absolutely flew by, and I was making very good progress. The marketing folks told the information technology management that they would like me to stick around for a while, which led to an agreement that I would stay for one more year. After two years, the same exercise occurred, and I stayed a third year, and then a

> *Basically, I worked myself out of a job. I was confident at that time that P&G would find something fun for me to do.*

fourth year, and on and on. By 1983 I was in charge of marketing for the packaged soap and detergent division, which was Procter & Gamble's largest division at that time. Consumer product marketing at P&G is a very quantitative discipline, and I absolutely loved it.

## P&G: Off to Market Research

Much to my surprise, in 1984 management explained that the vice president of market research was retiring and asked me if I would take that position. I had grown to love the world of brand management and marketing, so I was a bit surprised, but the move made all the sense in the world. This was a time when scanner technology was becoming the rage in supermarkets, and you could get market research panels that tracked all the purchases of individual households. This generated all kinds of new tools for understanding consumer behavior, but you needed massive amounts of computing capabilities in order to harness those data. Hence, my new job as the manager of market research was full of information technology challenges, marketing issues, and quantitative challenges.

## P&G: Back to Information Technology

After two years of running market research, I was asked to become vice president of the information technology organization at Procter & Gamble. This was a kind of "going home" for me in that I was going back to my roots in information technology. We did some fun

> *I am a great example of a company taking an individual and just pushing and pushing him to see just how much he can contribute and achieve.*

things during my two years as the head of IT, including setting up an electronic connection with Wal-Mart so that its computers and Procter & Gamble's computers communicated every evening. They figured out how much to ship to Wal-Mart for the next day's replenishment of shelves at the Wal-Mart stores. Those systems replaced a lot of salespeople, who tended to clog up the order replenishment cycle and generate large inventories for both Procter & Gamble and P&G's customers.

## P&G: Back to Marketing

In 1989, I was asked to become the senior vice president of marketing for Procter & Gamble, with the vice president of market research and the vice president of information technology reporting to me. In essence, this job took advantage of the collective experiences that I had had with the company to date. I held that position for five years, until 1994, when I became the chief operating officer of Microsoft under Chief Executive Officer Bill Gates.

Stepping back, what was really going on here with respect to my career at Procter & Gamble? It's a great example of a company taking an individual and just pushing and pushing him to see just how much he can contribute and can achieve. The cumulative breadth of experience makes such people very versatile and productive assets to the company.

In conclusion, your most valuable resource is your people. It is critical that you pay significant attention to issues like selecting personnel, setting high expectations, evaluating performance, and moving people around to maximize their impact and learning. The trap of mediocrity, which is essentially putting up with poor performance and underutilizing your stars, is a very serious one.

### PART VII

# TRAP #7
# LETHARGY: GETTING LULLED INTO A CULTURE OF COMFORT, CASUALNESS, AND CONFIDENCE

**When organizations** achieve success it often causes them to fall into the trap of nurturing a retirement-home culture. Its characteristics are slow, consensus-oriented decision making, comfort, ambiguity, casualness, confidence, and lack of aggressive behavior in general. This leads to the following four traits, which cause things to get even worse:

1. **Your company always adds projects and never eliminates any.** This kind of behavior comes about because the view is that this is a successful company, and successful companies dabble in a lot of things. Also, since our company is so good, of course it won't kill any projects, since our people clearly know what they are doing. In this kind of culture, all kinds of groups are off doing their own thing, and once projects emerge, they seem to be impossible to kill. You need a process for regularly inspecting the list of things happening in a group and cutting out the marginal things or those that have dragged on too long and never contributed to the business.

2. **Your company hires excessively.** Often the thinking is: if we are successful, of course we need more people so that we can do even better in the future. Groups come up with some remarkable reasons why they need yet more people. It's important to understand that once they get those additional people, they find things to do. It is surprising how

quickly those things become "mission-critical" and people get into the mode of protecting those practices. Head-count needs to be carefully managed, and new ideas should be staffed by killing old, stale projects.

3. **Your company lacks intensity about the competition.** When com-petition catches up with a company's previously unique and successful products, quite often the mentality is: our prod-ucts are fine—consumers know we are the best, and we will just lower our prices a bit, or launch a sales promotion, and this temporary nuisance—namely our competition—will go away. Your culture needs intensity, focused on the fact that business momentum is always created by distinctive-ness and uniqueness that has appeal to consumers. It's amazing how legacy practices strangle that kind of think-ing. You should always be rallying the troops around your latest distinctive product to continually create excitement.

4. **Your company fears change.** When organizations get complex, and things are very hard to execute and the organization is very bureaucratic, the fear of change increases. That's because everyone is worried that they are the one who will be affected by the change. This sort of organizational paralysis is a deadly disease. Managers need to be con-stantly reorganizing the troops around the big opportuni-ties. This helps create an agile and aggressive culture.

Now let's review some of the key steps a leader of an organiza-tion can take to make sure that the trap of a retirement-home culture is avoided and that you are constantly achieving the excitement and vigor of a start-up.

# 21

# CLARITY, SIMPLICITY, AND REPETITION ARE ESSENTIAL

An organization's values and culture are vitally important in determining its success. The overriding importance of values and cultures determines corporate success in both the short term and the long term. The following three guidelines are essential in institutionalizing those values and maintaining the organization's culture.

1. **Everyone should describe the culture in the same clear way.** If the troops hear confusing messages from various leaders, or if they notice that some leaders' behavior doesn't match the values, the culture weakens and fragments quickly. It's absolutely essential that everyone in the organization have the same clear understanding of the culture.

2. **The message should be simple.** Everyone in the organization should be able to immediately spout the organization's key values.

**3. The values need to be repeated over and over.** There is simply no substitute for employees hearing the management refer to the values on a regular basis and observing behavior that is consistent with those values.

Let's review a company that is an excellent example of an organization that has done a superb job regarding the clarity and simplicity of its core values and the continuous communication of those values to its employees.

## SOUTHWEST AIRLINES

In 1966, Herb Kelleher was practicing law in San Antonio when he was approached by a friend named Rollin King about the idea of starting up a local airline that would service the cities of Dallas, San Antonio, and Houston.[1] It took the two of them five years to get the legal entity called Southwest Airlines set up, and the airline began operations in 1971 with flights between Dallas and Houston for $20. That price was one-third of what its competitors were charging, and Southwest could do this because these flights had absolutely no frills. Also, the flights were able to turn around at a particular city in 20 minutes and get off to the next destination. Once it was up and running, Southwest's costs were 22 percent below the industry average, and its operating margin of 16.5 percent was triple the industry average.

Southwest quickly emerged as a real force in the airline industry, with its incredible efficiency and innovative point-to-point flight schedule. Kelleher's biggest contribution to Southwest Airlines over the years has been the incredible clarity, simplicity, and consistency of his message to employees concerning what Southwest was all about.[2] The culture was based on three values:

**1. Keep costs down.** Southwest clearly had the lowest cost structure in the airline industry, which enabled it to have fares that were 50 percent or more below those of the competition. It did smart things like buying only one kind of airplane (Boeing 737s), thus minimizing the amount of airplane maintenance training.

2. **Have fun.** Herb Kelleher himself is an incredible legend. The fun factor was extremely high with Herb, and it resonated throughout the organization. These folks are very outgoing, bordering on zany.

3. **Focus on the customer.** While Southwest wasn't giving its customers the frills that the big expensive airlines were, it was making up for this in friendliness and in fun. It treated each passenger with incredible respect, and it also got the humor going as soon as possible.

As Southwest has grown over the decades, it has been totally clear and consistent with respect to its culture. At the same time, the company has been very focused on maintaining its sound business model of point-to-point flights with one standard aircraft.

The "have fun" part of Southwest's culture also covers the fact that it really does operate as a big family. For example, when the Internet made it convenient to buy tickets at home off the Web rather than using reservation agents, Southwest closed down several reservation centers. But instead of letting those employees go, the company paid to relocate them to other areas so that all of them would have a job within Southwest. When asked why these people hadn't been let go in order to cut costs, Southwest's COO Colleen Barrett said, "We don't do those kinds of things. That's what our competitors do. At Southwest, our employees come first."[3]

When Colleen was asked why competitors have such a difficult time copying the Southwest model, she responded, "What we do is very simple, but it's not simplistic. We really do everything with passion. We scream at each other and we hug each other. We aren't uptight. We celebrate everything. It's like a fraternity, a sorority, a reunion. We are having a party!"[4]

## Southwest Airlines:
## The Champion of the Culture

Herb Kelleher was clearly the heart of this company, and he was constantly demonstrating to folks that they were part of the family; he was constantly driving for efficiency but having an incredible amount of fun. Katrina Brooker of *Fortune* magazine described it this way: "Southwest is like a family and Herb is the patriarch. They don't let ceremonies stand in the way of efficiency—or fun. Pilots, for instance, would help load bags or clean cabins, if necessary, to stay on schedule. Gate agents sometimes restocked planes. Flight attendants are famous for popping out of the overhead bins and telling jokes over the speakers. On Halloween employees throw raucous gate parties—complete with costumes, streamers, and cake."[5]

To get a sense of just how strong this culture is and how simple it is, back in February 2000, jet fuel went up to $1.00 per gallon, which was three times what it had been just a year earlier. Herb Kelleher sent a letter to all the employees talking about the fuel crisis and asking if each worker could help out by finding a way to save $5 cash for the company each day. He explained that this would save the company $50 million per year. Employees immediately moved into action and generated the dramatic results that Herb was targeting.

## Southwest Airlines: Preserving the Culture

Herb trained the organization to be incredibly selective in recruiting. Not everyone is comfortable with the extreme levels of fun these people have and also with the incredible focus on efficiency and making customers happy. Consequently, only 4 percent of the 90,000 people a year that apply for a job actually get one.[6] As Katrina Brooker of *Fortune* pointed out, "You've got better odds at getting in Harvard." ·

The key to Southwest's recruiting is a personality test that has the recruiter rate the individual on the traits of cheerfulness, optimism, decision-making skills, team spirit, communication, self-confidence, and self-starter skills. Each of those attributes is graded on a 1-to-5 scale. This test is applied to all applicants, no matter whether the person is applying to be a mechanic, a pilot, a flight attendant, or a ticket agent. Those seven traits were selected to give Southwest that consistency of culture that it clearly understands is of vital importance.

> *The key to Southwest's recruiting is a personality test that has the recruiter rate the individual on the traits of cheerfulness, optimism, decision-making ability, team spirit, communication, self-confidence, and self-starter skills.*

When recruits are hired, they are sent to Southwest's unique University for People. This is its training center in Dallas, where these new recruits get indoctrinated with the rigorous people skills and values that are the core of Southwest's culture. They study things like body language in order to get a better reading on which customers they need to cheer up, and they learn how to prop up other employees who may be facing work challenges or personal challenges.

For each airport that Southwest uses, it selects a group of employees at that facility to form a "culture committee." That group is responsible for making sure that the location carries the spirit of Southwest: the gate parties, the jokes, and the games.[7]

The consistency with which Southwest has carried out its business over the decades is amazing. Andy Serwer of *Fortune* magazine captured it well when he said, "Southwest hasn't really changed its original formula throughout the decades of battling big airlines. It enters markets in which traditional airlines dominate and then blasts them with much lower fares. Southwest flies 'point-to-point,' ignoring the hub-and-spoke model of most other airlines. It flies only 737's. It serves no meals, only snacks. It charges no fees to change same-fare tickets. It has no assigned seats and no electronic equipment on its planes, relying instead on relentlessly fun flight attendants to amuse passengers."[8]

> *There's no doubt that Southwest wins the clarity, simplicity, and repetition award in keeping its values and its culture absolutely constant.*

## Southwest Airlines: The Results

In 34 years, Southwest has grown to a company with about 35,000 employees, flying to more than 60 cities. It has a fleet of almost 400 Boeing 737s.

The first three years after the World Trade Center disaster in New York City on September 11, 2001, were very brutal for the airline business. During that period, the major carriers laid off thousands of people and collectively lost $22 billion. However, Southwest did not lay off a single employee during that three-year period, and it remained profitable each quarter. In the year 2004, the company earned $442 million, which was more than all other U.S. airlines combined. Its market capitalization stood at $11.7 billion, which was larger than all of its competitors combined. In May of 2004, Southwest became the leader in the number of domestic customers it carried per year, surpassing all other airlines in the United States.

From 2004 through the first quarter of 2006, the key challenge has been the incredible runup in oil prices. While other airlines such as United, US Airways, Northwest Airlines, and Delta Air Lines lost billions, Southwest had positive earnings per share in every quarter during this very difficult period.

Looking back at its incredible string of success over the decades, Brian Harris, an airline analyst with Smith Barney, was asked how Southwest can succeed where others fail. He said, "They have a huge competitive advantage; their culture." When Herb Kelleher was asked that question, he was very clear: "Our esprit de corps is the core of our success. That's most difficult for a competitor to imitate. They can buy all the physical things. The thing they can't buy is dedication, devotion, loyalty—feeling you are participating in a cause or a crusade."[9] Herb Kelleher stepped down as CEO in 2001, but remained as chairman. Most analysts believe that his strong spirit will continue to drive Southwest long after he is gone.

There's no doubt that Southwest wins the clarity, simplicity, and repetition award in keeping its values and its culture absolutely constant. It is the heart of the company, and it is amazing how much success it has generated in probably the toughest industry out there.

While Southwest Airlines teaches us a lot about maintaining a unique culture, often the task is to change the culture. Let's take a look at one of the world's greatest companies, and how it is using the basics of clarity, simplicity, and repetition to push its culture in a new direction.

## GENERAL ELECTRIC

The values that Jack Welch constantly reinforced throughout his long tenure as the CEO of General Electric were very clear: continually improve your operation, always make your targets, cut costs wherever possible, make smart deals, and achieve the number one or number two position in your industry. People moved in and out of jobs fairly quickly, reflecting the overall impatience of the organization to get superb results. That model was extremely successful for decades, and Jack Welch deserves a lot of credit for achieving those results.

On the other hand, as Diane Brady discusses in *BusinessWeek,* when Jeff Immelt moved into the CEO position in 2001 upon Welch's retirement, he soon recognized a big vulnerability in the culture.[10] Specifically, he was very concerned that the incredible focus on bottom-line results and on rewarding only those people who could achieve them was putting the company at great risk with respect to innovation. This led him to the conclusion that he had to launch a major effort to change the GE culture. To make the company grow, given its large size, he was going to need a lot of creativity and significantly more risk taking. Also, GE needed to be a lot better marketer than it was.

What Immelt had noticed as he began his new job was that his world was a lot different from that of Jack Welch. He had to deal

> *The difference between Immelt and Welch was that Jeff Immelt told the troops the value system at General Electric needed to change.*

with a slower-growing domestic economy, far more serious global competitors, and an environment in which investors asked a lot more questions.

Jeff Immelt spoke about the need for innovation over and over again to his management group, and to the entire company whenever he had a chance. His message is captured in the following quote from him: "Creativity and imagination applied in a business context is innovation. We're measuring GE's top leaders on how imaginative they are. Imaginative leaders are the ones who have the courage to fund new ideas, lead teams to discover better ideas, and lead people to take more educated risks."[11] In reacting to that comment, Bruce Nussbaum of *BusinessWeek* said, "It's hard to imagine former GE boss Jack Welch saying that." What Bruce was noticing was the difference between Immelt and Welch, namely, Jeff Immelt telling the troops the value system at General Electric needed to change.

### General Electric: Stating the Goal Clearly

Whenever Jeff Immelt had an opportunity to talk to any group of employees at General Electric, he would make sure that they understood that the world of 100 percent focus on Six Sigma was behind them; now the key task for the company was to develop some real skills in the area of creativity, strategy, and marketing.[12] While Six Sigma served the company well as a tool for perfecting processes, lowering cost, and driving simplicity and focus, seldom did it uncover large, innovation-based opportunities. Employees are being told repeatedly that they need to take educated risks, some of which may fail. Even the slightest hint of failure was clearly a no-no under the old regime.

Jeff is also not afraid to preach this gospel to his customers directly. After acquiring some gasification technology from Chevron Texaco, Jeff hit the road with the head of GE's energy business. The two of them made it very clear to key customers like public utility giant Cinergy Corporation (now Duke Energy) that the company needed to generate electricity with far fewer emissions. Jeff knew that the coal gasification technology could significantly cut emissions. He was out to make it clear to his customers that General Electric wanted to innovate in that area and make some good things happen. James Rogers, the CEO of Cinergy, said the following about Jeff: "He was unafraid to articulate a point-of-view that his customers might not share."[13] Cinergy was a company that burned 30 million tons of coal a year, and basically Immelt was calling into question the emissions record of coal-burning energy facilities and signing on to provide very significant improvements. Immelt's aggressive focus on innovation with customers helped him to make sure the GE employees knew that the boss was really serious about this. He was very clear and consistent internally and externally about GE's goals.

*Even the slightest hint of failure was clearly a no-no under the old Welch regime.*

## General Electric: Organize to Reflect the New Objectives

To send further signals within GE that innovation was key, Jeff Immelt formed a very high-profile organization within the company called the Commercial Council. This was a group of his top sales and marketing executives. The group met quarterly and held telephone conference calls once a month in order to work on making General Electric more innovative and generating more innovative products. In this particular group, he was very interested in focusing on the marketing and sales aspect of the business, where traditionally GE has not been stellar.

> *Bring in fresh, new talent in the area that you are focusing on.*

Another example of structuring the organization to send clear signals that things have changed was Immelt's appointment of a chief marketing officer. The person placed in the role was Beth Comstock, and her charge was to increase the company's marketing expertise. She began looking outside of GE at some of the organizations that were skilled in designing and generating innovative ideas and began pushing General Electric to embrace new practices.

Beth did all kinds of creative things to shake out some fresh, new ideas within General Electric. For example, she staged "dreaming sessions," where Immelt and his senior team reviewed and debated the trends in various markets, both some that GE currently participated in and some new ones.[14]

To further underscore how the values had changed at General Electric, Jeff Immelt formed what he called "Imagination Breakthrough" projects. His objective was to spend $5 billion on 80 or so of these kinds of initiatives.[15] As *BusinessWeek's* Bruce Nussbaum noted, Immelt instructed the leaders of these teams to "connect with consumers, learn to take risks, and place big bets."

## General Electric: Importing Talent

There's another way to communicate clearly to the troops that things are changing and to convey to them the new value system: bring in fresh, new talent in the area where you are trying to focus. Immelt did this at GE by bringing in Sir William Castell as a vice chairman. That was a rather shocking move to the folks at General Electric, and it was clearly noticed by the troops. Immelt had been telling the troops that GE was working on becoming more global and that he wanted people who knew their industries very thoroughly. Bill Castell really represented this. He had spent his entire career in the bioscience area, and he was heading up the diagnostic/bioscience firm Amersham PLC when GE acquired it. Immelt made Castell head of the new GE Healthcare unit and, surprisingly, located the organization's headquarters in the village of Chalfont St. Giles in England. This sent a very clear and visible message about the desired behavior.

### General Electric: Compensation System

To make sure that he was communicating to the troops that he wanted them to make bets and take risks that customers liked, Immelt modified the bonus system in 2005. The new system based 20 percent of the bonus on preestablished measures of how well a business was initiating fresh ideas to improve its ability to meet customer needs. As Immelt put it, "You're not going to stick around this place and not make bets."

### General Electric: Changing the Portfolio

Jeff Immelt took another action to make it clear that innovation was key: he significantly changed GE's portfolio of businesses. He launched a plan to sell $15 billion of less profitable businesses, including the insurance operation.[16] He also spent $60 billion on acquisitions in such areas as bioscience, cable, film entertainment, security, and wind power.

### General Electric: Benchmarking

One approach that Immelt used to make it clear that creativity was a key goal was to instruct various marketing groups to visit with companies that have been successful in these areas. For example, he sent a group to Procter & Gamble, which has had an unusually robust string of brilliant innovations over the last few years. He also sent a group to FedEx in order to understand just how it achieves the excellent customer service it has maintained for years.

### General Electric: Dealing with Weak Performers

One issue that GE employees watched very carefully was the entrenched practice of getting rid of the 5 to 10 percent of employees

> *Clarity, simplicity, and repetition—all three are your best tools to prevent a culture of comfort, casualness, and confidence.*

who were the weakest performers. Immelt has backed off a bit from making that an objective that he addresses regularly. As Diane Brady of *BusinessWeek* indicates, "There's more flexibility, more subjectivity to the process. Risking failure is a badge of honor at GE these days."[17] On the other hand, managers are clearly being held accountable. For example, each business leader has to come up with at least three "Imagination Breakthrough" proposals during the year that are robust enough that they ultimately go before the Commercial Council for discussion. The goal of these proposals is to get GE into new geographical areas or new lines of business or into a new customer base. There's also a minimum threshold of at least $100 million of growth for General Electric.

Change is never easy, and Jeff Immelt of GE knows that well. So do his people. As reported in *BusinessWeek*, Paul Bossidy, CEO of GE Capital, Commercial Equipment Financing, said: "This is a big fundamental structural change, and that can be tough." Susan Peters, GE's vice president for executive development, put it well when she said: "What you have been to date isn't good enough for tomorrow."[18]

Clearly, GE and Jeff Immelt are dead set on establishing a more innovative culture. Immelt clearly understands the need for clarity, simplicity, and repetition in establishing a culture of innovation at GE. Immelt also understands that this will all take time. The company is beginning to see some impact from the culture shift in areas such as wind power and solar power, but the stock price has yet to be significantly affected.[19]

Southwest Airlines and Jeff Immelt's efforts to change the culture at GE are great examples of the importance of clarity, simplicity, and repetition. All three are your best tools to prevent a culture of comfort, casualness, and confidence. Fight lethargy by making sure the troops understand the culture and what is expected of them.

# 22

## GET A PRODUCT EDGE AND USE IT TO OVERHAUL THE CULTURE

ere's one of the most powerful ways to quickly invigorate a culture and get an organization to shake off its legacy practices: seize a new product idea and use it to rejuvenate all aspects of the organization. This gets people to realize that it is all about success in the future instead of focusing on what has been done in the past.

### MOTOROLA

Motorola is an example of an immensely successful company that ran into hard times because it was committing a lot of the sins we have been discussing. Let's take a look in detail at how this came about and at how new management used an exciting new product idea to shake employees out of their legacy behavior and motivate them to create a new culture. This new culture focused on the basics and set high standards for what would be achieved in the future.

## Motorola: The Glorious Past

Motorola's incredible results in the 1980s and the early to mid-1990s put that company absolutely at the top of the electronics business.[1] In 1993, its earnings were over $1 billion, which represented a 127 percent increase versus a year earlier. Its revenues were up 27 percent, reaching $17 billion. The company's claim to fame at that time was its excellence in total quality management (TQM). In fact, Motorola was so revered that it gave courses on TQM to other companies. It was constantly singled out as being exceptional in its decentralized management approach, training, business reengineering, and self-directed work teams.

Motorola's technical contributions deserve to be mentioned because they are very significant. The company built some of the first car radios and first battery-powered household radios. The company used these technologies during World War II in providing walkie-talkies. It played a major role in putting a man on the moon, and it basically invented the cell phone business. In 1996, Motorola's introduction of the highly successful StarTAC cell phone helped it gain over half of the global cell phone market.

As Ronald Henkoff of *Fortune* magazine put it in 1994, "At issue is whether this huge decentralized, multi-national corporation with headquarters in Schaumburg, Illinois can avoid falling victim to the bureaucracy, complacency, and hubris that have afflicted so many other large American businesses."[2]

People had applauded Motorola's phenomenal results over several decades. But in the mid-1990s, the press turned skeptical and began questioning whether a company that had been dominated by engineers could be successful in the cell phone business, which required not only good technology but also great marketing. Marketing excellence was something that Motorola had not needed in the past and did not have.

## Motorola: Arrogantly Clinging to the Past

Motorola traditionally had had an incredible pride in its decentralization, and this led to many different product fiefdoms or silos—

that is, organizations that went off on their own and operated quite independently. In the mid-1990s, this was beginning to be a serious issue for Motorola because its business was so global. As it dealt with organizations such as the postal and telecommunications ministries in centralized countries, it ran into some serious challenges. For example, Rick Younts, the director of Motorola's Asian and Americas business at that time, said, "They expect one person to speak for Motorola with one point of view, not six or seven people with six or seven competing views." Younts was finding it very difficult to bring the very independent silos together into a unified dialogue with these key customers, which were becoming more important to Motorola.[3]

In the mid-1990s, a very high degree of comfort and overconfidence existed at Motorola. In 1994, Hector Ruiz, the general manager of the Paging Products Group, said the following: "Our technical people are bordering on being cocky. That keeps me awake at night. I've got to figure out how to keep these people unhappy."

## Motorola: The Problematic Culture

By 1997, it was clear that legacy practices were really being solidified within the organization, and that this was beginning to hurt results. There was probably no better example of being out of touch with the marketplace and the consumer than the tremendous effort that Motorola put behind smart cards.[4] These are small plastic cards that look like credit cards but have an embedded chip that carries data such as medical information or, say, $50 in cash value. Chris Galvin, the CEO, said: "Motorola's twenty years of experience with embedded silicon microprocessors, together with its radio frequency products and systems expertise, has given it a unique capability to elevate Smart Cards to a higher level."

What this smart card effort really pointed out was that Motorola was an incredibly engineering-oriented company, with little focus on the marketplace. As readers know, smart cards just never materialized in the United States, but the fanfare that Motorola made over this effort in the late 1990s says a lot about its culture.

*At a major communications conference, it showcased a strange collection of necklaces and armbands demonstrating how people could wear their StarTAC phones.*

The negative effect that this subdivided, engineering-heavy culture was having on Motorola began to have a serious financial impact in 1996 and 1997.[5] While in the early 1990s Motorola had matched the total return of companies such as Microsoft and Intel, it was beginning to stumble badly. Its 1996 earnings were off 35 percent versus a year earlier, and revenue was relatively flat. Most importantly, the stock price was stuck in the $23 range during the entire mid-1990s.

Motorola's clinging to legacy practices that had served it well in the past was really beginning to hurt on the product front as well. The company's slow-moving culture caused it to miss the movement of cellular phone technology from analog to digital. Its claim at the time was that it simply didn't have enough resources to devote to both technologies and that it had been highly successful with analog technology.

Another example was the Motorola PowerPC chip, which Apple used in the Macintosh computer. Motorola was criticized for not working with Microsoft to enable the Windows NT operating system to run on the PowerPC chip. The company was simply ignoring the marketplace, which was telling it that Windows was going to be a fairly successful product and that Apple was having serious problems.[6] Seeing the marketplace trends, the company should have developed PC chips for both the Apple and the Windows environments.

Motorola's culture, which lacked customer and market focus, was also causing it to stumble with its top customers. Motorola arrogantly required wireless networks to use a majority of Motorola cell phones; if they didn't, Motorola would not make the hot StarTAC phone available to them. Naturally, customers were angry, and they set out to find alternatives.

Motorola's unwillingness to develop any marketing expertise was never more obvious than in 1997, when it declared the StarTAC to be the first "wearable" phone.[7] At a major communications conference, it showcased a strange collection of necklaces and armbands demonstrating how people could *wear* their StarTAC phones. It was bad enough that the wearable phone idea was questionable. But to further demonstrate just how out of touch the company was with reality, while it was pushing this idea of "wearing" a StarTAC, Motorola had a billboard that featured Ryan O'Neal and Farrah Fawcett, with a headline that said, "The stars wear StarTAC." Motorola executives were highly embarrassed when the breakup of Ryan and Farrah was the cover story for *People* magazine. The company failed to understand the fragility of working with famous people in a marketing campaign.

## Motorola: Serious Business Problems

By 1998, Motorola was incurring some serious setbacks with key customers. For example, it lost a $500 million contract for digital wireless equipment in the first quarter of 1998 and missed its quarterly earnings estimate for that quarter as well. As Erick Schonfeld of *Fortune* put it in a March 1998 article, "The crux of Motorola's problem is that it has pinned its future on the legacy world of analog wireless telephony and it is late to market with new digital technology it needed to compete."[8] Its market share in cell phones had dropped from its traditional level of over 50 percent to 30 percent by 1998. About 50 percent of the phones that Motorola built were designed for analog networks, while the new digital technology was really taking off. In fact, in 1998, Nokia and Ericsson were already introducing their second and third generations of such phones.[9]

## Motorola: Moving Too Slowly

By 1999, Motorola's market share of wireless phones had slipped to 13 percent, and the press was full of stories about how Motorola seemed to be frozen in the past. One story about its advertising agency is very telling. In a 2001 *BusinessWeek* story, Geoffrey Frost, a

> *"The whole organization was in paralysis. You couldn't make a decision without needing 99 other people to make a decision. It was horrible."*
>
> —Motorola executive

fairly new marketing executive recruited from Nike, recommended to Motorola management that the company fire its current advertising agency, McCann Erickson.[10] After finally getting to argue his case with top management, Jeffrey was asked to go back and think about it some more and to challenge the current agency to put together a better campaign. After many months of effort, McCann didn't come forward with a campaign that impressed the marketing folks at Motorola. After a few additional months of anguishing over the possibility of a parting of the ways with its ad agency, management finally agreed to Frost's recommendation.

Later, Frost confided in the folks at *BusinessWeek* that he could not help but compare this experience at Motorola to his experience with Phil Knight of Nike.[11] At Nike, Frost confronted CEO Phil Knight about the performance of Wieden+Kennedy, its ad agency at the time. This took a lot of nerve on Frost's part, since that agency was run by a college friend of Knight's. When Frost put the issue on Knight's desk, it is reported that Knight said to Frost, "What the f— took you so long!"

The various articles about Motorola that were appearing in the press in 2001 were all about its indecisiveness, the hands-off style of its management team, and how strange this was for a company in the technology industry, where speed and conviction are key. Competitors were beating Motorola to the marketplace with new cell phone designs and new microprocessor capabilities, and it was really getting embarrassing. The stock price, which had moved positively to $60 per share with the Internet hype in the year 2000, was down to $17 by mid-2001. The company's first-quarter loss in 2001 was $206 million, its first loss from operations in 16 years.[12]

With the growing public criticism of Motorola, especially about its outdated practice of keeping its different businesses extremely separate from each other, the company took a bold move and merged the pager division, the cell phone division, and the semiconductor division all into one. The thinking was that all of these parts were now dependent on one another, given the new world of integrated technology. It called the organization the Communications Enterprise division, and it was gigantic, with more than 500 executives. This resulted in all kinds of infighting as organizations yearned to execute their business the way they had in the old days.[13] Julie Shimer, a vice president in Motorola's Internet unit at the time, said, "The last year I was there, you could get nothing accomplished. The whole organization was in paralysis. You couldn't make a decision without needing 99 other people to make a decision. It was horrible."

## Motorola: A New CEO Tackles the Culture Problem

As the company realized that it had gone from leading the industry to being viewed as an antiquated player, the board of directors made a bold move and hired a new CEO from the outside. The board knew that it needed to shake up the culture and get some vigor into the company, and in early 2004 it hired Ed Zander, the former president of Sun Microsystems, as the new CEO.

Ed quickly began to understand that Motorola was great at talking proudly about the past but was clearly having difficulty understanding and capitalizing on key trends. It had failed to notice the shift from analog wireless phones to digital, which had caused it to see its market share cut by a factor of 5. Motorola had moved from being number one in the wireless infrastructure equipment industry to a distant number four. Its revenues with cable companies had been cut in half as the company fell behind the competition in delivering new products. It spent 10 years and $2.6 billion on the Iridium satellite network, which required brick-sized phones and a high cost (several dollars a minute) for international calls. Iridium went bankrupt.[14]

Motorola also had problems in executing. When color-screen cell phones became popular in 2002, Motorola couldn't meet the demand and was beaten by its competitors. Samsung emerged as the number two cell phone player, behind Nokia. Motorola was late into the TV set-top box business; because of that, it lost out to rival Scientific-Atlanta. It had previously been the leader in chips for personal digital assistants (PDAs), but Intel overtook it in that business. Ericsson took the number one position from Motorola in the area of wireless infrastructure.[15]

## Motorola: Back to the Basics

With all of this happening, Ed Zander had his hands full. In a broad-ranging interview with Christopher Rhoads of the *Wall Street Journal* in 2005, Ed explained how he was tackling the problem. When asked how he needed to improve the company, he said, "Motorola's got a thick culture. I had to learn it, and it's been hard bringing things I think are valuable, such as a sense of urgency, fast decision-making, shareholder value, and competition."[16] In that interview, he laid out six key points that he was focusing on as he tackled that "thick culture."

1. **Create product excitement.** Zander believed that the most important first step was to get at least one product that was truly exciting. He immediately jumped on the RAZR cell phone when he arrived, and he really drove it hard. RAZR had a unique thin look. Motorola was successful with Cingular in getting people to buy the product, and it became very popular. Ed stated, "What it really did do was get Motorola in the minds of a lot of people around the world for being cool again. I also think it did a lot for our employees, because you start getting employees believing again that you can win."[17]

2. **Get back to putting the customer first.** It sounds like a trite statement, but Zander believed that Motorola was really committing the cardinal sin of ignoring customers. He said, "Why weren't we talking about Nokia every day? Why weren't we talking about Verizon every day? Why weren't we talking about shareholder value? Are we here to make money or not? Or are we here just to work and go home?"[18]

Ed started calling on Motorola's key customers regularly, and soon other executives were following the same pattern.

3. **Don't take no for an answer.** Ed has a great quote on this point, which is: "If you are a salesperson, you are not authorized to lose a deal." You go to the person who told you that you lost and say, "You've got to see my boss because I'm not allowed to lose this deal."[19] He put incredible intensity into winning with every customer every time.

4. **"Whack yourself before somebody whacks you."** This quote from Ed is powerful, and it says a lot about what Motorola needed. That long litany of where Motorola had been beaten in the marketplace, which included cell phones and wireless infrastructure, among other areas, was all about allowing the industry to move on, leaving you behind with your legacy practices and products. Ed believed that it has to be engrained in the culture that you are going to be ahead because you will not allow one of those competitors to get out in front.

5. **"Beware of clogged arteries."** Ed strongly believed that the real challenge for Motorola was to overhaul its vice president ranks. He believed that was where the bureaucracy and stagnation emanated from. He greatly reduced the number of vice presidents. He let many of them go, and some left of their own accord.[20] The broader point here is that you need an organization that is built for speed and agility. You can't have a bunch of layers, where each layer simply thinks up new questions that delay things.

6. **Don't go too fast.** Ed had a lot of work to do in the five areas just discussed. He emphasized the importance of being patient but also pushing hard for more customer focus, a leaner, tougher organization, and a sequence of exciting products that really would get Motorola on a roll again, both internally and externally.

> *The Motorola story shows the slow calcification of a culture that ends up stifling just about anything different from its legacy practices.*

The Motorola story shows the slow calcification of a culture that ends up stifling just about anything different from its legacy practices. Chris Galvin, the CEO from 1997 until 2003, worked hard to reinvigorate Motorola, but it just did not happen. Many people believed that the problem was that Chris had been born and bred in that culture. In fact, his grandfather had started the business, and his father was a prior CEO.

It's clear that Ed Zander understood that there was a huge problem with the culture, and that he was on the warpath. He spotted the new ultra-thin RAZR product that Motorola was working on, and he used it to show employees, and customers, how Motorola would act in the future.

After his first six months, Motorola began to regularly exceed Wall Street's expectations. While it had lost $1.78 per share in 2001 and $0.59 per share in 2002, it returned to profitability in 2003 with earnings of $0.38 per share, followed by $0.63 per share in 2004 and $1.81 per share in 2005. The company has regained the number two position in cellular handsets from Samsung, and revenue surged to $36.8 billion in 2005 compared with $23.4 billion in 2002. Unfortunately, in 2006, competition matched the slim, sleek Motorola RAZR cell phone. Motorola fought back with lower prices but not with innovation. That led to a 24 percent stock price decline and a nearly 50 percent profit decline in the fourth quarter of 2006. While Zander clearly made progress in restoring some start-up feel in Motorola culture, by late 2006, Motorola was facing the same challenges as the historically successful Dell, namely, the need for innovation in an ever more competitive environment.

To get an organization's culture to change dramatically, you need a rallying point from which to leverage. Using a bright new product idea that clearly has big potential is a great approach.

# 23

## AVOID THE CURSE OF AN INTERNAL FOCUS

The secret of success for any organization is to constantly produce products and services that clearly create excitement with its customers. What often happens in successful or stable organizations is that people become very comfortable with their current product or service offerings, and they lose a sense of paranoia about finding the next wave of innovation for their products. They also become very risk-averse. Along with success and stability comes the drive to hire more people and focus on internal things rather than on the customer.

It doesn't take long for the organization's real focus to be on avoiding disruptive change. Individuals in the organization simply work to keep their bosses happy and out of their hair. They also become very concerned about how they are being treated and how their work group is being treated, as opposed to what they are doing to surprise the marketplace with genuine innovation. Put another way, the focus becomes internal. To get a real feel for just how this occurs over time and how it seems to linger, let's take a look at a major corporation that had problems in this area recently.

# BOEING

In August of 1997, Boeing acquired McDonnell Douglas for $16.3 billion. McDonnell Douglas was the only American company competing with Boeing in the commercial airline business. McDonnell Douglas didn't really have any distinguishing features at the time of the acquisition. It didn't have a strong reputation for innovation or efficient manufacturing practices. The attitude reflected in the press was that the merger probably wouldn't help Boeing, since the company was bogged down with severe production problems that were eating it alive financially. As reported by Ronald Henkoff of *Fortune,* Boeing's internal operations were complex and a result of years of internal modifications and fragmentation.[1] He described it as follows: "Boeing executives had known for years—for decades even—that their factories were inefficient, their supply chains tangled, and their computer systems outdated. Ever since the late 1970's, they've tried in a piece-meal fashion to fix these problems but they never took the issues seriously."

To convey just how bad things had gotten, Henkoff stated the following: "Boeing's problem—and it's a big one—is that your humble service station probably operates more efficiently than the largest aerospace company on the planet."[2] Henkoff went on to describe how any alteration that a customer requested on a particular airplane consumed enormous amounts of engineering time, required hundreds of pages of detailed drawings, and cost hundreds of thousands, if not millions, of dollars to execute. Surprisingly, even with its sloppy internal processes, Boeing had managed to do fairly well. Most attributed that to the fact that Boeing's typical customers were airlines, which were protected by regulation, and the Department of Defense, which was not cost-conscious. In addition, Boeing didn't have a well-run competitor to race with during the 1990s.

## Boeing: The Crisis

In the fall of 1997, things got very bad. Attempts to install new production approaches were creating chaos in the plants. On two production lines, Boeing had to halt production for a full month.

> *Clearly, Boeing was its own worst enemy. For example, it offered 109 shades of white.*

This generated a $1.6 billion charge against third-quarter earnings. Plus, the company had to alert Wall Street that profits in 1988 would probably be $1 billion lower. It just couldn't seem to get airplanes out the door.

Clearly, Boeing was its own worst enemy. Whatever the customer wanted, Boeing would attempt to develop it.[3] For perspective, Boeing was offering 747 buyers as many choices of paint colors as you could possibly imagine. For example, the company offered 109 shades of white. At the plants, most things were done manually; there were no robots. It was all manual labor, with small teams of workers using primarily hand tools. As Henkoff mentioned, "It looks like a giant version of the repair bay in your local auto dealer's service department."[4]

Because of the lack of a competitor, the severe overstaffing, and the manual orientation of the company's production efforts, things at Boeing moved at an absolute snail's pace. For perspective, there were 990 pages of drawings that recorded every bulkhead configuration ever built for a 747.[5] Those drawings were used to order parts, and the manufacturing folks would depend on those drawings in their assembly of the plane. It was often said that the Boeing production process produced primarily paperwork rather than airplanes.[6]

The internal focus at Boeing was so intense that nearly all of the individual departments at each of the factories had their own computer systems, and the large majority of those systems didn't talk to one another. It was common knowledge that the parts list and sketches for a particular 747 were held in over 400 different databases.

## *Boeing: The Management Reaction*

By 1999, the company was in a severe tailspin. CEO Phil Condit had pulled his senior staff together for three days to develop a plan to turn around the situation.[7] As reported in the press, they concluded that they had to do four things: fix the production problems once and for all, develop some higher-margin defense and space division products and services, regain credibility on Wall Street, and scrap Boeing's paternalistic corporate culture. They also recognized that the culture issue was critical to achieving the first three goals.

Unfortunately, Phil Condit, who was the CEO, really didn't have much experience in how to achieve these four things. After all, as noted by *Fortune*'s Ken Labich, Condit was "a Boeing employee for more than 30 years, . . . steeped in the company's traditional warm and fuzzy management ethos."[8] As a result of the merger, Harry Stonecipher, who had headed up McDonnell Douglas, became the president of Boeing. He had quite a reputation for bluntness; as Labich put it, Stonecipher was "willing to break the eggs for Boeing's new cultural omelet." Just after the turnaround plan was announced, Condit and Stonecipher had the message down pat that they were putting a very high priority on "changing Boeing's culture from warm, familiar and somewhat insular to tough, lean and team-oriented."[9]

On the other hand, the two had drastically different approaches to achieving that new culture.[10] Condit made a big deal out of trying to eliminate the term "heritage employees," which was often used to refer to someone with deep Boeing experience. Naturally, that meant that they were probably also stuck in the old culture. Stonecipher, on the other hand, was known for acknowledging to anyone in the company who would listen that "it's about seniority, not performance around here" and that "in a family culture, you never throw out a bad performer." He would then make it clear that his view of the new culture wouldn't allow a bit of that.

## *Boeing: The Infighting*

By the year 2000, the tension at Boeing was incredible, primarily because of the style differences between Condit and Stonecipher.

Jerry Useem of *Fortune* noted that one Boeing insider described the Condit approach and that of Stonecipher as "the Boy Scouts versus the Mercenaries."[11] Useem summarized it by saying, "Whatever metaphor works best, the fact is that Boeing is a company at war with itself, fighting its own people, its own outmoded systems, and its own history in an attempt to rebuild itself from the inside. Forget Boeing versus Airbus. The future of this industry may hinge on Boeing versus Boeing."

Stonecipher took great pride in his gruffness. He often explained how much he admired Harry Truman, and he liked quotes such as, "I don't give 'em hell; I just tell them the truth and they think it's hell." When Stonecipher appeared before the Seattle Rotary Club in the late 1990s, he described Boeing as "arrogant" and its financial results as "absolutely dismal." He went on further to say, "Our problem is us."[12]

Condit's approach to fixing the problems couldn't have been more different from Stonecipher's. As Useem pointed out, "Condit's management style is one of consensus and what Condit terms 'aggressive listening.' In the mid-1990s, Condit had hundreds of managers attend a development program to improve their listening. This included such bizarre activities as listening to a jazz pianist, watching modern dance, and having a free-lance corporate poet read passages aloud from Beowulf."[13]

## Boeing: The Ethics Issues

The year 2003 was a very rough one for Boeing. In July, it was widely reported in the press, and confirmed by Boeing, that Boeing employees had stolen 25,000 pages of Lockheed Martin documents.[14] The Boeing managers who admitted to the theft said that they'd used those documents to shape Boeing's bids. The U.S. Air Force barred Boeing from bidding on a variety of contracts.

In November 2003, Boeing fired Chief Financial Officer Michael Sears.[15] The company found out that he had been having employment discussions with a Pentagon employee who was still overseeing Boeing contracts. Apparently what happened was that CFO Sears offered Air Force procurement officer Darleen Druyun

> *The backstabbing was widespread among the top brass.*

a job at Boeing while she was representing the U.S. Air Force in negotiating a $17 billion contract to replace aerial tankers with Boeing 767s. Druyun did accept the job at Boeing, but once the facts were uncovered, both she and Sears were dismissed. Also, the Pentagon put the tanker deal on hold.

## Boeing: Internal Politics

Looking at some of the details of how CFO Michael Sears behaved prior to being ousted gives some additional insights into Boeing's culture. As reported by Stanley Holmes in *BusinessWeek* in the summer of 2003, Sears began to wage an all-out war with then-CEO Condit.[16] He apparently got control of all public relations responsibilities, which is quite strange for a CFO, resulting in his being in charge of Boeing's access to both the media and the financial community. He also took control of Boeing's in-house leadership center, which was located in St. Louis. Sears excluded all the other top executives from meetings there. Most analysts viewed this move as an attempt on his part to create a high profile throughout Boeing's rank and file. One board member was quoted as saying, "It was clear to everybody that Sears was anxious to be the successor to Phil to the point that it got pretty disgusting." One of Sears's competitors for the CEO job was Jim Albaugh. As noted by Stanley Holmes, "While Sears was in charge of PR, there were leaks to the media implying that Albaugh withheld information about a $1.2 billion charge." Albaugh blamed Sears for all the nasty publicity he got because of the apparent leak.[17] As Holmes noted, "The back-stabbing was widespread among the top brass." Holmes also cites a former senior Boeing executive who was close to the situation as saying, "It was pretty destructive."

In December 2003, CEO Phil Condit resigned under the weight of all of the problems. In summarizing Condit's reign, Jerry Useem of *Fortune* said, "Condit didn't recreate Boeing during his seven year tenure so much as un-create it. He leaves behind a company that has lost its way and, more to the point, its nerve."[18] In replacing Condit, the board of directors reached for former Chief Operating Officer Harry Stonecipher, who had been retired for 18 months. We described some of Stonecipher's behavior earlier, but it was summarized well by Julie Cresswell of *Fortune* magazine when she said, "He's renowned for his blistering verbal attacks and once threw an empty soda can at a co-worker in a fit of rage." Stonecipher, in commenting on his mannerisms, said, "I'm not proud of my style. But it's been effective, and I'm probably too old to learn new tricks."[19]

## Boeing: A False Start

Once Stonecipher got into the CEO job, he launched a major effort to put a high priority on ethics at Boeing.[20] An internal governance organization was formed, and it reported directly to Stonecipher. An ethics statement was developed, and all employees had to sign a copy of it. In the Boeing in-house magazine in June of 2004, Stonecipher said, "Firing people who lack integrity is good business." Stonecipher seemed totally committed to cleaning up the many cultural issues that had caused so many major problems at Boeing.

In early 2005, Boeing held its annual executive retreat in Palm Springs, often referred to as the "Palm Springs Fling." *BusinessWeek* reported that at that session "CEO Stonecipher initiated a relationship with Boeing executive Debra Peabody."[21] Two months later, Boeing's board of directors announced that Stonecipher was being separated from the company because numerous e-mails between Stonecipher and Ms. Peabody had been made public, embarrassing the company very significantly. The board had no alternative but to ask Stonecipher to resign for ethics reasons.[22]

When you step back and look at Boeing's history over that 20-year period, going from being rated one of the most admired companies in the United States to the chaos that took place in 2003, 2004, and early 2005, it's very clear that the issue here is a culture that was focused internally and a company that was not really aware that it was competing in a free enterprise market. CEO Frank Schrontz had alerted the company in the mid-1990s that its decades of experience in a regulated industry were very poor training for it to compete in a free marketplace, and he certainly was right.

There is somewhat of a happy ending to this story. In 2005, Boeing began to develop terrific momentum behind a new airplane design called the 787 Dreamliner, scheduled to be available in 2008.[23] Specifically by spring 2006, it had 386 orders in hand for the $7 billion project, which incorporated such unique features as a plastic/carbon fiber fuselage.[24] Also, it hired a new CEO after a long period of search, and it chose Jim McNerney, who had previously been CEO of 3M and before that was in charge of the jet engine division of GE and a serious contender to replace Jack Welch when he retired.[25] McNerney is working hard to change this culture so that it focuses outwardly on its customers and to drive out the incredible insularity and infighting that Boeing had been experiencing.

The Boeing story shows us how a very successful organization can get incredibly internally focused, comfortable, and lethargic, and how destructive that behavior can be. Stepping back, it is very clear how critical culture can be in igniting the excitement, energy, and innovation that employees can generate.

### PART VIII

# TRAP #8

# TIMIDITY:
## NOT CONFRONTING TURF WARS, INFIGHTING, AND OBSTRUCTIONISTS

**Organizations** tend to fragment into fiefdoms. Management falls into the trap of ignoring the typical buildup of divisive turf wars and infighting. These entrenched division managements fight off any attempts to initiate significant change that might disrupt their fundamental comfort. They simply execute their legacy practices, and they believe they are quite good at what they do.

Attacking infighting and uncooperative but powerful division managers requires strong leadership that is keenly focused on a specific plan for progress. The leaders must have a strong commitment to that plan, and they need to be willing to reorganize the troops to achieve progress. They cannot be timid or shrink from the powerful division managers; instead, they must boldly move out individuals who are not willing to join the program.

The leaders need to be willing and anxious to make the tough decisions to keep things moving in the right direction. And it is the responsibility of the top brass to make it clear to everyone involved just what the plan is and why it is to their collective benefit to pursue it.

Infighting and turf wars can occur at many different levels. They may involve warring individuals within a group or a department, or they may involve warring groups. In the worst case, the whole organization, with its various divisions, groups, and individuals, is working to protect various turfs.

Now let's look at this nasty business trap in a bit more detail and outline some ways to circumvent these kinds of problems.

# 24

## BREAK UP FIEFDOMS AND LAUNCH YOUR PLAN

First, let's discuss fiefdoms. It doesn't take a lot of effort to find out if you have warring silos and impenetrable fiefdoms that are not cooperating. Just do a bunch of interviews at the lower levels of the organization. It's best to talk to the strong performers because they will be frustrated and thus more willing to tell you what is really going on. The average and below-average performers tend to really be comfortable in fiefdoms, and they will actually aggressively defend the current practices.

Once you have the information about where the silo and fiefdom problems are, the tough part is doing something about them. That requires nerves of steel and lots of leadership skills. However, the situation has to be confronted. There are two tools to reach for in breaking up fiefdoms:

> 1. **Place strong performers from outside the fiefdom in key jobs within the fiefdom.** This will not only provide some fresh new direction but also signal that "the party is over."
>
> 2. **Dismantle the fiefdoms by reorganizing.** This forces people to get back to basics and realize that changes are what will be required.

Over and over you see organizations struggling with this problem of fiefdoms. Let's take a look at a global corporate giant that had these kinds of problems. It is a classic case of an organization falling into the trap of turf battles and infighting, and the organization has had a very difficult time coming to grips with it.

# SONY

Back in the 1980s and 1990s, Sony was clearly the king of the consumer electronics industry. Its Trinitron TVs were absolutely state-of-the-art, and it had some incredible innovation in the Walkman and in its Sony PlayStation game player. But beginning in the year 2000, things started really heading south for Sony. By the end of its 2005 fiscal year, Sony had a net profit margin of 1.7 percent, which the press characterized as "a pitifully low figure."[1] Also, it was a far cry from the forecast made by Sony top management that the company would reach a 10 percent margin by the year 2007.[2] Over the four-year period ending in early 2006, its stock price had dropped over 50 percent.

During this period, significant competitors were emerging, such as Samsung from South Korea, which pulled ahead of Sony in the flat-panel television market. Having a Korean company pass it was very embarrassing to Sony. Apple probably did the most damage to the Sony franchise by launching its very successful iPod digital music player, making the Walkman look like an antique of the 1980s and early 1990s. Sony's digital cameras were also under attack by Canon and Nikon as digital photography became an incredibly active and innovation-driven market. While Sony PlayStation re-tained its leadership position, Microsoft introduced Xbox, which quickly became the number two player, and Microsoft clearly had its sights set on taking over the leadership position from Sony.

## Sony: The Issue

As Phred Dvorak discussed in the *Wall Street Journal,* the core issue for Sony was the fact that many of the new products that were emerging and embarrassing Sony required a variety of skills, such as hardware, software, content, and services.[3] These capabilities were in very well-guarded divisions or silos within Sony, and getting the divisions to work together to make things happen across these areas was very difficult.

Consequently, products like the iPod, which requires great hardware design, clever software, and great music download services, absolutely baffled Sony. The same was true of the TiVo digital video recorder. It had the same characteristics of needing a variety of talents to make it successful, not just hardware or just software. Put another way, the current organization just simply did not match up well with what was needed to develop attractive alternatives for the consumer.

## Sony: Reacting to iPod

Sony's Connect project vividly demonstrates the problems we are discussing here. As the Sony Walkman got buried by Apple and its iPod music player and iTunes Internet-based music store, Sony scrambled to develop a response. This effort, called Connect, was led by Howard Stringer, who was the head of Sony's U.S. operations at the time. This project was launched in early 2003—quite a slow response to Apple's November 2001 launch of the iPod.

Almost immediately, Stringer ran into huge problems simply because the various divisions that needed to participate in this project were off doing their own thing, making it very difficult for him to lead this effort to success, given that it cut across so many divisions.

For example, Sony's personal computer group, which resided in Tokyo, was to develop the software to organize the downloaded music.[4] Unfortunately, the software that was developed didn't work well with the new versions of the Walkman music player developed by the Japanese portable audio team. Even worse, it became clear that the Japanese portable audio team was really not well versed in the ways of teenagers and Web surfers, who were very involved with buying music online in the United States.

Stringer was working frantically to engage Sony's top management in Tokyo to help with these problems, but he caught Tokyo's attention only when the product failed in the marketplace. In essence, the company's real strengths with respect to hardware, software, and services all resided in separate warring divisions within Sony. From his base in the United States, Stringer was simply incapable of pulling the Japanese divisions together, given that there was no strong leadership at the top clearly stating the goal and reorganizing to achieve it.[5]

## Sony: Entrenched Fiefdoms

The level of infighting and lack of unity facing the Connect project was startling. Once it became clear that Connect had a lot of problems because of the jukebox software that was a key interface in its service, the Sony Japanese PC division was confronted and asked to fix the issues quickly. As reported in the *Wall Street Journal,* "A Sony spokesman in Tokyo says the division didn't have time to make changes given Connect's tight deadline" for achieving some significant improvement.[6]

At the same time, Sony's U.S. marketers were pushing hard for a Walkman that had a hard drive for storing music rather than relying on a high-capacity MiniDisc. While these removable cartridges were popular in Japan, they had not gone over well in the United States. It was only after extreme pressure that the Walkman division, run by Takashi Fukushima, finally relented and agreed to develop a hard-drive Walkman, but only after publicly stating, as we cited in Chapter 2, "Why Does This Happen?" that such hard drives "aren't interesting because anyone can make them."[7] Fukushima was also

*These problems of fiercely independent division managements and lack of consumer perspective were starting to be acknowledged at high levels of the company. Sony executive Rob Wiesenthal said: "I have 35 Sony devices at home. I have 35 battery chargers. That's all you need to know."*

the individual who dug in his heels with respect to enabling the Walkman to play MP3 files. He preferred Sony's proprietary technology called ATRAC, which was used in conjunction with the MiniDisc.[8]

The lack of unity, leadership, and proper reorganization were also evident in the way Sony mishandled its efforts in online music. As early as 1998, Sony was considering launching online digital music services. Unfortunately, there were huge arguments within the company. The Japanese PC unit and the Walkman unit had their own ideas about what should be done, while Sony's U.S. music unit greatly feared all of these activities because it was worried about piracy issues. Sony Chairman and CEO Nobuyuki Idei decided to just suspend the whole subject and see if a compromise could be developed. Unfortunately, this opened the floodgates for competitors to enter what was to become one of the fastest-growing parts of the consumer electronics industry. Again, Sony management was demonstrating incredibly weak leadership and an unwillingness to organize around the task and get it done quickly.

In 2005, Sony launched the PlayStation Portable (PSP), a small portable game console that not only is a game player but also can be used for music and photos. Having no real interaction with the music folks within Sony, the PSP was launched with memory slots that supported only Sony's proprietary Memory Stick Duo format. As noted in the press, most people viewed this as "a subtle attempt to get consumers to buy expensive Memory Stick cards from Sony."[9] This further demonstrates just how insular Sony's various divisions were and how they had ignored learning from other areas of their company. These problems of fiercely independent division management and lack of consumer perspective were starting to be acknowledged at high levels of the company. For example, executive Rob Wiesenthal commented; "I have 35 Sony devices at home. I have 35 battery chargers. That's all you need to know."[10]

> *It doesn't matter whether you are managing a group of five or six people or running the whole thing. The people under you need to know what the game plan is. Where are you trying to go?*

## Sony: Action Taken

Given all of these problems, the board finally acted. In mid-2005, Howard Stringer was picked to replace Idei as the CEO. *Business-Week*'s Brian Bremner summarized the situation well with regard to what Howard would face: "Stringer has to convince skeptical insiders and outside investors that its warring fiefdoms can be finally quelled and forced into a coherent company."[11] On the other hand, as reported in the *Wall Street Journal* recently, Stringer seems to fully understand what he needs to do, as he stated, "All great companies want the status quo to remain long after the quo has lost status."[12] He is off to a good start. It was reported in early 2006 that Stringer had already eliminated 5,700 jobs, closed nine factories, and sold $705 million of assets, including 1,220 cosmetic salons and a chain of 18 restaurants.[13]

It's also encouraging to see that in October 2006, Sony finally introduced an up-to-date Walkman with a hard drive that should be able to compete with the iPod. Unfortunately, the iPod has about 75 percent of the market and is well accepted by tens of millions of users after having been available for almost five years.

Sony represents a classic example of an organization falling into the infighting/silos trap. It is very clear that Howard Stringer must break up the fiefdoms and organize around the opportunities as he launches his future plans for success.

Now let's discuss the importance of having a clear plan for progress. It doesn't matter whether you are managing a group of five or six people at the low end of an organization or whether you are running the whole thing. The people under you need to know what the game plan is. Where are you trying to go? What are you trying to achieve? How does that differ from where we are today? Those are the kinds of questions that people will constantly be asking if they are in a situation where a plan for progress is lacking. Here are a few guidelines that are extremely important in this area:

1. **All of your people should be able to provide a unified and clear answer to the question, "Where are we going and why?"** People hunger to know what it is they are heading for and how they can assist. If the future is unclear, internal debates will begin, and if these are not dealt with, they will simmer into major organizational unrest.

2. **When faced with an uncertain future and the resulting organizational problems, analyze thoroughly, but put a high priority on speed.** The longer people are left in the dark as to what is going on, the more time they waste debating, and, most importantly, you stand a good chance of losing your really good people.

3. **Once you launch the plan, listen carefully to what the troops are saying and what customers are saying, adjust your plan appropriately, and then listen again.** People who are close to the situation have very good ideas. A good manager will take full advantage of that and really work to understand what people are experiencing and what their suggestions for modifications are as they implement the plan.

In the 2000 to 2005 time frame, there was a great example of a major company falling into the trap of warring factions and having no agreed-upon plan to unite those factions with a shared vision. Let's review it.

# MORGAN STANLEY

Back in 1999, Morgan Stanley had major issues concerning what it should do in the future because the consolidation of the banking industry was happening fast.[14] President John Mack wanted Morgan Stanley to merge with Chase Manhattan. Phil Purcell, the CEO, acknowledged that a merger should be considered but favored J. P. Morgan & Co. The two of them resolved their differences by doing nothing. Ironically, just one year later, Chase bought J. P. Morgan. This, plus other frustrations, led John Mack to quit.

Things went on for a few more years with basically no clear direction at Morgan Stanley. By the end of 2003, the board of directors had finally reached the point where they demanded a plan that would generate significant positive momentum for Morgan Stanley.[15] The board asked that this plan be unveiled to the board in July 2004.

## Morgan Stanley: Needed A Plan

CEO Phil Purcell assigned a small team to work on this task, but just as the team began its work, it was announced that JPMorgan Chase had purchased Bank One. This caused the discomfort level at Morgan Stanley to go even higher because it was clear that Morgan Stanley had missed another great opportunity.

The team working on Morgan Stanley's direction came up with the idea of merging with Wachovia. It was a regional bank that was just beginning to spread its wings. As Emily Thornton of *BusinessWeek* put it, "New Yorkers were still learning how to pronounce its name."[16]

For six months, there were internal debates about Wachovia and whether a merger with it should be pursued.[17] By the time of the board meeting in July 2004, when the directors were expecting a plan to be unveiled, Phil Purcell and the internal committee he formed had not developed any good, sound ideas for the future. Consequently, Purcell's recommendation to the board was simply to take the current business and improve its performance. The board of directors avoided a confrontation with Purcell and accepted his recommendation. This set off all kinds of bombshells, since the general consensus was that Morgan Stanley was floundering.

## Morgan Stanley: Internal Chaos

In the biggest bombshell of all, a group of eight former Morgan Stanley executives got together and sent a letter to the board calling for Phil Purcell's resignation.[18] This group even took out ads crying for a plan and urging that Phil Purcell be fired. Obviously, the group felt that the board and the management were letting Morgan Stanley down. The group believed that the bank deserved an aggressive plan for progress, and that no such plan was being generated.

Believe it or not, the story gets even worse. Purcell thought the head of investment banking at Morgan Stanley, Vikram Pandit, was behind the letter. Purcell then reorganized the company, but did not provide positions for Pandit and some of the other key players at the bank. This led to a quick exit of some incredibly talented individuals. By this time, the whole affair was a soap opera that was discussed daily in all the key Wall Street publications. As you would guess, this house of cards eventually collapsed, and in June 2005, Phil Purcell announced that he would retire.[19]

There was a great quote by Phil Purcell concerning all of this. As reported in *Fortune,* a former Morgan Stanley executive said he heard Purcell complain, "At Dean Witter, I told people to turn left and they turned left. At Morgan Stanley, they looked at me and asked why."[20] It's a very telling statement in that even Phil Purcell could see that the troops wanted to know not only the plan but why the company was going in that direction. It's a reasonable request, but Purcell was viewing it as unnecessary.

*Newsweek* reported in June 2005 that Phil Purcell sought advice from a consultant about how he could improve his image.[21] According to a senior Morgan Stanley executive, the consultant apparently said, "Go public with your plan to improve the firm's finances." The consultant then went on to explain that this plan should be not only aired internally but given to the press and discussed on business TV channels so that all the world would know and, most importantly, the employees would know where Purcell was going and why. As noted in the *Newsweek* article, "Purcell never fully acted on the advice."

This whole Morgan Stanley situation was summarized by veteran Wall Street executive Michael Holland, who runs his own investment firm, when he said, "And the big problem here was that there was no message from the top."[22]

> *"At Dean Witter, I told people to turn left and they turned left. At Morgan Stanley, they looked at me and asked why."*
>
> —Phil Purcell

If you go back to the guidelines we discussed, what is needed is obvious. People want to know where you're going and why it's a smart thing to do. When that is not known, you need to get with the troops, sort out the best thinking, hash things out, thoroughly learn the situation, and then stake your bets and get on with it. Speed is important through that whole process because you will have people churning around wondering where things are going. Without such a plan for progress, you are almost guaranteed to get infighting, turf wars, and fiefdoms, because everyone is uncertain about the future.

# 25

## ASSEMBLE A TEAM YOU BELIEVE IN

Once you have a plan for progress, you need to know that the individuals on the team are believers in the plan and can make it happen. Anything less should not be tolerated. This may mean that you have to let some people go as you reorganize to maximize your chances of success. Legacy people protecting legacy practices can be major stumbling blocks in pulling off significant change, and this is where they lose out big from a career perspective if they continue to hold on to those practices.

Too often in organizations, we think that certain people have deep expertise and experience, and we are afraid to move them out. This is usually a gigantic mistake. Naturally, there are exceptions to this rule, such as certain narrow and deep specialists who are not involved in operating or leading, but provide unique expertise or a historical perspective, but even in those cases, beware. In most business settings, I have seldom seen a situation in which a smart, enthusiastic employee with a lot of common sense and energy can't master the basics in just about any area in a remarkably short time. More importantly, new people are not weighed down by the history of how things have been done in the past and the drive to defend the ways of the past. Consequently, they come up with some startlingly fresh ideas.

The automobile business again provides a rich example. In this case, we see a once successful company that developed major problems because of the lack of an aggressive, energized leadership team.

# PORSCHE

In the 1950s and 1960s, Porsche established itself as *the* thoroughbred luxury sports car brand. Starting in the early 1970s, however, it had a very difficult time, and by the early 1990s, Porsche was a company in deep distress. It had an antiquated, legacy production system that was very inefficient, and it had experienced two decades of failure to broaden the appeal of its product line.

In the 1970s and 1980s, Porsche tried hard to create new models that were less expensive and hopefully more broadly appealing. It built a mid-engine car with Volkswagen called the 914. It also produced a front-engine car with Audi called the 924. Each of these met with limited success and was eventually discontinued. In 1978, Porsche brought out the 928, which was a front-engine V-8-powered car that was supposed to replace the classic rear-engine 911 that had been in production for 15 years. Porsche enthusiasts were turned off by these mid-engine and front-engine vehicles, and these models really languished.[1]

These failures made Porsche somewhat gun-shy in making additional moves, and by the early 1990s, the company was on the brink of collapse. For perspective, car sales, which had been 53,000 in 1986, were down to fewer than 12,000 in 1993.[2] It's clear that Porsche didn't really understand what its brand was all about, namely, being *the* thoroughbred luxury sports car. It was completely out of date with respect to production techniques, and there was no strong leadership to pull the organization together to tackle these problems.

*In most business settings, I have seldom seen a situation in which a smart, enthusiastic employee with a lot of common sense and energy can't master the basics in just about any area in a remarkably short time.*

## Porsche: A Fresh Leadership Team

In 1993, the Porsche board of directors moved into action and set out to assemble a new executive team. It named Wendelin Wiedeking as the new CEO. He was well seasoned in the automobile business; in fact, he had worked for Porsche in the early 1980s. He recruited several individuals from BMW in developing his new team of direct reports. He selected these people carefully because he knew what kind of strength was going to be needed to turn this nasty situation around. It was clear that Porsche needed some fresh thinking and new personnel looking at the problem, and that is exactly what the board and Wiedeking provided.

One of Wiedeking's primary strengths was his ability to make principled but unpopular decisions. For perspective, at one point, the German government offered to provide a $98 million subsidy to assist in the construction of a new Porsche plant. Wiedeking turned it down because he feared that taxpayers would be critical of their government using their hard-earned funds to help an enterprise such as Porsche.[3]

As Alex Taylor described in a *Fortune* article, Wiedeking was famous for speaking his mind and following his instincts.[4] He was quoted as saying, "Those who make concessions will lose. If we were just a small copy of a major player, our continued existence would certainly be unjustified." Clearly this guy understands the need for fresh approaches and distinctiveness in products.

## Porsche: Tackling the Problems

In the legacy-driven organization that Wiedeking inherited, one of the hardest things to do was to kill projects that hadn't been productive. He made the hard decision to kill both the front-engine 928 and the less-expensive 968 in order to reduce complexity and cost. The only model remaining was the classic 911, but that represented vintage Porsche, and Wiedeking believed that he could build the company around it.

The next thing he tackled was the poor-performing legacy manufacturing processes. It took three years of constant assault to generate significant improvement, but by 1997, Porsche workers took only 45 hours to build a 911, compared to 120 hours in 1991. The time required to develop a new model shrank to three years from seven, and finished cars drove out of the plant after just three days of work, compared with six weeks previously.

Achieving those manufacturing results was not easy. Wiedeking began the task of attacking Porsche's legacy practices by making numerous trips to Japan to study Japanese production techniques. This led to his hiring a group of Japanese manufacturing consultants known as Shingijutsu. Alex Taylor of *Fortune* reported that the stories about Shingijutsu trying to help Porsche have become company legend.[5] For example, a consultant found a poorly glued piece of carpet in a 911 and shrieked, "Bring me the person responsible for this!" Another consultant observed a pile of parts near the assembly line and asked: "Where is the car factory? It looks like a mover's warehouse." It was also reported that Wiedeking himself grabbed a circular saw as he was walking down the parts aisle and sawed off the metal shelving in order to encourage the troops to move faster in achieving the Japanese minimum-inventory approach to production.

In revamping its production processes, Porsche was extremely aggressive in outsourcing so that the company could minimize the amount of capital spent on manufacturing. It made only one-fifth of the car's parts; the rest were produced by outsiders. Wiedeking's views in this area were clear: "I hate fixed costs."[6] In the end, the number of suppliers was cut from 950 to 300, and production costs were reduced by 30 percent.

## Porsche: Creating Excitement

Once the production problems were sorted out, management turned its attention to modernizing the product line. It updated the 911 to make it more luxurious and began using water-cooled, instead of air-cooled, engines. The purists really raised their eyebrows at that change, but Wiedeking knew that it was a dead-right move from a technology perspective. In addition, they created a mid-engine roadster, the Boxster. It was a smaller, less expensive version of the 911 with a very sporty look and great performance. Producing the Boxster was certainly a very risky move, given Porsche's lack of success in the 1970s and 1980s when it attempted to broaden its product line. Taking further risk, Porsche decided to use a Finnish supplier and to build the Boxster at its factory, making it the first Porsche assembled outside of Germany. Talk about breaking a legacy practice!

The Boxster was hugely successful. By 2003, it accounted for 40 percent of Porsche's unit sales worldwide and 50 percent of its sales in the United States, Porsche's largest market.

Next came the most difficult decision Porsche probably ever made: to launch a sport utility vehicle. As Alex Taylor put it, "The idea of Porsche making an SUV is only slightly less jarring than Lafite Rothschild producing a blush wine, or Brioni applying its Italian stitching to a pair of overalls. This is a company that thrives by building cars that go faster than most people can drive them—and that cost more than most people can afford. Irrational though it sounds, Porsche has refined this formula to perfection."[7]

Such thinking did not discourage CEO Wiedeking. The idea was to produce the thoroughbred luxury sports car of SUVs. As Porsche's marketing boss, Hans Riedel, put it: "This will be good for all those fathers who don't want to sacrifice their sports cars to parenthood."[8]

Porsche knew that it had to make its SUV distinctive. It chose the name Cayenne, and it knew that it was very late to the SUV market. Hans Riedel was quoted as saying, "We come in at the eleventh hour, but we're not going to do the 365th SUV. We're doing the sports car of sport utilities with on-road performance that is comparable to our other cars."[9]

In planning for the production of the Cayenne, all kinds of legacy thinking were thrown out the window. First, Porsche developed the car in cooperation with Volkswagen, which would market its own version of the Cayenne with a VW body and engine. Volkswagen would build Cayenne bodies at its factory in Slovakia and ship them to a new Porsche plant in Leipzig, Germany, where the Porsche engine, suspension, and interior would be installed.

*The Carrera GT is truly the heartthrob of any red-blooded male. Its eye-popping price of over $400,000 sends a clear signal that this is the very best sports car in the world.*

The Leipzig factory produced more cars with fewer workers than just about any other auto plant in the world. Because 88 percent of the Cayenne's parts are provided by suppliers and arrive at the plant in preassembled modules, Porsche needed just 300 workers to assemble 25,000 vehicles annually.[10] This compares with 3,500 employees producing 32,000 Boxsters and 911s in the company's Zuffenhausen plant in Germany. One analyst estimated that Porsche is able to break even when the Leipzig plant is running at only 20 percent of capacity, compared with 70 percent or so for your typical automobile manufacturing plant.

To help make sure that the Cayenne didn't spoil the Porsche image of being *the* thoroughbred luxury sports car, Porsche created a new super sports car, the Carrera GT, which was shown for the first time at the Paris motor show in September 2001. The Carrera GT is essentially a racing car built for street use. It is made of lightweight carbon fiber and generates 550 horsepower from a 10-cylinder engine behind the driver's head. It accelerates from zero to sixty in under 4 seconds. The Carrera GT is truly the heartthrob of any red-blooded male. Its eye-popping price of over $400,000 sends a

> *Looking back to 1993, this is a clear example of the value of getting some new talent to look at the problem and letting these people build a unified team to achieve great things.*

clear signal that this is the very best sports car in the world. Its reviews say that it is clearly in a league of its own.

## Porsche: The Results

By the end of 2004, Porsche was absolutely in high gear. The 911 was as healthy as ever, the Boxster was a raging success, and so was the Cayenne SUV. The financial rewards were enormous. Porsche had the highest full-year pretax margin in the industry, 17 percent.[11] That made Porsche clearly the most profitable automobile company in the world.

Looking back to 1993, this is a clear example of the value of getting some new talent to look at the problem and letting these people build a unified team to achieve great things. Led by Wiedeking, Porsche burst through the status quo in virtually all aspects of its business. As with Toyota, the contrast between what Porsche has done since 1993 compared to the performance of General Motors over the past 30 years is staggering. Porsche put in fresh talent at the top; it tackled its legacy manufacturing practices; it launched exciting, bold new products with the Boxster and the Cayenne; and it strengthened its brand with the Carrera GT. This led to phenomenal growth. It is an incredibly rich case study of the benefits of tackling the problems of legacy people and practices head on with a fresh team and giving that team the authority to make things happen.

# 26

## BEWARE OF VAGUE ACCOUNTABILITY AND ISOLATIONISTS

uccess often leads organizations to hire more people than they should and to create a lot of managers and a lot of staff groups. This often results in overlapping and vague responsibilities. Even worse, the complicated organization is often burdened with excessive checks and balances that can make decision making very slow and complicated, with no one specifically accountable. Here are some ways to avoid such wasteful situations:

1. **Make individuals accountable; don't turn them into comment collectors.** Many organizations operate with what I call the "layers of wisdom" model. In this situation, an individual or a small group gets a bright idea, and the first layer of management immediately swoops down and gives the individual or group advice as to what should be changed. Those with the idea also get input from the various staff groups. They make the changes that all these people are suggesting; then they go to yet another level of line and staff management and get the same kind of treatment. By

265

the time they have gone up and down all these chains of command and attempted to reflect everyone's point of view, they've eaten up too much time, and they've also probably had all the creative and distinctive elements of the plan taken out.

What should happen when we assign a project to an individual or a small group is simple: let the people responsible know that their job is not to just reflect input from others. They need to do the proper homework to make the effort successful. If they don't get it right, their performance appraisal and career progress should reflect that.

**2. Don't allow compromises to be made at low levels. Put an experienced person in charge.** In organizations with excessive layers, we see situations where two or three groups at a fairly low level will come together, and relatively inexperienced people will be making important decisions that lack a broad perspective. This can lead to a lot of frustration on the part of project teams, but, worse, it can also lead to some bad decision making. The best design is to equip that project team with the seasoned personnel and capabilities that it's going to need and then let it run. While management should check in frequently, you don't want to be putting constraint after constraint on the group as it sorts through the basic issues and attacks its particular project.

Here is an example of an impressive global company that has had problems in this area.

## UNILEVER

In 2004, many folks believed that Unilever had a serious problem because of its very unusual dual-CEO situation. The co-chairmen of the company, who functioned as joint CEOs, were Antony Burgmans and Patrick Cescau. These two CEOs even lived in different areas: one in Rotterdam and the other in London. The general consensus in the financial community was that Unilever not only had too many CEOs, but also had too many people and too many managers.[1]

## Unilever: The Dove Example

One example of a situation where extra staff and vague accountability really hurt Unilever involved its brand Dove. While Dove has been one of Unilever's most successful brands, many people believe that the company really hasn't tapped its full potential. For example, even though skin care and facial

> *This is a perfect example of not delegating responsibility and accountability to a specific product group, such as a separate Dove, Pond's, and Lux group, and charging each group to be the best.*

care is a huge market in China, and Dove's positioning is tailor-made to be successful in that environment, Unilever has not performed well there. The basic reason is that Unilever really doesn't delegate responsibility for driving the brand's success to one group. Issues go up the chain of command and get debated between the Rotterdam and London groups, and you end up with compromises.

In the case of Dove, Unilever didn't decide to market Dove strongly in China because of a perceived risk that strong marketing of Dove would cannibalize the sales of Unilever's Pond's and Lux brands.[2] This is a perfect example of not delegating responsibility and accountability to groups, such as creating separate Dove, Pond's, and Lux groups and charging them to be the best they can be. Clearly, what should happen is that Dove, Pond's, and Lux should all compete with one another in China and each achieve its maximum amount of impact.

Richard Tomlinson of *Fortune International* described it this way: "The lesson here is that Unilever's execution problem stems from a lack of firm, strategic guidance at the top. Too often the company's ability to respond to market developments gets lost in the five-year plans, revised growth targets, and action programs that are stuffed in the briefcases of dozens of senior executives who shuffle

> *Slow decision making like this is what you typically find when people don't really feel accountable for their business. If they feel accountable, they will be embarrassed by such a problem, and they won't let it happen.*

everyday between London and Rotterdam."[3] Sylvian Massot of Morgan Stanley sums it up this way: "It's a problem of complexity. There's too much management, so they don't know where to start to fix the business."[4] When you have excess complexity and management, too many people need to be involved in decisions, and that creates a lack of accountability.

## Unilever: The Slim-Fast Example

A clear example of lack of responsibility and accountability, and the slow movement that results, involves Unilever's brand Slim-Fast. It was riding a wave of success until 2003, when Americans went crazy over the Atkins diet. They demanded low-carb offerings from all of their vendors, and Slim-Fast simply didn't deliver. In 2003, Slim-Fast revenue dropped by one-third. James Amoroso of Banque Pictet in Geneva summarized it this way: "They weren't quick enough to react to the fad."[5] Slow decision making like this is what you typically find when people don't really feel accountable for their business. If they feel accountable, they will be embarrassed by such a problem, and they won't let it happen. On the other hand, if they simply float proposals up a complicated chain of command and those proposals get debated and debated by the multiple levels of excess management, all sense of urgency disappears pretty quickly.

Many shareholders believe that Unilever's two-headed, binational structure is at the root of its problems. One British investor says, "If you have two people responsible for everything, nobody is responsible for anything." The reason why these investors and shareholders are so upset is that Unilever keeps disappointing them. Specifically, as of early 2005, it had alerted Wall Street that it wouldn't make its first-quarter 2005 profit forecast, Moreover, that was the seventh such negative alert in the prior nine quarters. By early 2006, the stock was still struggling and was 20 percent below its 1998 levels.

It's incredible how large, successful organizations can get so bureaucratic, leading to vague accountability and slow movement. They get to a point, as you see with Unilever, where they can hardly fix things on their own. In the case of Unilever, it's been a huge issue for years.

It is encouraging to see that in early spring 2006, Unilever ended its 75-year-old structure of having two chairmen, one in London and one in Rotterdam. The company announced that Patrick Cescau, former co-chairman, would be chief executive and Anthony Burgmans, former co-chairman, would become chairman of both operations.[6] The investment community seems encouraged by this, since by the fall of 2006, the stock price was back to its 1998 levels, although long-term investors will get little nourishment from that achievement.

## THE VULNERABILITIES OF INFORMATION TECHNOLOGY

An area in which a lack of clear responsibility can really hurt is information technology. In many organizations, the IT group operates the central computing facilities, runs the telecommunications network, and has groups of people who serve the various business units. Often these business units grab hold of IT resources and take them over to such an extent that they are spending far too much money on information technology. But more importantly, these business units are building all kinds of systems that don't work together with other systems that the corporation runs and other systems that other business units build and run. That can make it extremely difficult to pull together reports that summarize the activity of selected business units or the entire corporation.

## The CIO Job Risk

Often the chief information officer (CIO) is at the heart of this traffic jam. If that person allows all kinds of duplication to go on in the different business units and allows those units' budgets to continue to grow, spawning more developers and more systems, a major train wreck is guaranteed to happen.

What needs to happen in organizations is that the CIO needs to really be held accountable for the entire organization having first-class information technology services. He should dictate what things are going to be organization-wide, and then he should allow business units to do certain things that are unique to a particular business unit. However, he should also demand that the business units participate in the organization-wide system in common areas such as financial reporting, procurement, and human resources systems.

Here's why many CIOs get fired. They tell their top management they will be effective in the information technology area; yet they allow the business units to do anything they want. Sooner or later, everyone is going to be disappointed. Management won't like the cost and won't like the fact that it can't summarize the business across the business units. The business units will want more and more autonomy and more and more independence from the CIO and will constantly be pulling that organization apart to gain control over more and more IT capabilities. I have seen this happen over and over again, and what it means is that you need a very strong CIO, backed by management, who sets the guidelines with regard to the company's information technology architecture, how systems will be built, which systems will be organization-wide, and what can be delegated to the business units to meet their local needs.

The same issues apply to the heads of human resources, finance, procurement, manufacturing, and other staff units. You don't want those functions to fragment. For an area like HR, you have to give the head of HR the accountability to do things right organization-wide and then judge him accordingly. If his job responsibilities are vague, and he allows each of the divisions to do its own thing, sooner or later HR will fragment. Each of the business units will develop its own HR group, overstaff it, and create its own HR practices unique to that business unit, causing problems when you need to address some people issues on an organization-wide basis.

Clear responsibility and accountability can really simplify an organization, and they are an absolute necessity if you are to be able to constantly fight off legacy practices. Legacy people and legacy practices flourish in a world where consensus is needed to do things and compromises are common.

> *Here's why many CIOs get fired. They tell their top management they will be effective in the information technology area; yet they allow the business units to do anything they want. Sooner or later, everyone is going to be disappointed.*

Now let's discuss isolationists. Success often leads to people believing that they are really good, and that often leads to a desire to be independent. In this case you often end up with egocentric behavior and the fragmenting of the organization as individuals and groups go off and pursue their own interests, constantly patting themselves on the back. They tend to become isolated from the challenges of the broader organization and become very protective.

These characteristics can emerge at any level within the organization. Here are two guidelines you need to practice on a regular basis:

1. **Require your people to dive in and get to know the issues in detail.** You can teach your people what kind of behavior you want by being a good role model. It sends a great signal when you, as the manager of a group, mix it up thoroughly with your people. You should ask all the naïve questions in order to become really aware of the key issues and the strengths and weaknesses of the group. This also sends a

message to your people that objectivity is crucial and that superficiality is not acceptable. This kind of behavior requires a fair amount of humility on your part because you need to regularly raise your hand and say, "I don't understand; can you explain?" Lots of folks who have gained some degree of success are reluctant to do this because they believe it is harmful to their reputation as being one of the elite. That kind of isolationist behavior encourages your people to also be isolationists.

2. **Make it clear that you want to hear the bad news right away and that the messenger doesn't get punished.** When fear exists in an organization, truth has a difficult time emerging. It's up to the manager of the group to make sure that employees know that they are all in it together, they are all human, and mistakes are great learning opportunities.

While these kinds of problems can happen at any level of an organization, they can even happen at the very highest levels. Let's take a look at such an example.

## HEWLETT-PACKARD

The Hewlett-Packard board of directors brought in Carly Fiorina as its new CEO in 1999. She had a huge challenge in turning around the very troubled HP franchise. Six years later, in February 2005, the board relieved her of her duties, and it had been a truly wild ride. At the end of her tenure, Louis Lavelle of *BusinessWeek* summarized her efforts: "She was a sales whiz known for high-profile marketing events and a fondness for global gatherings packed with A-list politicians, celebs, and CEO's. Problem is, many who spent time around her came away with the impression that she was as interested in burnishing her own image as she was in turning the company around."[7]

## HP: The Comparison to IBM

In early 2005, when Carly was relieved of her duties, *BusinessWeek* published an article that made direct comparisons between Carly's behavior at HP and Lou Gerstner's behavior during his tenure at IBM.[8] They pointed out that both were high-profile, successful executives prior to their taking on their new responsibilities, and both were marketing specialists from outside the computer industry. Here's what *BusinessWeek* said about Lou: "He gained the respect and loyalty of IBMer's early by going to the IBM research labs upon taking office, recognizing and celebrating IBM's core technology culture." Lou also gets credit for a massive orientation program to all parts of the business in the first several months of his tenure, and he reported on his findings via e-mail to all employees, making it clear that he was rolling up his sleeves and getting into the details, and that he wanted input from everyone. In contrast, *BusinessWeek* reported, "Carly was never able to win the loyalty of HP employees, who mostly resented and resisted her until the day she was ousted by the board of directors."

Soon after Gerstner took the CEO position at IBM, he publicly disparaged the "vision thing," but he quickly followed with a powerful, new overarching strategy for IBM that was extremely simple to explain to the employees.[9] Specifically, he concluded from his massive orientation efforts with customers as well as with employees that IBM needed to focus all of its great technical capabilities on solving customers' problems and enabling customers to run their business better. He put tremendous muscle behind the IBM services organization, which was focused on specific customers and was charged with leveraging all the capabilities of IBM to improve those customers' businesses through the use of information technology.

In contrast, that same *BusinessWeek* article summarized Carly's work the following way: "Fiorina's strategy of merging with a low-end computer maker, Compaq, failed to create a focused strategy for HP. She tried to serve too many customers in too many markets; consumer electronics, commodity PC's, high-valued enterprise businesses, and of course, printing."[10]

In a nutshell, Lou dove in, got his employees thinking about the

> *In a nutshell, Lou dove in, got his employees thinking about the future, came up with a strategy of helping customers, and went to work. Carly never generated a clear picture of the future that would excite her employees and get them to follow her.*

future, and came up with a strategy of helping customers, and they went to work. Carly never generated a clear picture of the future that would excite her employees and get them to follow her. When a manager isn't out in front of the troops with a game plan that has been actively vetted with them, a gulf between them and the manager quickly forms, leading to the troops backing away and becoming risk-averse and the manager becoming more and more isolated.

### HP: Carly's Fame

Soon after Carly was named CEO of HP, *Fortune* magazine published its first-ever ranking of the 50 Most Powerful Women Executives in America, and Carly was on top of the list. As *Fortune* magazine described it in 2005: "Her reputation bloomed, heading toward rock star celebrity. She became one of the few business people identifiable by her first name: she was just 'Carly.' Totally poised, she gave countless speeches; she became the only woman who never had a bad hair day; she was the subject of endless rumors that she might move on to politics."[11] It was clear to everyone how much Carly enjoyed the high-profile aspect of her job, but the business continued to suffer.

### HP: Turnover and Business Problems

By 2005, HP was suffering from a fairly significant "brain drain." As reported in *Fortune,* of the 11 direct reports that Carly had in October of 2003, 6 were gone by 2005.[12] An additional 20 highly placed

HP executives also departed, with a few of them going to direct competitors Dell and EMC.

All of this came to a head at the end of HP's third fiscal quarter in July 2004. HP missed its earnings target badly, and that hadn't been the first time. Coincident with the announcement of the poor results, three key executives were let go, with Carly explaining that they were responsible for the miss.[13] This set off all kinds of news stories discussing how Carly had separated herself from the bad news and blamed employees instead. There is nothing that causes a manager to get isolated from the employees like having the manager blame his or her people publicly when bad news comes along.

> *There is nothing that causes a manager to get isolated from the employees like having the manager blame his or her people publicly when bad news comes along.*

Through all of this, the HP shareholders were the losers. At the time of Carly's departure, the stock stood at about $20 per share, which was 13 percent below its price before the much-celebrated and controversial merger of Compaq and Hewlett-Packard. Embarrassingly, HP's chief competitor in printers, Lexmark, was up by 60 percent and Dell was ahead by 90 percent in the same period.[14] At that point, the directors decided it was time for Carly and HP to part ways.

In fall 2006, Carly launched a book entitled *Tough Choices,* in which she summarizes her career. In his review of the book, George Anders of the *Wall Street Journal* really captures the isolationist aspect by noting: "There is little evidence she made friends or even found reliable allies during her five years as HP's boss. She became a leader without followers, frustrated with various subordinates, most of her board, and all the media."[15]

It is interesting to note that in fall 2006, the HP board also uncovered a few examples of isolationist behavior within its own group. There were accusations that certain board members were leaking board information to the press, and that some board member or company executive was launching private investigations. This all led to a public soap opera in the press centering around possible privacy violations in obtaining the phone records of individual directors. The immediate fallout was the resignation of some board members, lawsuits, congressional hearings, and court activities.

The lessons from our discussions of Sony, Morgan Stanley, Porsche, Unilever, and HP are quite robust. As a leader of a group, be it large or small, you need to work actively with your employees to map out a plan for progress, get the right organization in place, give your employees clear responsibilities, hold them accountable, and make sure that both you and they dive in and learn the details. If fiefdoms or isolationists are discovered along the way, deal with them.

### PART IX

# TRAP #9
# CONFUSION: UNWITTINGLY PROVIDING SCHIZOPHRENIC COMMUNICATIONS

**Many leaders** of successful organizations fall into the trap of schizophrenic communications. They will describe a direction one day, then change their position the next day; or they will say one thing, but their actions don't support it. This is because they really haven't given the situation adequate thought. Why should they? They are successful. The typical behavior is no acknowledgment of any serious problems or major opportunities but a lot of self-congratulations and pointing out the highlights of their own work.

When problems start to emerge, the leaders of previously successful organizations are often slow to engage in dialogue about the key issues. They give random, offhand reactions when there is a need to address problems directly. A leader's failure to acknowledge any difficulties and lack of clarity of direction is immediately clear to the troops, and debates begin at the lower levels about the issues and what should be done. Also, internal silos and fiefdoms thrive in such an environment because the confusion takes the focus off the fact that these groups are doing whatever they want.

These kinds of communication issues happen at all levels of the organization. The problem can be a first-level group manager who constantly confuses his six direct reports about the direction of their efforts. The reason is that he has not internalized the need to change anything. It can be a division vice president who doesn't have a clear direction for the people in his organization, even though the problems are mounting, a competitor is thriving, or an opportunity is being mismanaged.

So the question is: what should a manager do to avoid these kinds of problems? I have two approaches to discuss in this part that will be valuable guidelines for steering clear of the schizophrenic communications trap.

# 27

## WHERE ARE WE GOING AND HOW ARE WE DOING?

People know when things aren't right in an organization. In the absence of a leader who is clearly communicating where the organization is going and how they are doing, people get very protective of their turf and their practices, and anarchy takes hold. First, let's discuss the critical issue of "where are we going?" Here are three things that the leader should do to make sure that there is a sound plan for progress and that the troops are fully aware of that plan.

1. **No matter whether you are a first-level manager or a CEO, find out what is going on and why.** Too many people, when they get into a managerial role, think that their job is to manage people. Their job is actually to be the thought leader of the group and to not only be responsible for their people but also lead their group in constantly improving its contribution to the overall greater good of the organization. By

thought leader I mean the person who confronts the tough issues and leads the dialogue and debate about what to do.

2. **Develop a plan to tackle the problems and opportunities.** Action is very important. It's also wise to get moving based on 80 percent of the information and make course corrections as you progress and learn more. Without a plan or strategy to attack the future, the organization will waste a tremendous amount of time debating what it should do. This causes morale problems and productivity problems. Most importantly, it solidifies the legacy practices even further because people fear that change is coming.

3. **Tell everyone frequently and directly, not by trickle-down communications, what the crisis is and what the plan to attack the problem is.** Frequent communication to all of the troops at the same time is vitally important. Assuming that your story can trickle down level by level is unrealistic. Managers at each level will put their own twist on it to help protect their current world. They will attempt to soften any bad news associated with the message and to downplay any change that the message tries to put in place in their part of the organization.

There is a great example from the early 1990s of this need to clearly communicate the crisis and the strategy. Here are the details.

# IBM

As we saw in Chapters 4 and 5, global giant IBM was in a critical state by late 1992. It was clearly on its way to complete financial disaster. The CEO had devised a plan to break up the company into multiple components and spin them off as separate businesses. The plan was debated extensively, but nothing ever happened. At this point, the board stepped in and, after an extensive search, named Lou Gerstner as the new CEO.

I described in Chapter 5 how Gerstner quickly went to work to develop a new business model. He visited all the parts of IBM to find out what was going on and why. He then developed the plan. Here I will discuss the masterful job he did in clearing up all the schizophrenic communications and getting a laserlike focus on the new strategy.

## IBM: Communicating the Crisis

Having collected extensive information on the basic problems at IBM and, as we saw in Chapter 5, developing the new strategy of solving the customers' information technology–related business problems, Gerstner launched a major employee communications effort to describe what the problems were and where IBM would be going. As Gerstner mentions in his book, "It is the job of the CEO to define and communicate that crisis, its magnitude, its severity, and its impact. Just as important, the CEO must be able to communicate how to end the crisis—the new strategy, the new company model, the new culture."[1]

It was at this point that Lou Gerstner discovered the power of e-mail for the first time in his life. As he put it, "I also discovered the power of IBM's internal messaging system, so I began to send employees 'Dear Colleague' letters. They were a very important part of my management system at IBM." Six days after he came on board, Gerstner sent a message to all employees, showing respect for them, but also making it clear that his job was to help the company become successful again and that he was confident that if they worked together, they could do that. It was a real confidence builder for the company, and the feedback that Gerstner received directly from hundreds of IBM employees encouraging him was very satisfying to him.

## IBM: Communicating the Strategy

After collecting information for the first few months, Gerstner sent an e-mail to all employees indicating that the company's major focus would be on solving customers' information technology problems and that an IBM services organization would be put in place to help customers use information technology properly to move their business ahead. He emphasized that IBM products were very important and that he was expecting continuing innovation on the product front, but that the core thrust had to be making all that worthwhile by truly satisfying customers and solving their information technology problems. Gerstner sent e-mails on this subject over and over again, and he includes a 50-page appendix in the back of his book that is filled with the e-mails that he used to make sure that at every point, the organization knew what he was thinking and what he was trying to achieve at IBM.[2]

> *When you step back, what Gerstner did should be done by every manager, no matter what their level. Gerstner went out and learned what was really going on.*

When you step back, what Gerstner did should be done by every manager, no matter what the level. Basically, Gerstner went out and learned what was really going on. He talked to a lot of people about what should be done, with particular emphasis on understanding the customer. He then outlined a game plan and checked it with a variety of people internally and with customers. Then he clearly communicated to everyone what the new direction was and why it made sense.

Now let's talk about the need to regularly communicate "how we are doing." When you are trying to drive change or implement a strategy, the participants need to be kept up to date on what's going well and what isn't. The reason is simple: people really don't enjoy tackling change. If a status report is sent once or twice, but then the troops hear nothing for a while, their conclusion will be that things are fine and it's business as usual. Here are a couple of pointers that I want to emphasize in this particular area:

1. **Have a regular vehicle for describing how it's going.** Seek out some kind of continuous communication device that you will utilize on a regular basis. Use it to constantly reinforce the change that you are working to institute and to report on results to date. Sometimes this is a monthly all-hands meeting; sometimes it's a weekly newsletter; sometimes it's frequent e-mails that lay out the key measures that demonstrate how close you are getting to achieving the objective. Having a regular vehicle gives the troops the impression that there is a scorecard that you are watching closely and that they can expect to constantly be told how things are going.

2. **When you make course corrections in the plan you are pursuing, clearly explain the change and the reason for the change.** At the time of the modification, some additional communication will definitely be needed to make sure that people understand that it's not business as usual, but the plan has changed a bit. What's vitally important at these junctures is to make sure that the troops understand why the change is being made and what you expect the ramifications of that change to be.

Here is a great example of a leader clearly communicating the plan and regularly reporting on results while also collecting key information from employees at all levels and from the marketplace, and adjusting the plan accordingly. This kind of continual two-way communication is very effective.

# WAL-MART

Back in the early days of Wal-Mart, Sam Walton personally designed a process that was used every week to continually collect information on Wal-Mart and competitive stores. It was done to find out what was and was not working, as a basis for modifying plans accordingly. After all, Sam would point out, the customers and the employees in the stores know best what it will take to keep Wal-Mart on top. The whole communications process was focused on tackling missed opportunities promptly and getting them fixed within days. The repetition of this process week after week sent a clear signal that store execution was absolutely king at Wal-Mart.

## Wal-Mart: The Process

Let's take a look at that weekly cycle. Back in 1992, *Fortune* published an article in which one of its writers, who had spent a week with a Wal-Mart regional vice president, discussed that communication cycle in detail.[3] It begins on Monday morning, when each of the regional vice presidents climbs into one of the Wal-Mart airplanes to fly to his or her region. From the moment they land until the end of the day on Wednesday, the vice presidents are moving around their region, visiting as many Wal-Mart stores and competitive stores as possible. They are continually telling the Wal-Mart associates, which is the term that Wal-Mart uses for its employees, that they are the ones who are important and that they are the ones who really make it happen. That message came straight from Sam Walton, who had repeated it literally thousands of times during his career at Wal-Mart, and it is continually reinforced by his regional vice presidents every week as they go out into the field. The intent is to make sure that these employees understand that their management really does want to hear the bad news and wants to hear where significant opportunities exist.

In some cases the vice presidents are visiting a new store to do the official ribbon cutting, and in other cases they are checking on new store managers to see how well they are doing in their first few weeks in their new role. Most importantly, they are walking the aisles with the associates, who describe what would enable their particular department to do better than it's currently doing. They take copious notes, and particular emphasis is placed on items that are out of stock, which often generate an immediate phone call to the distribution center and to the buyers at headquarters in Bentonville, Arkansas. They also learn of the hot items and can immediately

> *Key issues for Wal-Mart include ensuring the delivery of increased quantities of a new Garth Brooks T-shirt, given that Garth Brooks will be doing a tour in a particular regional vice president's area.*

call the distribution center and the appropriate Wal-Mart buyer to make sure that adequate amounts of these items are in stock, since they are moving much faster than was first estimated.

During a three-day period, each regional vice president will typically visit 10 to 12 Wal-Mart stores and two or three competitive stores. As noted in *Fortune,* these regional vice presidents represent a "traveling core of inspectors, scouts, trend spotters and market researchers."[4] Also, they provide great inspiration to the troops on the ground by continually reminding them of their importance and making sure that all associates know that management really does want to hear about any problems.

It's also important to note that those individuals at store level who are running various departments have all the financial information they need to run their department like a small business. For example, if you are in charge of the toy department in a particular store, you have at your fingertips all the data concerning what your sales are, what your profit margins are, what your inventory is, and what your goals are for that particular week.[5] The fabulous information system that provides all this detailed information to the departments within each store is a great enabling device in communicating clearly the results that are being achieved.

## Wal-Mart: Pulling Together the Learning

Going back to our visit, on Thursday, the various regional vice presidents head back to Bentonville, and as soon as they arrive, they go to their sparsely outfitted cubicles to begin collecting their thoughts about issues that they want to bring up in the next two days in an important series of meetings with the top management of the company. Key issues are such things as ensuring the delivery of increased quantities of a new Garth Brooks T-shirt, given that Garth Brooks will be doing a tour in a particular regional vice president's area. A vice president may also be pushing hard on a pricing issue. For example, why is Wal-Mart in South Sacramento offering a 75-foot garden hose for $12.99 when Target's price in a nearby store is $11.99?

> *It is clear to every employee that his job is to spot missed opportunities quickly and then use the company's very responsive system to get them addressed.*

On Friday morning, each regional vice president is armed with loads of information for the 7:00 a.m. operations meeting. The morning is filled with sales and merchandising reports from each of the regions and, most importantly, a review of problems and of revenue opportunities that are being inadequately addressed. The afternoon sessions are focused on particular products. This is where a regional vice president can take advantage of the opportunity to drive home his point about the Garth Brooks T-shirts or garden hose pricing. The buyer in charge of clothing will be specifically told to order thousands more of these T-shirts by the end of the day and be given a target of a few days to get them into stores.

The meetings have a somewhat random nature. In the afternoon, they will bounce from vitamins to fertilizers to marketing flyers, all with the intent of understanding what is selling or working and what isn't and how the company is doing at stocking the stores for maximum revenue. In mid-afternoon, the session ends, and each regional vice president goes back and dictates a memo that is sent via voice mail to all of the district managers and store managers in the region telling them about the actions that were taken and what to expect in the next few days.[6] Notice that what has happened is instantly communicated to the field. Consequently, those associates who have made a point about the need for improvement typically get that issue addressed within two or three days of the regional vice president's visit. That really makes them feel a part of the system, and, most importantly, it prevents legacy practices from getting entrenched.

## Wal-Mart: The Ultimate Communication Tool

On Saturday, the top management of Wal-Mart, all the regional vice presidents, the buyers, and key marketing personnel of the company all get together for the famous Wal-Mart "Saturday Morning Meeting." The entire focus of this session is on the core mission of excellent success at store level. They also go through detailed revenue and profit reviews of how they've been doing during the last week and what is going well and what needs to be fixed promptly. This meeting leverages the learning of the prior day, when the problems were reviewed in detail based on the absolutely up-to-date information on what is going on in the field. It often has an inspirational speaker or a customer who imparts some kind of wisdom to the group.

Right after the Saturday Morning Meeting, the key messages are broadcast on TV from Bentonville to all stores over the company's six-channel satellite system, which also collects store data for the master computer, executes credit card approval within five seconds, and handles all logistics data for the company's complex distribution system.[7] With the satellite, Wal-Mart managers can talk to every store at the same time as many times a day as they want to, and it has dramatically reduced the response time on key issues. Wal-Mart trains people by using the satellite system, and, most importantly, it shares merchandising information about what seems to be working and what isn't working immediately upon learning it from some regional vice president, district manager, or store manager.

When you step back, what is really happening? The entire system is geared to continually telling Wal-Mart employees where they are going and how they are doing. It continually reinforces the idea that the expectation is that employees will find any problems quickly and make significant changes to improve their business. It is clear to every employee that his job is to spot missed opportunities quickly and then use the company's very responsive system to get them addressed. This system is designed to prohibit the growth of any kind of legacy practice that causes stagnation, and to keep Wal-Mart constantly on top. It's clear that this communication system is one of the reasons for Wal-Mart's superior performance over recent decades, and it's absolutely amazing how it has enabled the company to continue to operate like a small organization although it has become one of the largest companies in the world. This tool makes it very hard for a legacy practice to develop and is tailor-made to drive continual improvement.

IBM and Wal-Mart provide two very positive examples of organizations that have communicated very well with their employees. Making it clear where the organization is going, creating a system to regularly report how it's going, and modifying your direction if needed go a long way in maintaining success.

# 28

# MAKE EXPECTATIONS CRYSTAL CLEAR

When driving change, the leader needs to describe specifically what the goal is and how progress will be judged. Here are three guidelines to keep in mind that will help in the communication of clear expectations.

**1. Simplicity.** You need to tell the troops what you are asking for and why you are asking for it. Your message had better be succinct, understandable, and sensible.

**2. Standardized measures.** It's ideal if you can develop an exhibit or two showing the data or charts that you are using to determine whether you've achieved the goal or not. If you do not think through the reporting tool before efforts are launched, what happens is a lot of creativity on the part of the organization to convince you that progress is being made. Positive anecdotes become the way the project gets managed when there is an absence of crisp measures and standardized tracking tools.

> **3. Continual inspection.** People need to know that management really cares and that it is using specific measures to determine whether success is being achieved. There is nothing that reinforces this better than randomly diving down into the organization and talking to people who are carrying out the change. It's important that you not take the responsibility away from them; in fact, you want to reinforce their responsibility. What you're doing is simply making sure that things are happening along the lines of your expectations. Word gets out quickly among employees that the boss is serious about this effort and that he's randomly swooping down to see how it's going.

We have a great example of a top-notch company falling into some bad legacy practices that really put it in a bad business situation and then having a leader come in and make it absolutely clear what was to be achieved. Let's take an in-depth look.

## GILLETTE

If you go back to 1996, it would be hard to find a company that was in a stronger position than Gillette. It was viewed as one of America's best corporate innovators. Over the prior five years, 40 percent of its revenue had come from new products. During the period from 1990 to 1996, earnings grew at an annual rate of 17 percent, and return on equity grew to almost 33 percent. The company's profit margin was 12 percent, which was the second best in the consumer products industry; only Coca-Cola was better, at 17 percent.[1]

In the period from 1986 to 1995, Gillette ranked tenth among all companies with respect to shareholder return. This put it ahead of such stellar companies as Merck and Disney.[2] During that 10-year period, it increased shareholder value by $13.8 billion. There is a famous quote by Warren Buffett, who owned 10.8 percent of the stock at the time. He said, "I go to bed happy at night knowing that hair is growing on the faces of billions of males and on women's legs around the world while I sleep. It's more fun than counting sheep."

Besides being in the razor and blades business, the company was also marketing Braun electrical appliances; Gillette toiletries and cosmetics, such as Right Guard and Soft & Dri antiperspirants; stationery products such as Parker, PaperMate, and Waterman pens; and Oral-B toothbrushes. All of these consumer products were among the worldwide leaders in their markets, and they were profitable and fast growing, with good technology as the basis for their success.

It was very clear back in 1996 that the continued future success of Gillette depended on continued innovation.[3] This was traditionally Gillette's core strength, and the company really prided itself on bringing significant improvements in its products to the marketplace. The Gillette management at the time encouraged people to invent products that clearly cannibalized the existing successful products. A very important value within the company at that time was the overt practice of not penalizing individuals whose innovations were rejected by the marketplace. This value was very important in unleashing the creativity needed to keep Gillette moving ahead.

Gillette's tremendous success in the early to mid-1990s was primarily driven by its Sensor razor and blades. This product was introduced in 1990, and an improvement was launched in 1993. By 1996, Gillette had 68 percent of the U.S. market in wet shaving, 73 percent in Europe, and 91 percent in Latin America. The Sensor and its improved version, the Sensor Excel, generated very high profit margins and were absolutely the key ingredient in Gillette's success during this period.

## Gillette: Self-Inflicted Problems Emerge

While Gillette was clearly one of the top performers in the consumer products business in 1996, during the next three years the business softened significantly. In the first nine months of 1999, net income was down 7 percent, and sales were flat. The company's stock price had dropped to $35 per share, which was a 45 percent decrease from nine months earlier. Operational problems were clearly becoming an issue at Gillette. Its inventories were bulging as salespeople forced product into retail stores in an attempt to bring the financial numbers to a more satisfying level. For perspective on the inventory situation, at the end of June 1999, Gillette had $1.3 billion of finished goods inventories, which was 43 percent higher than the inventory levels in 1996, even though Gillette's revenues were about the same in 1999 as they were in 1996. While its business in razor blades, batteries, and toothbrushes was acceptable, the rest of the business was really hurting.[4]

> *Gillette had simply overhired and overbuilt during the early to mid-1990s. It's as if all the positive press back in 1996 had caused the company to step back and assume that it would always be successful in the future.*

Just before the end of the July–September quarter of 1999, Gillette announced that it would once again miss its quarterly sales targets.[5] This was the fourth miss in the past five quarters. The next day, the stock price dropped yet another 9 percent.

In trying to analyze why this stellar company was now having major problems, the Asian crisis of 1999 was often pointed to. While this did create some softness on a global basis in industries such as consumer products, as an analyst for Bear Stearns pointed out at the time, "There are companies with greater exposure to international markets that have been making their estimates, like Colgate." Jeremy Kahn of *Fortune* magazine described the situation in a late 1999 article by saying, "The real damage Asia inflicted on Gillette was to expose the company's underlying weaknesses; a culture plagued by inertia, inefficiency, nostalgia; mismanaged inventories and receivables; a super complicated corporate structure cobbled together over years of acquisitions; and most important, three-decade-old divisions that have consistently—and badly—underperformed."[6]

Assuming that it would always be successful, Gillette had simply overhired and overbuilt during the early to mid-1990s. It's as if all

> *Then he asked the division chiefs to raise their hand if they thought costs were too high in their organizations. Nobody raised their hand. It was a clear sign that all of the divisions were lying in the weeds, protecting their legacy practices and blaming others for the core problem.*

the positive press back in 1996 had caused the company to step back and assume that it would always be successful in the future.

In the late 1990s, Gillette launched an effort to overhaul its structure.[7] In 1999, the company announced a reorganization designed to save $535 million by shutting down 14 factories and 12 distribution centers around the world, consolidating 30 offices, and cutting 4,700 jobs, which was 11 percent of Gillette's workforce. Part of this reorganization reconfigured the sales organization to provide simpler interactions with its customers. In the past, for a specific customer, each Gillette division had a salesperson assigned. None of them knew anything about the other divisions' business, and so the customers had to deal with many different Gillette perspectives.

By the end of the year 2000, Gillette had reached even further lows. The stock price was down at the $28-per-share level, and there was investor unrest and takeover talk. There was tremendous pressure on the board of directors to do something, and analysts complained that the board "has been sleepy." Gillette badly needed to revitalize its various businesses.[8]

Wall Street experts were blaming a lot of the problems on the fact that most Gillette executives had come up through the ranks at Gillette. Most of them had backgrounds in the razor-shaving business, but they were trying to manage industries that were quite different, such as hair care, deodorants, batteries, and pens. In the shaving market, where the company had been enormously successful for decades, executives were thoroughly trained about the importance of engineering expertise to develop truly superior products for which a premium price could be charged.

When executives trained in the shaving business were transferred to other parts of Gillette to manage other areas, the formula used in the shaving business really didn't apply, but they didn't realize that. They were trying to apply legacy practices of "big engineering steps forward" in categories that primarily require great marketing, such as hair care and stationery products. As Don Stewart of Cannondale Associates put it in late 2000, "They need a large infusion of fresh blood." Gillette was really trapped in its legacy practices.[9]

## Gillette: The New CEO Tells It Like It Is

In January 2001, Jim Kilts, the former head of Nabisco, was brought in as the new CEO of Gillette.[10] He had a tough job in front of him. As Jeremy Kahn of *Fortune* magazine had put it, the new CEO would have to tackle "its clunky sales management structure, its insularity, and its general lameness." The stock price in early 2001 was at a five-year low, and Gillette was in real trouble.

Two weeks after Jim Kilts took over as CEO, he sent out his letter to the shareholders as part of the year's annual report. He pointed out that the company's results "have come short of original consensus estimates for the past fourteen quarters," and "while Wall Street expects volatility in the high tech sector, they do not treat it kindly in consumer products. In fact, they penalize it severely." At last, there was some frank communication from the head of Gillette.

Kilts went on to explain that the organization needed to focus on each and every one of its brands and to make sure that the right thing was being done to build total brand value in each case. His communications were clear and concise. He was speaking to the entire shareholder community, as well as all the employees.[11]

Kilts also publicly stated that Gillette had been losing market share in products accounting for more than two-thirds of its sales, including batteries, toothbrushes, and disposable razors. He noted that profit margins had been dropping and that the stock market price was an embarrassment. He also openly admitted that employee

> *Kilts produced a pamphlet called "Escaping the Circle of Doom" and made sure his division heads understood that they were going to make their estimates and that Gillette absolutely needed to recover its credibility.*

morale was at a low point and that employee turnover was unacceptable.

During this period, Kilts was also getting a lot of advice from the press. Rosabeth Moss Kanter of the Harvard Business School suggested that Kilts would have to take a sharp knife to "a sloppy, undisciplined organization that has let bureaucracy get out of control."[12] Wendy Nicholson, an analyst with Smith Barney, pointed out that neither sales nor earnings had grown in five years and that "management has let the company go haywire."[13]

It didn't take Jim Kilts long to begin talking candidly about the approach he would use to fix Gillette. Kilts had been selected because he had turned around tough situations before and had a lot of battle scars from the experiences. As Katrina Brooker of *Fortune* pointed out in late 2002, "Rather than rally the troops with big speeches on how Gillette can change the world, Kilts presented slides on how their market shares, gross margins, SG&A (selling, general and administrative) expenses and operating profits compared with those of competitors. It's not glamorous; it's not sexy; it's a buttoned up, old school approach to business. And it works."[14]

Brooker also pointed out that in the first few months of Kilts's effort at Gillette, he held a meeting with all of Gillette's key managers. At that meeting, he asked all of the division chiefs how many thought the company's costs were too high. All indicated that they were. Then he asked the division chiefs to raise their hand if they thought costs were too high in their organizations. Nobody raised their hand. It was a clear sign that all of the divisions were lying in the weeds, protecting their legacy practices and blaming others for the core problem.

Kilts openly described the problem as a "circle of doom."[15] He would elaborate that businesses got themselves into trouble by setting unrealistic targets and then making bad decisions in their attempt to reach those unrealistic targets. This made the situation even worse.

Kilts also talked openly about Gillette's tendency to stuff product into its customers' warehouses at the end of the quarter. He personally visited one of the company's big retail customers and learned that the customer would constantly wait to the end of the quarter "because I know you will always cut a deal" to attempt to make Gillette's quarterly numbers.

## Gillette: Clear Expectations and Communications

All of this valuable learning during his first few months of employment at Gillette enabled Jim Kilts to make it clear to all employees that things were going to change dramatically. People were going to be held accountable for making goals, with serious implications if they didn't. Gillette needed a leaner and more agile internal structure, and it needed to get back its innovation skills in order to put its products in an exciting position versus their competitors. Everyone knew that holding the individual divisions responsible for achieving goals was a clear culture change that needed to be made.

To make sure that he was being clear and communicating properly, at the beginning of each quarter, Kilts's direct reports were required to give him a list of written objectives that they expected to achieve.[16] Each week they had to submit a brief document outlining the progress that they had made toward achieving those objectives, and at the end of the quarter Kilts gave them a grade from 1 to 100. He also communicated clearly that their pay and promotions were dependent on their grades. He made it clear that anything consistently below 80 would be unacceptable. He produced a pamphlet called "Escaping the Circle of Doom" and made sure that his division heads understood that they were going to make their estimates and that Gillette absolutely needed to recover its credibility.

Kilts also tackled the operational aspects of the company.[17] Over the years, Gillette had evolved to the position of being the fastest in its industry at paying its bills and the slowest at collecting debts. This resulted in working capital as a percentage of sales being at the lofty level of 36 percent by the end of the 1990s. This statistic is basically an indicator of how well the company is managing its assets and liabilities. Compared to Gillette's 36 percent, P&G was at around 1 percent and Colgate about 3 percent. Things were equally chaotic with regard to financial reporting. No one in the company really knew whether Gillette was having a good quarter or a bad quarter until the end of the quarter. Also, the number of different product extensions that the company had generated and not managed properly had absolutely exploded. It had 24,000 SKUs, each representing a different variation of one of its products.

Kilts tackled these financial reporting problems with gusto, and within six months, both he and his senior management team got a daily report that recorded how many razors, batteries, and toothbrushes Gillette had sold the day before. Also, Kilts required every division head to benchmark her costs against the top industry competitor and to get her division into a leadership position with respect to the industry. This was a very embarrassing exercise, as most of Gillette's divisions had a cost structure that was 30 to 40 percent higher than their competitors'.

Jim Kilts was a real shock to the old-timers at Gillette. As Katrina Brooker stated in her 2002 *Fortune* article, "The company has long had a gentle, paternalistic culture, and until Kilts arrived all of its top managers had been with the company for decades. Kilts grading system—which he implemented throughout the company—made some feel they were being treated like naughty school children."[18] On the other hand, most people recognized that the company needed the kind of clarity and accountability that Kilts was demanding.

### Gillette: At Last, Some Results

By the end of 2002, things were beginning to pay off for Kilts.[19] Gillette's revenue had grown an average of 5 percent each quarter for the prior three quarters. Its profits were up 20 percent, and working capital as a percentage of sales had dropped to 14 percent.

While that was still above the industry norm, it was a clear signal that the company was beginning to handle its balance sheet properly. Its free cash flow for the past 12 months had increased to $1.3 billion, compared with $815 million a year earlier. Also, since Kilts arrived, Gillette had paid down $1.8 billion in debt.

*It is very simple. Always give the employees a description of the current status of things, the desired outcome, and clear expectations of what should take place in the future.*

Things continued to go well for Kilts and Gillette for the next three years, and in February 2005, it was announced that Procter & Gamble and Gillette had made a deal and that P&G would acquire Gillette for $55 a share. Kilts had served the shareholders well during his period as CEO, and he did it with absolutely clear communication of what was expected of the various organizations within the company, measuring that carefully, and making changes if goals were not met. This really shook up the company from its comfortable legacy world and put Gillette back on track, which eventually led to a good reward for the shareholders with the P&G acquisition.

Employees get very confused and quite nervous when the leader is schizophrenic about what the group is trying to achieve. It touches off debates and defensive attitudes as the confusing messages accumulate. It sounds very simple to always have in front of the employees a description of the desired outcome, the current status of things, and clear expectations of what should take place in the immediate and longer-term future. The stories in this part from IBM, Wal-Mart, and Gillette are valuable reminders that doing these things well is harder than you think, but it has big payoffs in achieving and sustaining success.

### PART X

# THE KEY
# TO CONTINUAL
# SUCCESS:
# A QUESTIONING
# ATTITUDE

**A key lesson** that you should take away from this book is that no matter what the history of the organization is, once any degree of success has been achieved, the three human tendencies that we talked about in Chapter 2, "Why Does This Happen?" take hold. Success breeds a culture of lack of urgency, satisfaction, excessive pride, a protective attitude toward the way things have been done in the past. Success also encourages an entitlement mentality that assumes that since you've done well in the past, that will always be the case.

The humbling part of business is that just as soon as you have achieved some degree of success, the word gets out. Your competitors are observing you, and they are hungry and anxious. They are plotting aggressively to move ahead of where you are. That means that you are actually in a foot race. But these human tendencies cause you to ignore all that and sit back and enjoy the comfort of finally arriving.

If you take anything away from this book, I hope it is the following two guidelines, which you should practice at all times, but that are exceptionally important once you reach the point of success or stability:

1. **When you are a winner, be as aggressive as you were when you were lagging behind.** Remember the high sense of urgency when the competition was ahead of you and you were hustling with the bright idea that you believed could put you out in front. In any organization, that same degree of urgency needs to exist at all times.

2. **Develop a culture that constantly questions all practices at all times.** You need to become a student of your areas of responsibility and the areas around you, and you should constantly be probing for new and better ways to do things, while continuing to execute your current responsibility with excellence.

We have one final chapter that clearly exhibits the ups and downs that an organization can go through. This is a good way to get sharply focused on the final point: you are never finished avoiding those nine nasty traps.

# 29

# RESTING ON YOUR LAURELS IS NEVER AN OPTION!

The information technology business is full of valuable business lessons, primarily because the very high innovation rate in the technology industry drives continual change. This requires people in this business to never get overly confident and never believe that they have everything figured out. In this fast-paced industry, it is almost guaranteed that new technology and new ideas will emerge to challenge any success that you may be enjoying. With surprising speed, a competitor will grab an idea and run with it, all in the split second that you are taking to pat yourself on the back.

Because things happen so fast, some information technology companies are very useful case studies of doing things right. We can also learn from other companies that do things wrong, because you see the ramifications of their behavior so quickly in the marketplace.

There is one company whose ups and downs over the years provides a great example of an organization that has lost momentum because of all the success-induced traps we have been discussing, regained its luster, then lost it again and, incredibly, regained momentum once again. Let's take a closer look.

# APPLE

In the early 1980s, Apple was truly on top of the new and exciting personal computer industry. Its unique Apple II provided a completely new set of capabilities for individuals and became wildly popular. Steve Jobs, Apple's cofounder, was heaped with lavish praise.

By 1983, Apple's business was softening, and Jobs took the very unusual step of hiring someone from outside the computer industry to join Apple to help. He chose John Sculley, former president of Pepsi-Cola USA, the beverage subsidiary of PepsiCo. Sculley got off to a slow start, and it was clear that Jobs and Sculley were having difficulty figuring out who should do what. This was a classic case of two people trying to do one job.

## Apple: Major Problems

By 1985, things were in very rough shape. In May of that year, Apple reorganized, reduced its workforce by 20 percent, and experienced its first-ever quarterly loss; its stock hit a three-year low of $14 per share.[1] While there were marketplace forces that were causing some of its problems, such as a downturn in the personal computer business, Jobs had been spending most of his time developing and launching the Macintosh computer. Meanwhile, no one was minding the store with regard to the company's most important product at the time, which was the Apple II. Additionally, you just didn't sense the urgency around the Macintosh effort that had been observed during the incredible launch and success of the Apple II.

Given all the bad news in mid-1985, the board of directors decided that Sculley should take over as president and chief executive officer. As a result, all the operating authority was taken out of the hands of Steve Jobs. Sculley reorganized things and put Jobs in charge of the Macintosh division as its general manager.

As you would imagine, this was a particularly difficult situation for everyone. Jobs was the chairman and owned over 11 percent of the company but he wasn't running things. He was the leader of the Macintosh group, and he was very protective about that division's work. A member of the Mac staff at that time said, "He was so protective of us that whenever we complained about someone outside the division, it was like unleashing a Doberman."[2] He ignored the fact that the Apple II was carrying the company.

> *The problem was that the Macintosh was built with the expectation that the world would come to it. That's called an entitlement mentality.*

As the Macintosh business got worse and worse, Sculley and Jobs started to really get into it with each other. It was an impossible situation, and the board took way too long to resolve it. Eventually, the board asked Jobs to give up his position as Macintosh general manager and to simply remain as chairman of the company.

The problem was that the Macintosh was built with the expectation that the world would come to it. That's called an entitlement mentality. For example, each Mac was loaded with special proprietary software that made it extremely difficult for software developers to write new software for the Mac.[3] Also, unlike the IBM PC and the Apple II, the Macintosh had no slots that outside manufacturers could use for printed circuit boards that would slide into the computer to expand its memory, add mathematical processors, or otherwise add to its usefulness. Jobs didn't seem to really be paying attention to what the customer wanted and what would be needed to make this thing sell. By fall 1985, Jobs had left Apple.

### Apple: The Revival

This gave John Sculley an open field, and he dived into the challenge with gusto.[4] He quickly brought a real sense of urgency as he closed plants, slashed costs, and laid off one-fifth of Apple's six thousand employees. He brought in new talent to fix the Macintosh problem with fairly obvious solutions. Apple needed to work extensively

> *"Allowing Apple to guard its technical breakthroughs jealously rather than licensing other computer makers to build Macintosh clones trapped Apple in a niche." It was a classic case of being proud and protective.*

with software partners who would develop tools that would run on the Macintosh. Additionally, expansion ports were designed that allowed peripheral hardware to be plugged into the Mac to perform such specialized tasks as networking and data communications.

One of the software companies that Apple was working with at the time was Aldus, which developed software that enabled someone to use the Macintosh and a laser printer to produce fantastic-looking brochures, newsletters, and a variety of other marketing materials, which organizations had previously had to ship out to an independent printer.[5] The Macintosh and Aldus became quite the rage in the area of desktop publishing. The incredible ease of use of the Macintosh had always been there, but now there was some exciting software and a more flexible piece of hardware that users could really incorporate into their work very productively.

So what had happened? Apple had just been too proud of its incredible success with the Apple II. At the outset, the company believed that the Macintosh's unique characteristics automatically entitled it to instant success. It didn't do all the hard work of figuring out just how it would fit into the consumer's work flow and what kind of partnerships would be needed in order to really make it a success. The lack of urgency concerning those issues was what caused the core problems that led to the exit of Jobs and the emergence of Sculley.

The late 1980s were truly a glory period for Apple because it had focused leadership and an urgency to make the Macintosh friendly to software developers and useful to customers. The Macintosh became a world-class tool, particularly in the area of desktop publishing.

## Apple: The Next Tailspin

By 1990, Apple had hired a ton of people, and its technology advantage had eroded.[6] You could see the signs of entitlement and pride taking hold. The company launched a series of long-term projects, including the Newton personal digital assistant. Meanwhile, it passed up one of the biggest opportunities a technology company had ever had: it did not license the right to make Macintosh clones, something that Sculley later admitted he deeply regrets. Macintosh clones would be Mac-like computers manufactured by other companies that would run the Macintosh operating system and applications. As Alan Deutschman of *Fortune* put it, "Allowing Apple to guard its technical breakthroughs jealously rather than licensing other computer makers to build Macintosh clones trapped Apple in a niche."[7] It was a classic case of being proud and protective.

By 1993, Apple was missing its profit forecasts, and its share price was sinking. The word on the street was that Sculley was positioning himself to become U.S. secretary of commerce. He had no urgency about the business and would make weird statements publicly that must have confused the employees, such as "I can see the day when Apple won't be in the personal computer business."[8] Sculley abruptly resigned as CEO in June 1993 while remaining with the company as chairman. Mike Spindler was put in his place.

Looking at this period in the early 1990s, the core reason for Apple's problems was that its pace of innovation simply couldn't keep up with what was going on in the PC clone business, where Microsoft's software was providing a rich platform for application developers to exploit. Microsoft was bending over backward to work with software developers and made sure changes were made to its operating system to accommodate developer needs. Put another way, Microsoft was hungry and Apple was proud.

The period between 1993 and 1997 was really rugged for Apple. It had two new CEOs during this period, and by the fourth quarter of 1996, sales were dropping at a 30 percent rate and the company turned in a loss of $120 million.[9] The core problem was that no new innovations were coming out the door. Apple badly needed to update its operating system, and it spent an enormous amount of time hiring different kinds of people to get insight into what direction to go in. Meanwhile, after Jobs left Apple, he had formed a software company called Next. Its operating system was quite novel, but it really never reached any level of success. When Gil Amelio was put into the Apple CEO job in February 1996, his clear challenge was to develop a new operating system, or Apple was going to lose all credibility and would probably go out of business.

Steve Jobs, whose heart had never really left Apple, saw the company's dilemma and approached Apple about using his Next operating system for the Macintosh. He was elegant in his argument to CEO Amelio, and subsequently to the board, that the Next operating system would be just what Apple needed. Meanwhile, Apple's revenue was still dropping 30 percent from the level a year earlier, and the crisis was very significant.[10]

Apple bought Jobs's argument and paid almost $400 million to acquire Next; the advisory services of Steve Jobs came with it.[11] While Apple acquired some new and progressive thinking in that operating system, little did it know that it had also acquired a highly motivated Steve Jobs, who wanted to get back into the Apple game. Within months, after some tumultuous organizational and board maneuverings, he took over as interim CEO in September 1997. He had his work cut out for him, given that Apple had lost $1 billion in the previous 12 months.[12]

### Apple: A Second Revival

Jobs moved with incredible speed and announced to the troops that "Apple's future is in the consumer market. There's no company doing a great job serving that market. Apple has the opportunity. What's that worth in the future? I don't know. It could be big."[13] The incredibly energized Steve Jobs made quick and decisive decisions to deal with Apple's core problems. Apple was supporting 15 product lines, and that was simply too many. Jobs moved quickly to kill Apple's printer business and the Newton.

Apple had become highly decentralized and inefficient, with 22 marketing groups scattered around the company.[14] Jobs reorganized the company, creating companywide departments for marketing, sales, manufacturing, and finance and eliminating many of the fragmented legacy practices and people. The distribution channel was a mess. Jobs made the decision to sell Macs only through resellers and through stores that were committed to Apple. Less-than-enthusiastic retail outlets were dumped. Bruce Chizen, who was running Adobe Systems' products and marketing, observed: "In the last few years it was impossible for any developer to work with Apple." Since the arrival of Jobs, "it's been a 180 degree turnaround."

> *During this period, I was COO at Microsoft, and I remember vividly our finance people returning from a meeting with Jobs and reporting how fired up and cooperative the guy was.*

During this period, I was COO at Microsoft, and I remember vividly our finance people returning from a meeting with Jobs and reporting how fired up and cooperative the guy was. Shortly after that session, Microsoft agreed to a deal with Jobs where we would launch a new version of the Microsoft Office suite for the Mac and supply Apple with much-needed cash of $150 million, and Apple agreed to several Microsoft requests. This helped Apple start to regain Wall Street's confidence.

In his first 10 months after being named interim CEO, Jobs had Apple develop and launch a new iMac.[15] This was an elegant-looking, small-size personal computer that was extremely user-friendly. He selected his trusted confidant Avie Tevanian, who was with him at Next, as Apple's top software engineer.[16] They quickly went to work on generating the future operating system for Apple, which would be called OS X.

The iMac did quite well because it directly addressed some key consumer needs.[17] The iMac's consumer software tools were a big hit. The iPhoto tool was viewed as the best photo management program at the time. The iMac also had great digital music capabilities through its iTunes software. It also had sensational digital video editing capability with a tool called iMovie. You could also create DVDs

> *In the early 1980s, Apple and Jobs were flying high. Then Apple tanked because of Jobs's proud and protective attitude toward the Macintosh.*

via a tool called iDVD. Apple was also working on the early stages of a music player that it called iPod. These products created quite a buzz for Apple, and, as we all know, the iPod emerged as an incredible success.

In March 2006, Apple sold its billionth song from its iTunes Store.[18] The iPod had a 73 percent market share of the 30 million MP3 players sold in the United States. On the other hand, experts worry a bit about the proprietary nature of the Apple music system, which is similar to the Macintosh's problems of being too proprietary. Songs purchased from iTunes are protected by Apple's Fair Play approach, causing them to be playable only on an iPod.

Stepping back, the difference between Steve Jobs's behavior during those last painful months in the mid-1980s and his incredible energy and innovation in the late 1990s and early 2000s is amazing. In the early 1980s, Apple and Jobs were flying high, and then they tanked because Sculley and Jobs did not rally around a focused plan and because of Jobs's proud and protective attitude toward the Macintosh. In the late 1980s, Sculley really got things back on track, but he then developed an entitlement mentality and began to pursue a broad array of distractions. Jobs then got Apple going again by reorganizing the legacy-ridden organization and launching some tremendously exciting products.[19]

Apple's volatile history is an extremely rich reminder of the need to constantly be vigilant in your efforts to improve.

In summary, no matter how many times you have been up or down, watch out for the wicked traps that success creates.

# NOTES

### The Issue: Success Is a Serious Business Vulnerability

1. Lee Smith, "Rubbermaid Goes Thump," *Fortune*, vol. 132, no. 7, Oct. 2, 1995, p. 90.
2. Ibid.
3. Matthew Schifrin, "The Big Squeeze," *Forbes*, vol. 157, no. 5, Mar. 11, 1996, p. 45.
4. "How Rubbermaid Managed to Fail," *Fortune*, vol. 138, no. 11, Nov. 23, 1998, p. 32.
5. Ibid.
6. Smith, "Rubbermaid Goes Thump."
7. "Thoughts," *Forbes*, vol. 175, no. 13, June 20, 2005.
8. Alex Taylor III, "Can the Germans Rescue Chrysler?""*Fortune*, vol. 143, no. 9, Apr. 30, 2001, p. 106.
9. "Thoughts."
10. Peter Drucker, *The Essential Drucker* (New York: Harper Business, 2001).

### Chapter 1

1. "Last Tango in Detroit?" *The Economist*, Apr. 8–14, 2006, p. 57.
2. Carol Loomis, "The Tragedy of General Motors," *Fortune*, vol. 153, no. 3, Feb. 20, 2006, p. 60.
3. Charles Burck, "Will Success Spoil General Motors?" *Fortune*, vol. 108, Aug. 22, 1983, p. 94.
4. Ibid.
5. Ibid.
6. Ibid.
7. "GM in Low Gear," *Fortune*, vol. 114, Sept. 29, 1986, p. 7.
8. Anne B. Fisher, "GM Is Tougher than You Think," *Fortune*, vol. 114, Nov. 10, 1986, p. 56.
9. Ibid.
10. Alex Taylor III, "The Tasks Facing General Motors," *Fortune*, vol. 119, no. 6, Mar. 13, 1989, p. 52.

11. Ibid.
12. Alex Taylor III, "Can GM Remodel Itself?" *Fortune*, vol. 125, no. 1, Jan. 13, 1992, p. 26.
13. Jonathan Fahey, "Idling," *Forbes*, vol. 176, no. 8, Oct. 17, 2005, p. 110.
14. David Welch, "The Good News about America's Auto Industry," *BusinessWeek*, no. 3971, Feb. 13, 2006, p. 32.
15. "GM Sold Lots of Cars, and Lost $1,227 Each," Reuters, Aug. 29, 2005.
16. Joann Muller, "Surviving Globalism," *Forbes*, vol. 177, no. 4, Feb. 27, 2006, p. 44.
17. Ibid.
18. Ibid.
19. Taylor, "Can GM Remodel Itself?"
20. Alex Taylor III, "GM: Time to Get in Gear," *Fortune*, vol. 135, no. 8, Apr. 28, 1997, p. 94.
21. "GM's Big Decision," *Fortune*, vol. 141, no. 4, Feb. 21, 2000, p. 100.
22. Ibid.
23. Bernard Simon, "GM Discounts Cause Confusion," *Financial Times*, Nov. 14, 2005.
24. Alex Taylor III, "GM Hits the Skids," *Fortune*, vol. 151, no. 7, Apr. 4, 2005, p. 71.
25. David Welch, "Running Out of Gas," *BusinessWeek*, no. 3926, Mar. 28, 2005, p. 28.
26. Ibid.
27. James Womack, "Why Toyota Won," *Wall Street Journal*, Feb. 14, 2006, p. 13.
28. David Welch, "The Other Club Battering GM," *BusinessWeek*, no. 3974, Mar. 6, 2006, p. 38.
29. David Welch, "Why GM's Plan Won't Work," *BusinessWeek*, no. 3932, May 9, 2005, p. 84.
30. Justin Fox, "A CEO Puts His Job on the Line," *Fortune*, vol. 151, no. 9, May 2, 2005, p. 17.

31. "GM Sold Lots of Cars, and Lost $1,227 Each."

## Chapter 2

1. Joseph White, "How U.S. Auto Industry Finds Itself Stalled by Its Own History," *Wall Street Journal*, Jan. 7, 2006.
2. David Welch, "Why GM's Plan Won't Work," *BusinessWeek*, no. 3932, May 9, 2005, p. 84.
3. Andrew S. Grove, *Only the Paranoid Survive* (New York: Doubleday, 1999).
4. Linda Grant, "Missed Moments," *Fortune*, vol. 136, no. 8, Oct. 27, 1997, p. 188.
5. Joseph Nocera, "Kodak: The CEO vs. the Gadfly," *Fortune*, vol. 149, no. 1, Jan. 12, 2004, p. 84.
6. Joann Muller, "The Impatient Mr. Ghosn," *Forbes*, vol. 177, no. 11, May 22, 2006, p. 104.
7. Ibid.
8. Julie Pitta, "Where Is DEC Going?" *Forbes*, vol. 147, no. 1, Jan. 7, 1991, p. 41.
9. Richard Rapaport, "Culture War: Route 128," *Forbes*, vol. 152, no. 6, Sept. 13, 1993, p. 54.

## Chapter 3

1. Chester Dawson, "Blazing the Toyota Way," *BusinessWeek*, no. 3884, May 24, 2004, p. 22.
2. Clay Chandler, "Full Speed Ahead," *Fortune*, vol. 141, no. 3, Feb. 7, 2005, p. 78.
3. Ibid.
4. Ibid.
5. Ibid.
6. Alex Taylor III, "Why Toyota Keeps Getting Better and Better and Better," *Fortune*, vol. 122, no. 13, Nov. 19, 1990, p. 66.
7. Ibid.
8. Ibid.
9. Stuart Brown, "Toyota's Global Body Shop," *Fortune*, vol. 149, no. 3, Feb. 9, 2004, p. 120.
10. Ibid.
11. Ibid.
12. Taylor, "Why Toyota Keeps Getting Better and Better."
13. Jathon Sapsford, "Toyota's Chief Bets on Hybrids, Squeezing Rivals," *Wall Street Journal*, July 13, 2005, p. B1.
14. Chester Dawson, "Proud Papa of the Prius," *BusinessWeek*, no. 3938, June 20, 2005, p. 20.
15. Ibid.

16. "Gentlemen, Start Your Engines," *Financial Times*, Jan. 21, 2006, p. 77.
17. Ian Rowley, "Toyota Revs into the New Year," *BusinessWeek Online*, Jan. 5, 2007.
18. Chandler, "Full Speed Ahead."
19. "The Driver Who's Passing GM," *BusinessWeek*, no. 3942, July 11, 2005, p 54.

## Chapter 4

1. Norm Alster, "IBM as a Holding Company," *Forbes*, vol. 148, no. 14, Dec. 23, 1991, p. 116.
2. Graham Button, "Early, and Then Some," *Forbes*, vol. 151, no. 1, Jan. 4, 1993, p. 12.
3. Carol Loomis, "The Hunt for Mr. X," *Fortune*, vol. 127, no. 4, Feb. 22, 1993, p. 68.

## Part I
## Chapter 5

1. Louis V. Gerstner, *Who Says Elephants Can't Dance?* (New York: HarperCollins, 2002).
2. Robert Slater, "Without Gerstner, This Story Goes Untold," *BusinessWeek*, no. 3646, Sept. 13, 1999, p. 17.
3. Gerstner, *Who Says Elephants Can't Dance?*
4. Daniel Lyons, "Dancing Lessons," *Forbes*, vol. 175, no. 5, Mar. 14, 2005, p. 100.
5. Steve Hamm and Spencer Ante, "Beyond Blue; Never Mind Computers and Tech Services," *BusinessWeek*, no. 3929, Apr. 18, 2005, p. 68.
6. Robert Hof, "PayPal Spreads Its Wings," *BusinessWeek*, no. 3934, May 23, 2005, p. 105.
7. "Meg and the Power of Many," *The Economist*, June 11, 2005, p. 65.
8. Hof, "PayPal Spreads Its Wings."
9. "Meg and the Power of Many."
10. Brian Bremner, "Sony's Dilemma; Can It Afford to Spin Off Its Insurance Unit?" *BusinessWeek*, no. 3926, Mar. 28, 2005, p. 50.

## Chapter 6

1. Julie Cresswell, "Fidelity Comes Out Swinging," *Fortune*, vol. 150, no. 9, Nov. 1, 2004, p. 192.
2. Ibid.
3. Aaron Pressman, "The Busiest Broker on Earth," *BusinessWeek*, no. 3929, Apr. 18, 2004, p. 84.
4. Ibid.
5. Cresswell, "Fidelity Comes Out Swinging."

6. Ibid.
7. Robert Barker, "Fidelity's Help for Mutual Fund Investors," *BusinessWeek*, no. 3784, May 27, 2002, p. 106.
8. Brian Bremner, "Fidelity: Leader of the Pack," *BusinessWeek*, no. 3797, Sept. 2, 2002, p. 54.
9. Cresswell, "Fidelity Comes Out Swinging."
10. Aaron Pressman, "Fidelity's Heir Apparent," *BusinessWeek Online*, May 5, 2005.
11. Adrian Slywotzky, *Value Migration.* (Boston: Harvard Business School Press, 1995).
12. Nanette Byrnes, "The Art of Motivation," *BusinessWeek*, no. 3982, May 1, 2006, p. 57.

### Part II

1. "Oldsmobile," *Wikipedia Encyclopedia*, Wikimedia Foundation, Inc.
2. "Lessons Learned from Olds Woes," *Advertising Age*, vol. 73, no. 9, Mar. 4, 2002, p. 30.
3. Bob Garfield, "Once a Giant, Olds Struggles to Find a Niche," *Advertising Age*, vol. 63, no. 40, Sept. 28, 1992, p. 52.

### Chapter 7

1. Alex Taylor III, "Chrysler's Great Expectations," *Fortune*, vol. 134, no. 11, Dec. 9, 1996, p. 101.
2. "Gentlemen, Start Your Engines," *Fortune*, vol. 137, no. 11, June 8, 1998, p. 138.
3. Alex Taylor III, "Can the Germans Rescue Chrysler?" *Fortune*, vol. 143, no. 9, Apr. 30, 2001, p. 106.
4. Ibid.
5. Gail Edmondson, "Stalled; Was the Daimler-Chrysler Merger a Mistake?" *BusinessWeek*, no. 3851, Sept. 29, 2003, p. 54.
6. Taylor, "Can the Germans Rescue Chrysler?"
7. Kathleen Kerwin, "Chrysler Puts Some Muscle on the Street," *BusinessWeek*, no. 3886, June 7, 2004, p. 72.
8. Kathleen Kerwin, "A Breakthrough for Chrysler?" *BusinessWeek*, no. 3884, May 24, 2004, p. 113.
9. Ibid.
10. Kerwin, "Chrysler Puts Some Muscle on the Street."
11. Neal Boudette, "Chrysler's Storied Hemi Motor Helps It Escape Detroit's Gloom," *Wall Street Journal*, June 17, 2005.
12. Joann Muller, "The Engine That Could," *Forbes*, vol. 176, no. 1, July 4, 2005, p. 52.
13. Boudette, "Chrysler's Storied Hemi Motor."
14. Kathleen Kerwin, "The Zoom Machine at Chrysler," *BusinessWeek*, no. 3925, March 21, 2005, p. 40.
15. Boudette, "Chrysler's Storied Hemi Motor."

### Chapter 8

1. Julie Cresswell, "Ivan Seidenberg, CEO of Verizon, Vows to Overpower the Cable Guys," *Fortune*, vol. 149, no. 11, May 31, 2004, p. 120.
2. Jon Fine, "An Ugly Battle for the Clicker," *BusinessWeek*, no. 3959, Sept. 5, 2005, p. 26.
3. Tom Lowry, "Verizon's Video Vision," *BusinessWeek*, no. 3931, May 2, 2005, p. 77.
4. Cresswell, "Ivan Seidenberg."
5. Ibid.
6. Ibid.
7. Ibid.
8. Scott Woolley, "Xbox," *Forbes*, vol. 175, no. 12, June 6, 2005, p. 62.
9. Ibid.
10. "Way Beyond the PC," *The Economist*, Nov. 26, 2005.
11. Peter Lewis, "Not Just Playing Around," *Fortune*, vol. 151, no. 12, June 13, 2005, p. 126.
12. "Inside Microsoft's Consumer Strategy," *BusinessWeek Online*, Dec. 7, 2004.
13. Cliff Edwards, "Who's Got Game Now?" *BusinessWeek*, no. 3933, May 16, 2005, p. 40.
14. "The Meaning of Xbox," *The Economist*, Nov. 26, 2005.

### Chapter 9

1. Erick Schonfeld, "Stetsons Off to Texan Technology," *Fortune*, vol. 131, no. 7, Apr. 17, 1995, p. 20.
2. Erick Schonfeld, "Hotter than Intel," *Fortune*, vol. 140, no. 7, Oct. 11, 1999, p. 179.
3. Ibid.
4. Ibid.
5. Ibid.
6. "TI's Strategy in the Slump," *BusinessWeek Online*, Nov. 26, 2002.
7. Olga Kharif, "Texas Instruments' Power Sources," *BusinessWeek Online*, Oct. 27, 2003.
8. Jeffrey Liker, *The Toyota Way* (New York: McGraw-Hill, 2004).

9. Brian Hindo, "Squeezing Out Oil, Gas, and Profits," *BusinessWeek*, no. 3931, May 2, 2005, p. 79.

**Part III**

1. David Stires, "Fallen Arches," *Fortune*, vol. 145, no. 9, Apr. 29, 2002, p. 74.
2. Grainger David, "Can McDonald's Cook Again?" *Fortune*, vol. 147, no. 7, Apr. 14, 2003, p. 120.
3. Stires, "Fallen Arches."
4. Kate MacArthur, "Big Mac's Back," *Advertising Age*, vol. 75, no. 50, Dec. 13, 2004, p. S1.
5. David Stires, "McDonald's Keeps on Cooking," *Fortune*, vol. 149, no. 10, May 17, 2004, p. 174.

**Chapter 10**

1. Kate MacArthur, "Big Mac's Back," *Advertising Age*, vol. 75, no. 50, Dec. 13, 2004, p. S1.
2. John Helyar, "Will Harley-Davidson Hit the Wall?" *Fortune*, vol. 146, no. 3, Aug. 12, 2002, p. 120.
3. Joseph Weber, "He Really Got Harley Roaring," *BusinessWeek*, no. 3925, Mar. 21, 2005, p. 70.
4. James D. Speros, "Why the Harley Brand's So Hot," *Advertising Age*, vol. 74, no. 11, Mar. 15, 2004, p. 26.
5. Helyar, "Will Harley-Davidson Hit the Wall?"
6. Speros, "Why the Harley Brand's So Hot."
7. Diane Brady, "Cult Brands; The BusinessWeek/Interbrand Annual Ranking of the World's Most Valuable Brands Shows the Power of Passionate Consumers," *BusinessWeek*, no. 3894, Aug. 2, 2004, p. 64.
8. Speros, "Why the Harley Brand's So Hot."
9. Weber, "He Really Got Harley Roaring."

**Chapter 11**

1. Cora Daniels, "Mr. Coffee: The Man Behind the $4.75 Frappuccino Makes the 500," *Fortune*, vol. 147, no. 7, Apr. 14, 2003, p. 139.
2. Jennifer Reese, "Starbucks: Inside the Coffee Cult," *Fortune*, vol. 134, no. 11, Dec. 9, 1996, p. 190.
3. Richard Teitelbaum, "Starbucks Corp.," *Fortune*, vol. 126, no. 4, Aug. 24, 1992, p. 133.

4. Diane Brady, "Cult Brands; The BusinessWeek/Interbrand Annual Ranking of the World's Most Valuable Brands Shows the Power of Passionate Consumers," *BusinessWeek*, no. 3894, Aug. 2, 2004, p. 64.
5. Reese, "Starbucks: Inside the Coffee Cult."
6. Teitelbaum, "Starbucks Corp."
7. Ibid.
8. Patricia Sellers, "Starbucks: The Next Generation," *Fortune*, vol. 151, no. 7, Apr. 4, 2005, p. 30.

**Chapter 12**

1. Kate MacArthur, "McDonald's Salads," *Advertising Age*, vol. 75, no. 44, Nov. 1, 2004, p. S8.
2. Kate MacArthur, "Salad Days at McDonald's," *Advertising Age*, vol. 75, no. 50, Dec. 13, 2004, p. 50.
3. Jack Ewing, "A Cold Shoulder for Coca-Cola," *BusinessWeek*, no. 3931, May 2, 2005, p. 30.
4. Ibid.

**Part IV**
**Chapter 13**

1. Michael Hammer, "Making Operational Innovation Work," *Harvard Management Update*, vol. 10, no. 4, Apr. 2005, p. 6.
2. Ibid.
3. Ibid.
4. Ibid.
5. Angela Key, "Dimon in the Rough: The Problem Solver," *Fortune*, vol. 142, no. 1, June 26, 2000, p. 292.
6. Emily Thornton and Joseph Weber, "A Made-to-Order Megamerger; Bank One Will Supply J.P. Morgan Chase with the Top Talent It Needed," *BusinessWeek*, no. 3867, Jan. 26, 2004, p. 48.
7. Key, "Dimon in the Rough."
8. Thornton and Weber, "A Made-to-Order Megamerger."
9. Shawn Tully, "The Jamie Dimon Show: He's Tough. He's Loud. He's Irrepressible. And He's Just What Bank One Needed," *Fortune*, vol. 146, no. 2, July 22, 2002, p. 88.
10. Joseph Weber, "J.P. Morgan Is in for a Shock; Jamie Dimon Won't Take Charge Until 2006, but His Influence Will Be Immediate," *BusinessWeek*, no. 3868, Feb. 2, 2004, p. 66.
11. Tully, "The Jamie Dimon Show."

12. Thornton and Weber, "A Made-to-Order Megamerger."
13. Patricia Sellers, "The New Breed: The Latest Crop of CEO's Is Disciplined, Deferential, and Even a Bit Dull. What a Relief," *Fortune*, vol. 146, no. 10, Nov. 18, 2004, p. 66.
14. Tully, "The Jamie Dimon Show."
15. Emily Thornton, "Dimon's Grand Design," *BusinessWeek*, no. 3926, Mar. 28, 2005, p. 96.

### Chapter 14

1. Patricia Sellers, "P&G: Teaching an Old Dog New Tricks," *Fortune*, vol. 149, no. 11, May 31, 2004, p. 166.
2. Bruce Nussbaum, "Get Creative! How to Build Creative Companies," *BusinessWeek*, no. 3945, Aug. 1, 2005, p. 62.
3. Ibid.
4. Peter Lewis, "A Perpetual Crisis Machine," *Fortune*, vol. 152, no. 6, Sept. 19, 2005, p. 58.
5. "Sony and Samsung Company Profiles," *Wall Street Journal*, Jan. 3, 2006.
6. Lewis, "A Perpetual Crisis Machine."
7. Andy Serwer, "The Education of Michael Dell," *Fortune*, vol. 151, no. 5, Mar. 7, 2005, p. 72.
8. Ibid.
9. Ibid.
10. Andy Serwer, "Dell Does Domination," *Fortune*, vol. 145, no. 2, Jan. 21, 2002, p. 70.
11. Sewer, "The Education of Michael Dell."
12. Daniel Roth, "Dell's Big New Act," *Fortune*, vol. 140, no. 11, Dec. 6, 1999, p. 152.
13. Serwer, "The Education of Michael Dell."
14. Adam Lashinsky, "The Hard Way," *Fortune*, vol. 153, no. 7, Apr. 17, 2006, p. 92.
15. Peter Burrows, "Stopping the Sprawl at HP," *BusinessWeek*, no. 3986, May 29, 2006, p. 54.
16. Elizabeth Corcoran, "A Bad Spell for Dell," *Forbes*, vol. 177, no. 13, June 19, 2006, p. 42.

### Part V
### Chapter 15

1. Linda Grant, "Missed Moments," *Fortune*, vol. 136, no. 8, Oct. 27, 1997, p. 188.
2. "Fisher's Photofinish," *BusinessWeek*, no. 3634, June 21, 1999, p. 34.
3. Ibid.
4. Andy Serwer, "Kodak: In the Noose," *Fortune*, vol. 145, no. 3, Feb. 4, 2002, p. 147.
5. Ibid.
6. William Symonds, "The Kodak Revolt Is Short-Sighted," *BusinessWeek*, no. 3856, Nov. 3, 2003, p. 38.
7. Joseph Nocera, "Kodak: The CEO vs. the Gadfly," *Fortune*, vol. 149, no. 1, Jan. 12, 2004, p. 84.
8. "Another Kodak Moment," *The Economist*, May 14, 2005, p. 69.
9. William Bulkeley, "Kodak Shifts to Loss as Revenue Slips," *Wall Street Journal*, Apr. 25, 2005.
10. William Bulkeley, "Kodak Posts Loss, Sets More Job Cuts as Film Sales Sink," *Wall Street Journal*, July 22, 2005.
11. Bernard Condon, "Globetrotter," *Forbes*, vol. 175, no. 8, Apr. 18, 2005, p. 68.
12. Ibid.

### Chapter 16

1. Daniel Roth, "Can Nike Still Do It without Phil Knight?" *Fortune*, vol. 151, no. 7, Apr. 4, 2005, p. 58.
2. Lane Randall, "You Are What You Wear," *Forbes*, vol. 158, no. 9, Oct. 14, 1996, p. 42.
3. Roth, "Can Nike Still Do It?"
4. Ibid.
5. Ibid.
6. "Can Nike Still Do It?" *BusinessWeek*, no. 3669, Feb. 21, 2000, p. 120.
7. Roth, "Can Nike Still Do It?"
8. Ibid.

### Chapter 17

1. Peter Burrows, "Why HP Is Pruning the Printers," *BusinessWeek Online*, Apr. 28, 2005.
2. Tam Pui-ing, "HP Looks beyond Ink Sales for Growth," *Wall Street Journal*, June 20, 2005.
3. Burrows, "Why HP Is Pruning the Printers."
4. "Intel," *BusinessWeek*, no. 3753, Oct. 15, 2001, p. 80.
5. Ibid.
6. Adam Lashinsky, "Is This the Right Man for Intel?" *Fortune*, vol. 151, no. 8, Apr. 18, 2005, p. 110.
7. "Intel."
8. Lashinsky, "Is This the Right Man?"

**Part VI**
**Chapter 18**

1. Betsy Morris, "The Real Story: How Did Coca-Cola's Management Go from First-Rate to Farcical in Six Short Years?" *Fortune*, vol. 149, no. 11, May 31, 2004, p. 84.
2. Ibid.
3. Ibid.
4. Ibid.
5. Ibid.
6. Fred Vogelstein, "Search and Destroy," *Fortune*, vol. 151, no. 9, May 2, 2005, p. 72.

**Chapter 19**

1. Joe Saumarez Smith, "Why Harvard Lost Out to Vegas," *Financial Times*, Apr. 8, 2005.
2. Julie Schlosser, "Teacher's Bet," *Fortune*, vol. 149, no. 5, Mar. 8, 2004, p. 158.
3. Smith, "Why Harvard Lost Out to Vegas."
4. Ibid.

**Chapter 20**

1. Adam Lashinsky, "eBay's Management Merry-Go-Round," *Fortune*, vol. 150, no. 13, Dec. 27, 2004, p. 32.

**Part VII**
**Chapter 21**

1. Katrina Brooker, "Can Anyone Replace Herb?" *Fortune*, vol. 141, no. 8, Apr. 17, 2000, p. 186.
2. "Southwest after Kelleher, More Blue Skies," *BusinessWeek*, no. 3726, Apr. 2, 2001, p. 45.
3. Barney Gimbel, "Southwest's New Flight Plan," *Fortune*, vol. 151, no. 10, May 16, 2005, p. 93.
4. Andy Serwer, "Southwest Airlines: The Hottest Thing in the Sky," *Fortune*, vol. 149, no. 5, Mar. 8, 2004, p. 86.
5. Brooker, "Can Anyone Replace Herb?"
6. Ibid.
7. Ibid.
8. Serwer, "Southwest Airlines."
9. Brooker, "Can Anyone Replace Herb?"
10. Diane Brady, "The Immelt Revolution," *BusinessWeek*, no. 3926, Mar. 28, 2005, p. 64.
11. Bruce Nussbaum, "How to Build Creative Companies," *BusinessWeek*, no. 3945, Aug. 1, 2005, p. 62.
12. Brady, "The Immelt Revolution."
13. Ibid.
14. Diane Brady, "The Transformer, Beth Comstock, General Electric Company," *BusinessWeek*, no. 3945, Aug. 1, 2005, p. 77.
15. Nussbaum, "How to Build Creative Companies."
16. Brady, "The Immelt Revolution."
17. Ibid.
18. Ibid.
19. Nussbaum, "How to Build Creative Companies."

**Chapter 22**

1. Ronald Henkoff, "Keeping Motorola on a Roll," *Fortune*, vol. 129, no. 8, Apr. 18, 1994, p. 67.
2. Ibid.
3. Ibid.
4. Rick Tetzeli, "And Now for Motorola's Next Trick," *Fortune*, vol. 135, no. 8, Apr. 28, 1997, p. 122.
5. Ibid.
6. Ibid.
7. Ibid.
8. Erick Schonfeld, "Hold the Phone: Motorola Is Going Nowhere Fast," *Fortune*, vol. 137, no. 6, Mar. 30, 1998, p. 184.
9. Ibid.
10. "Motorola," *BusinessWeek*, no. 3741, July 26, 2001, p. 72.
11. Ibid.
12. Ibid.
13. Ibid.
14. Adam Lashinsky, "Can Moto Find Its Mojo?" *Fortune*, vol. 149, no. 7, Apr. 5, 2004, p. 126.
15. Ibid.
16. Christopher Rhoads, "CEO Zander Shakes Up VP's, Pushes Cool Phones and Vows to Leave Rivals in the Dust," *Wall Street Journal*, June 23, 2005.
17. Ibid.
18. Ibid.
19. Ibid.
20. Ibid.

**Chapter 23**

1. Ronald Henkoff, "Boeing's Big Problem," *Fortune*, vol. 137, no. 1, Jan. 12, 1998, p. 96.
2. Ibid.
3. Ibid.
4. Ibid.
5. Ibid.
6. Ibid.
7. Kenneth Labich, "Boeing Finally Hatches a Plan," *Fortune*, vol. 139, no. 4, Mar. 1, 1999, p. 100.

8. Ibid.
9. Ibid.
10. Ibid.
11. Jerry Useem, "Boeing vs. Boeing," *Fortune*, vol. 142, no. 7, Oct. 2, 2000, p. 148.
12. Ibid.
13. Ibid.
14. Jerry Useem, "Boeing to Pieces," *Fortune*, vol. 148, no. 13, Dec. 22, 2003, p. 41.
15. Julie Cresswell, "Boeing Plays Defense," *Fortune*, vol. 149, no. 8, Apr. 19, 2004, p. 90.
16. Stanley Holmes, "Why Boeing's Culture Breeds Turmoil," *BusinessWeek*, no. 3925, Mar. 21, 2005, p. 34.
17. Ibid.
18. Useem, "Boeing to Pieces."
19. Cresswell, "Boeing Plays Defense."
20. Holmes, "Why Boeing's Culture Breeds Turmoil."
21. Ibid.
22. Ibid.
23. Alex Taylor III, "Boeing Finally Has a Flight Plan," *Fortune*, vol. 151, no. 12, June 13, 2005, p. 27.
24. Mark Tatge, "Global Gamble," *Forbes*, vol. 177, no. 8, Apr. 17, 2006, p. 78.
25. Stanley Holmes, "I Like a Challenge—And I've Got One," *BusinessWeek*, no. 3943, July 18, 2005, p.44.

### Part VIII
### Chapter 24

1. "Behind the Smiles at Sony," *The Economist*, Mar. 12–18, 2005.
2. Ibid.
3. Phred Dvorak, "At Sony, Rivalries Were Encouraged; Then Came iPod," *Wall Street Journal*, June 29, 2005.
4. Ibid.
5. Ibid.
6. Ibid.
7. Ibid.
8. Ibid.
9. "Behind the Smiles at Sony."
10. Marc Gunther, "The Welshman, the Walkman, and the Salarymen," *Fortune*, vol. 153, no. 11, June 12, 2006, p. 70.
11. Brian Bremner, "Sony's Sudden Samurai," *BusinessWeek Online*, Mar. 10, 2005.
12. Walt Mossberg, "Shaking Up Sony," *Wall Street Journal*, June 6, 2006.
13. Gunther, "The Welshman."
14. Emily Thornton, "Morgan Stanley Lost Its Way," *BusinessWeek*, no. 3942, July 11, 2005, p. 68.
15. Ibid.

16. Ibid.
17. Ibid.
18. Ibid.
19. Ibid.
20. Bethany McLean, "Brahmin's at the Gate," *Fortune*, vol. 151, no. 9, May 2, 2005, p. 58.
21. Charles Gasparino, "Out on the Street," *Newsweek*, June 27, 2005, p. 36.
22. Ibid.

### Chapter 25

1. Alex Taylor III, "Can You Believe Porsche Is Putting Its Badge on This Car?" *Fortune*, vol. 143, no. 4, Feb. 19, 2001, p. 168.
2. Alex Taylor III, "Porsche's Risky Recipe," *Fortune*, vol. 147, no. 3, Feb. 17, 2003, p. 90.
3. Ibid.
4. Ibid.
5. Ibid.
6. Taylor, "Can You Believe?"
7. Ibid.
8. Ibid.
9. Ibid.
10. Taylor, "Porsche's Risky Recipe."
11. Richard Milne, "Porsche Unveils Record Profits," *Financial Times*, Nov. 16, 2004, p. 30.

### Chapter 26

1. Richard Tomlinson, "One Company, Two Bosses, Many Problems," *Fortune International*, vol. 151, no. 1, Jan. 24, 2005, p. 56.
2. Ibid.
3. Ibid.
4. Ibid.
5. Ibid.
6. Beth Carney, "Unilever's Many Woes," *BusinessWeek Online*, Feb. 11, 2005.
7. Louis Lavelle, "Three Simple Rules Carly Ignored," *BusinessWeek*, no. 3922, Feb. 28, 2005, p. 46.
8. "Now Who'll Save Hewlett-Packard?" *BusinessWeek*, no. 3921, Feb. 21, 2005, p. 96.
9. Ibid.
10. Ibid.
11. Carol Loomis, "Why Carly's Big Bet Is Failing," *Fortune*, vol. 151, no. 3, Feb. 7, 2005, p. 50.
12. Ibid.
13. Carol Loomis, "How the HP Board KO'd Carly," *Fortune*, vol. 151, no. 5, Mar. 7, 2005, p. 99.

14. Loomis, "Why Carly's Big Bet Is Failing."
15. George Anders, "Bitterness and the Boardroom," *Wall Street Journal*, Oct. 16, 2006.

**Part IX**
**Chapter 27**

1. Louis Gerstner, *Who Says Elephants Can't Dance?* (New York: Harper Business, 2002).
2. Ibid.
3. "A Week Aboard the Wal-Mart Express," *Fortune*, vol. 126, no. 4, Aug. 24, 1992, p. 77.
4. Ibid.
5. Hank Gilman, "The Most Underrated CEO Ever," *Fortune*, vol. 149, no. 7, Apr. 5, 2004, p. 242.
6. "A Week Aboard."
7. John Huey, "Wal-Mart: Will It Take Over the World?" *Fortune*, vol. 119, no. 3, Jan. 30, 1989, p. 52.

**Chapter 28**

1. Linda Grant, "Gillette Knows Shaving—and How to Turn Out Hot New Products," *Fortune*, vol. 134, no. 7, Oct. 14, 1996, p. 207.
2. Ibid.
3. Ibid.
4. "The Big Trim at Gillette," *BusinessWeek*, no. 3654, Nov. 8, 1999, p. 42.
5. Jeremy Kahn, "Gillette Loses Face," *Fortune*, vol. 140, no. 9, Nov. 8, 1999, p. 147.
6. Ibid.
7. Ibid.
8. "Most of Gillette's Bleeding Is Self-Inflicted," *BusinessWeek*, no. 3701, Oct. 2, 2000, p. 56.
9. "A Fresh Face Could Do Wonders for Gillette," *BusinessWeek*, no. 3706, Nov. 6, 2000, p. 52.
10. Andy Serwer, "An About-Face for Gillette? It's About Time!" *Fortune*, vol. 143, no. 9, Apr. 30, 2001, p. 181.
11. "Razor Burn at Gillette," *BusinessWeek*, no. 3737, June 18, 2001, p. 37.

12. Ibid.
13. Katrina Brooker, "Jim Kilts Is an Old-School Curmudgeon. Nothing Could Be Better for Gillette," *Fortune*, vol. 146, no. 13, Dec. 30, 2002, p. 94.
14. Ibid.
15. Ibid.
16. Ibid.
17. Ibid.
18. Ibid.
19. Ibid.

**Part X**
**Chapter 29**

1. Bro Uttal, "Behind the Fall of Steve Jobs," *Fortune*, vol. 112, Aug. 5, 1985, p. 20.
2. Ibid.
3. Ibid.
4. Brian O'Reilly, "Apple Finally Invades the Office," *Fortune*, vol. 116, no. 11, Nov. 9, 1987, p. 52.
5. Ibid.
6. Alan Deutschman, "Odd Man Out," *Fortune*, vol. 128, no. 2, July 26, 1993, p. 42.
7. Ibid.
8. Ibid.
9. Brent Schlender, "Something's Rotten in Cupertino," *Fortune*, vol. 135, no. 4, Mar. 3, 1997, p. 100.
10. Ibid.
11. Ibid.
12. David Kirkpatrick, "The Second Coming of Apple," *Fortune*, vol. 138, no. 9, Nov. 9, 1998, p. 86.
13. Ibid.
14. Ibid.
15. Ibid.
16. Schlender, "Something's Rotten in Cupertino."
17. Peter Lewis, "Apple Jacks It Up," *Fortune*, vol. 145, no. 4, Feb. 18, 2002, p. 139.
18. Devon Leonard, "The Player," *Fortune*, vol. 153, no. 5, Mar. 20, 2006, p. 54.
19. Brent Schlender, "How Big Can Apple Get?" *Fortune*, vol. 151, no. 4, Feb. 21, 2005, p. 66.

# INDEX

# ABOUT THE AUTHOR

Robert J. (Bob) Herbold, retired executive vice president and chief operating officer of Microsoft Corporation, is the Managing Director of Herbold Group, LLC, a consulting business focused on profitability, operational, and marketing issues. Herbold serves on the Board of Directors of Agilent Technologies, Indachin Ltd. Hong Kong and First Mutual Bank. Also, in 2001 he was appointed by President Bush to the President's Council of Advisors on Science and Technology and currently chairs the Education Subcommittee of the Council.

Herbold joined Microsoft in November 1994 as executive vice president and chief operating officer. During his tenure in this position until spring 2001, he was responsible for finance, manufacturing and distribution, information systems, human resources, corporate marketing, market research, and public relations. During his 6½ years as COO, Microsoft experienced a fourfold increase in revenue and a sevenfold increase in profits. From spring 2001 until June 2003 Herbold worked part time for Microsoft as executive vice president, assisting in the government, industry, and customer areas.

Prior to joining Microsoft, Herbold spent 26 years at The Procter & Gamble Company. In his last five years with P&G, he served as senior vice president of advertising and information services. In that role, he was responsible for the company's worldwide advertising/brand management operations as well as all marketing related services such as media and television program production. He was also responsible for management information systems and market research on a worldwide basis.

Herbold's experiences at Microsoft and Procter & Gamble were the basis of an article he authored in the January 2002 issue of the *Harvard Business Review* entitled "Inside Microsoft: Balancing Discipline and Creativity," which focuses on how companies can improve their profitability and agility. In 2004 he authored the book *The Fiefdom Syndrome* (Doubleday), which focuses on the turf battles that undermine careers and companies and how to overcome them.

Herbold has a Bachelor of Science degree from the University of Cincinnati and both a Master's degree in mathematics and a Ph.D. in computer science from Case Western Reserve University. Herbold is a member of the Board of Trustees of The Heritage Foundation, Nanyang Technological University and the Hutchinson Cancer Research Center, and the Board of Overseers of the Hoover Institution at Stanford University and is senior executive in residence at INSEAD, Singapore campus. He is also the president of The Herbold Foundation, which is primarily focused on providing college scholarships to science and engineering students.

TY VAGUENESS NEGLECT PRIDE BO
RGY TIMIDITY CONFUSION NEGLEC
Y LETHARGY TIMIDITY CONFUSION
MEDIOCRITY LETHARGY TIMIDITY
Y BLOAT MEDIOCRITY LETHARGY T
COMPLEXITY BLOAT MEDIOCRITY L
BOREDOM COMPLEXITY BLOAT ME
CT PRIDE BOREDOM COMPLEXITY
NEGLECT PRIDE BOREDOM COMP
NFUSION NEGLECT PRIDE BOREDOM
TY CONFUSION NEGLECT PRIDE BO
RGY TIMIDITY CONFUSION NEGLEC
Y LETHARGY TIMIDITY CONFUSION
MEDIOCRITY LETHARGY TIMIDITY
Y BLOAT MEDIOCRITY LETHARGY T
COMPLEXITY BLOAT MEDIOCRITY L
BOREDOM COMPLEXITY BLOAT ME
CT PRIDE BOREDOM COMPLEXITY
NEGLECT PRIDE BOREDOM COMP
NFUSION NEGLECT PRIDE BOREDOM
TY CONFUSION NEGLECT PRIDE BO
RGY TIMIDITY CONFUSION NEGLECT
Y LETHARGY TIMIDITY CONFUSION
MEDIOCRITY LETHARGY TIMIDITY
Y BLOAT MEDIOCRITY LETHARGY T